Prosperity and Justice

'With its calls for a rebalancing of economic power, a more activist state, a new industrialization model, and managed automation, this report is nothing if not bold. What makes it especially distinctive and valuable is that this big-picture reform agenda is backed up by detailed proposals – on a national investment bank, increased public investment, a social dividend, expansion of collective bargaining, worker representation on company boards, regulation of digital platforms, and much more. The report is an inspiration for all those in the UK and elsewhere who are trying to chart a new course for inclusive prosperity.'

Dani Rodrik, Ford Foundation Professor of International Political Economy, Harvard University

'The Commission makes an irrefutable case that British economic performance must improve, and then suggests a suite of original initiatives aimed at doing just that. There will be challenges on particular recommendations, but overall this is the most impressive, authoritative and compelling economic analysis and accompanying prescriptions in recent times. It deserves to change the terms of economic debate.'

Will Hutton, Principal of Hertford College Oxford, *Observer* columnist and co-author of *Saving Britain*

'If we are going to rescue democracy and our way of life, we need to reform capitalism so that it conspicuously serves the interests of the majority and not just the lucky privileged few. Some of the IPPR Commission's proposals are perhaps too idealistic and impractical, but most are serious and important contributions to the debate of our age.'

Robert Peston, Political Editor, ITV News

'It is shameful that the fifth largest economy in the world is not already oriented towards producing sustainable prosperity for all its citizens but, sadly, the UK is so far from this that we really do need a "new economy". The Commission on Economic Justice makes a thoughtful, mature and significant contribution to thinking on what that "new economy" should look like – they give us not only a strong and positive vision, but a pragmatic roadmap for how to get there.'

Kate Pickett, Professor of Epidemiology, University of York
and co-author of The Spirit Level and The Inner Level

'Over the last ten years policymakers have failed to respond to the challenges the UK has faced, and have created additional home-grown problems. We need a complete rethink to avoid another lost decade. This report provides exactly that, with lots of innovative, sensible and well-researched ideas across the whole spectrum of economic policy from industrial policy to taxes, the environment to distribution. In my own area, it provides the best prospectus for future UK macroeconomic policy that I have seen.'

Simon Wren-Lewis, Professor of Economic Policy,
Blavatnik School of Government,
University of Oxford

'Left unaddressed, conflicts between finance and production, the rich and the poor, the state and the market, have historically heralded costly economic crises and political instability. Ten years after the global financial crisis, the UK faces the unresolved legacy of several such conflicts. Focusing on the origins of these vulnerabilities, the IPPR Commission on Economic Justice has analysed the political economy of ownership, distributive governance, competition, industrial policy, investment and financial stability. The comprehensive volume summarizing these efforts is a product of substantial comparative work. Informed by this research, the Commission's proposed reform programme is future-orientated yet realistic. It is an urgent read for those who strive to find workable solutions to the increasingly apparent crises in the UK's economic model.'

Anastasia Nesvetailova, Professor of International Political Economy and Director, City Political Economy Research Centre, University of London

'An excellent platform to start a serious debate about how bold and imaginative government policy can offer a serious alternative to simplistic populist recipes. Urgent reading!'

Carlota Perez, Visiting Professor of International Development at the LSE and author of *Technological Revolution and Financial Capital: The Dynamics of Bubbles and Golden Ages*

'When countries face challenges on the scale of those testing the UK today, they are just as likely to retreat into apathy and disengagement as they are to embark on an informed search for solutions. Fortunately this book has arrived just in time to provide a framework for rethinking how and where such solutions might be identified and to set out new directions for public policy beyond the paralysing terrain of Brexit. It's a must-read for anyone interested in alternative futures for the UK economy and indeed for others facing similar challenges of slowing productivity, rising inequality and a labour market undergoing fundamental change.'

Roy Green, Emeritus Professor, University of Technology Sydney

Prosperity and Justice

About IPPR

The Institute for Public Policy Research (IPPR) is the UK's pre-eminent progressive think tank. Founded in 1988, our purpose is to conduct and promote research into the economic, social and political sciences, science and technology, the voluntary sector and social enterprise, public services, and industry and commerce; and to educate the public in these subjects. We are an independent charitable organisation with our main offices in London. IPPR North, IPPR's dedicated think tank for the North of England, operates out of offices in Manchester and Newcastle, and IPPR Scotland, our dedicated think tank for Scotland, is based in Edinburgh.

For further information on IPPR and to contact us please visit www.ippr.org.

Prosperity and Justice

A Plan for the New Economy

The Final Report of the IPPR Commission on Economic Justice

polity

First published in 2018 by Polity Press in association with the Institute for Public Policy Research

Polity Press
65 Bridge Street
Cambridge CB2 1UR, UK

Polity Press
101 Station Landing
Suite 300
Medford, MA 02155, USA

ISBN-13: 978-1-5095-3498-2
ISBN-13: 978-1-5095-3499-9(pb)

A catalogue record for this book is available from the British Library.

Typeset in 10/16.5 Utopia by Servis Filmsetting Limited, Stockport, Cheshire
Printed and bound in Great Britain by Clays Ltd, Elcograf S.p.A.

The publisher has used its best endeavours to ensure that the URLs for external websites referred to in this book are correct and active at the time of going to press. However, the publisher has no responsibility for the websites and can make no guarantee that a site will remain live or that the content is or will remain appropriate.

Every effort has been made to trace all copyright holders, but if any have been overlooked the publisher will be pleased to include any necessary credits in any subsequent reprint or edition.

For further information on Polity, visit our website: politybooks.com

Contents

Preface

The IPPR Commission on Economic Justice was established in autumn 2016 in the wake of Britain's vote to leave the European Union. The referendum result was a stark repudiation of the status quo and crystallised profound feelings of economic injustice felt in many parts of society. The Commission was founded in the belief that it was insufficient simply to argue that economic change was necessary. The country needed to see how it could be achieved. The purpose of the Commission was, therefore, broadly conceived: to examine the challenges facing the UK economy and to make recommendations for its reform.

The members of the Commission come from all walks of life and different political viewpoints. They voted on different sides of the EU referendum, and the Commission is independent of all political parties. Given the breadth of Commissioners, we have reached a remarkable degree of agreement, which we hope can be reflected in a wider national consensus about a new direction for the UK economy. Our proposals are deliberately ambitious. Taken together, we believe they offer the potential for the most significant change in economic policy in a generation.

The report is wide-ranging, but not comprehensive: some fields, such as specific reforms to the welfare system and education, have been beyond our scope. It is UK-wide: while we propose greater devolution of economic powers, we have not sought to write detailed plans for any of the individual nations of the United Kingdom. We have not taken a position on Brexit; our analysis shows that the UK's economic problems are of long standing. The economy needs reform no matter what happens. We do not attribute blame to any particular politicians or parties, since our economic problems have developed under successive governments of all colours.

The Commission met ten times and has overseen 18 months of research, conducted by a team at the IPPR led by the Commission's Director Michael Jacobs. We called for and received evidence from a wide range of sources, and engaged in extensive consultation with stakeholders and experts. We are very grateful to the many organisations and individuals who contributed to the development of our ideas. We are particularly grateful to those whose financial support for the Commission made it possible. They are listed in the acknowledgements that follow.

Our Interim Report was published in September 2017, setting out our analysis of the condition of the economy and the causes of its weak performance. The Commission has also published 17 discussion and policy papers to inform its work and to stimulate public debate. These papers provide more detail on the analysis and proposals made in this report. The Interim Report and full set of papers are available at ippr.org/cej.

This book constitutes the final report of the Commission. But it is by no means the last word. Economic change is not simple; there are no 'silver bullets' or magical solutions to remedy deep and longstanding problems. We hope that we can spark a national conversation on why we need a change of direction, and what that direction should be. We can bridge the gap between the country we are and the country we would like to be. We hope our report contributes to that task.

Tom Kibasi

Chair of the Commission and Director of the IPPR

The IPPR Commission on Economic Justice

Dominic Barton
Global Managing Partner, McKinsey and Company

Sara Bryson
Community Organiser, Tyne & Wear Citizens, Citizens UK

Matthew Clifford MBE
Co-founder and CEO, Entrepreneur First

Charlie Cornish
Group Chief Executive, Manchester Airports Group plc

Claire Dove OBE, DL
Chief Executive, Blackburne House Group

Lord John Eatwell
President, Queens' College, University of Cambridge

Grace Gould
Entrepreneur in Residence, LocalGlobe

Sandra Kerr OBE
Race Equality Director, Business in the Community

Lord Bob Kerslake
Chair, Peabody Trust

Tom Kibasi
Director, IPPR, and Chair of the Commission

Catherine McGuinness
Chairman, Policy and Resources Committee, City of London Corporation

Mariana Mazzucato
Professor in the Economics of Innovation and Public Value, University College London

John Mills
Founder and Chairman, JML

Dame Helena Morrissey DBE
Head of Personal Investing, Legal & General Investment Management

Frances O'Grady
General Secretary, Trades Union Congress

Stephen Peel
Founder and Chairman, SMP Policy Innovation

Mary Senior
Scotland Official, University and College Union

Hetan Shah
Executive Director, Royal Statistical Society

Mustafa Suleyman
Co-founder and Head of Applied Artificial Intelligence, DeepMind

Sally Tallant
Director, Liverpool Biennial Festival of Contemporary Art

Neera Tanden
President, Center for American Progress

The Most Revd and Rt Hon. Justin Welby
Archbishop of Canterbury

Note

The IPPR Commission on Economic Justice presents its final report in order to stimulate vital public debate. Individual members of the Commission agree with the broad thrust of the arguments made in this report, but they should not be taken to agree with every word or recommendation. Commissioners serve in an individual capacity, and this report should not be taken as representing the views of the organisations with which they are affiliated.

Acknowledgements

This report has been prepared by Tom Kibasi (Chair of the Commission) and Michael Jacobs (Director of the Commission), with research and writing by the IPPR Economy team: Catherine Colebrook (Chief Economist), Mathew Lawrence, Carys Roberts and Grace Blakeley, Laurie Laybourn-Langton, Lesley Rankin and Alfie Stirling.

Many other IPPR colleagues also contributed to the research, including Ed Cox, Joe Dromey, Phoebe Griffiths, Russell Gunson, Izzy Hatfield, Jona de Jong, Loren King, Sarah Longlands, Marley Morris, Luke Murphy and Luke Raikes. The Commission would like to express their appreciation to them all, along with Tim Woodward for editing, Emma Killick and Louise Rezler for project management, and the IPPR publications and communications team, including Jade Azim, Florri Burton, Katherine Gibney, Abi Hynes, Richard Maclean, Olivia Vaughan and David Wastell.

The Commission has benefited greatly from the contributions of a wide range of individuals and organisations with whom we have engaged and who have responded to our calls for evidence. These are listed at www.ippr.org/cej. A literature review to support the Commission's work was undertaken by the Sheffield Political Economy Research Institute. We would especially like to thank the members of the Commission's Panel of Economic Advisers (listed at www.ippr.org/cej) who have provided guidance and reviewed material. They should not, however, be held responsible for the contents of this report.

Funding for the Commission was generously provided by the Friends Provident Charitable Foundation, the City of London Corporation, the TUC, GMB and TSSA, and by Sir Trevor Chinn, John Mills, Stephen Peel and Martin Taylor. We are extremely grateful to all those whose generosity made the Commission's work possible.

FRIENDS PROVIDENT Foundation

Fairer economy, better world

CITY OF LONDON

Introduction and Overview

Travel across the UK today and it is impossible to escape a palpable feeling that the economy is not working for most people. Earnings that have been stagnant for a decade are combined with greater insecurity at work. Young people have been hit particularly hard – many unable to afford a home of their own, and on course to be poorer than their parents. Whole communities feel left behind. Many people feel powerless and fatalistic.

It isn't all bleak. Some parts of the economy – and some people – have been doing well. Unemployment is at historic lows, and fewer older people are living in poverty than in the past. We have global success stories in sectors such as car manufacturing, life sciences, finance and creative industries. The problem is that there aren't enough of them and too few people have been sharing in them.

The central argument of this report is that a fairer economy is a stronger economy. We do not have to choose between prosperity and justice: the two can, and must, go hand-in-hand. But without fundamental reform, our economy will continue to fail large numbers of people. We have to 'hard-wire' justice into the economy, not treat it as an afterthought.

This means rethinking the way the UK economy works: what it produces and how, and the rules and institutions that govern it. It will require governments to take a different approach to economic policy, and demand change of businesses, workers and investors alike. But the prize will be great: an economy where all can flourish, in a country that can be proud of its success.

The report is structured in two parts. In part I, we set out our overall arguments; in part II, we present our 10-part plan for economic reform.

We begin by describing the UK economy today. While it has some impressive strengths, it is not working well for most people. In recent years it has been growing, but despite this, most people have not been getting better off. Inequality of income is too high and inequality of wealth is even greater. The economy is divided by both age and geography, with wide regional disparities; too many once-thriving communities now offer few good jobs and little hope. Most households living in poverty are also in work. It is apparent that we need to rethink what counts as a successful economy.

We argue that economic policy should aim for both prosperity and justice. In chapter 2, we offer a broader definition of what prosperity means: the quality and security of work as well as income; time with family and community as well as money; and the common good as well as individual wellbeing. We offer six principles of economic justice aimed at making sure that all people, places and generations share in prosperity. We explain how a fairer economy generates greater prosperity, with stronger and more stable growth and lower social costs. Everyone – from top to bottom – is better off when the economy's rewards are more fairly shared. But redistributing the results isn't good enough to confront the depth of the challenges we face today. Justice must be 'hard-wired' into the processes of production and consumption. We conclude by setting out our vision for a good economy – one we believe most people will share.

In chapter 3, we explain some of the economy's longstanding weaknesses and set out five fundamental shifts in economic understanding and policy that are needed to tackle them. First, the economy has an unbalanced pattern of demand, overly reliant on household debt and ever-rising property prices. We need to shift from short-termism in finance to investment-led growth. Second, the UK economy is internationally uncompetitive, with an unsustainable imbalance between imports and exports. So we need to shift from trade deficits to what we call 'new industrialisation' across the UK. Third, many sectors are stuck in a rut of low productivity and low wages, with too many poor quality and insecure jobs. This requires a shift from overly flexible labour markets to a focus on raising productivity in the 'everyday economy' where most people work. Fourth, the economy has fallen behind in adopting new technologies, weakening productivity. We must shift from being technology laggards to embracing 'managed automation'. Last, many sectors of the UK economy are highly concentrated and governments have been complacent about competition policy. So we should shift from excessive market power to more open markets. Each of these five shifts, we argue, would promote prosperity and economic justice at the same time.

To achieve the change we seek, we will need fundamental reform of the way the economy is governed and policy made. Chapter 4 argues that we need a purposeful and active state, with its role in wealth creation better understood and actively embraced. Greater devolution of economic power is the necessary precondition of this change. We argue for greater partnership across the economy: within firms, among businesses, between businesses and trade unions, and in the way that economic policy and economic change are managed. The common thread running through all our proposals is a rebalancing of power: from corporate management towards workers and trade unions, from short-term finance towards long-term investors, from Whitehall towards the nations and regions of the UK.

In the concluding chapter of part I, we argue that the UK must now embrace change on a sufficient scale to achieve 'escape velocity' from an economy that delivers neither prosperity nor justice, to one that achieves both. We face a decade of disruption ahead, in which doing nothing will drag us further backwards. Change of this magnitude is possible: it has happened twice before in the past century and other countries pursue different policies with better results. A new economic settlement will require a programme of fundamental reform across the economy.

Part II offers a concrete plan to achieve this through ten areas of policy. Each of its chapters offers an analysis of the issues and sets out the Commission's specific proposals for change.

In chapter 6, we set out how the economy can be reshaped through industrial strategy: raising productivity and boosting exports, and creating more, better-paying jobs across the whole country. In chapter 7, we explain how the UK can create such jobs, improve the quality of work and fairer access to it, and support a better work–life balance. Chapters 8 and 9 propose new ways to strengthen business and markets. We propose wide-ranging reforms to corporate governance to create more purposeful companies focused on long-term success. And we set out reforms to create more open and competitive markets, including a new regulatory framework for the digital economy.

Chapter 10 proposes a boost to public investment alongside reforms to fiscal and monetary policy. Chapter 11 sets out new measures to improve financial stability. In chapter 12, we show how financial wealth, housing and company ownership can be more fairly shared. Chapter 13 describes our proposals to make the tax system for both individuals and businesses simpler and fairer.

The final chapters propose the measures needed to underpin an economy of prosperity and justice. We describe a new framework to put the economy onto an environmentally sustainable footing. And we propose a new 'economic constitution' for the UK, to shift economic power away from Westminster and widen participation and consultation in economic decision-making.

This is a long-term plan for the country, not for one parliament nor any single party. The economy belongs to all of us, and change is in our hands. We can have an economy where prosperity is joined with justice, if we have the courage to create it. In this report, we seek to show how.

PART I

BUILDING THE NEW ECONOMY

1

The Economy Today

How well is the UK economy doing? In the continuing arguments around the consequences of Brexit, it is sometimes hard to get a handle on what is actually happening. Forecasts may be wrong; short-term headlines can disguise long-term trends. Perhaps most of all, national-level statistics can never tell the full story of the real-life economy that ordinary people experience themselves.

Strengths and success stories

The UK economy – still the world's fifth largest[1] – possesses some impressive strengths. It has world-leading sectors characterised by extraordinary innovation, high productivity, strong exports, highly skilled jobs and good pay.

After the US, the UK is the most successful exporter of services in the world.[2] Our trade surplus in services is around £100 billion per year, or a little over 5 per cent of GDP.[3] Our country is home to the world's leading financial centre in the City of London, with Edinburgh another, and financial services are well distributed across the nations and regions of the UK. The financial sector employs 1.1 million people, generates a trade surplus of £51 billion and contributes £27.3 billion in tax revenues for the exchequer.[4]

We have leading positions in key areas of modern manufacturing. Our aerospace industry is the second largest in the world, accounting for more than 10 per cent of all UK exported goods.[5] It employs more than 90,000 people and has been an arena for cutting-edge innovation for more than a century. A more recent success has been the revival of the motor manufacturing industry, following a major restructuring after the financial crisis. Since 2009, annual automotive exports have more than doubled from £19 billion to £44 billion, making it the UK's largest goods exporting sector.[6] This is a remarkable turnaround for an industry that had been in steady decline since the 1970s.

The UK is a scientific superpower. Our life sciences sector has a turnover of £64 billion a year, employs a quarter of a million people nationwide, and accounts for more than 9 per cent of goods exports. It achieves higher levels of productivity than its competitors in the US and Germany.[7] The vibrant tech start-up ecosystem in London has developed world-leading collaborations with other sectors, from finance to fashion to pharmaceuticals. Home to more than 300,000 developers, London attracted £2.2 billion of tech investment in 2016, more than Paris, Berlin and Amsterdam combined.[8] Job creation in the digital sector is twice the pace of other fields, and across the UK it contributes £97 billion to the economy.[9]

Our creative industries have thrived in recent decades. Now worth nearly £100 billion, they employ nearly 2 million people, and have grown at twice the rate of the economy as a whole since 2010.[10] Creative industries exports are worth over £21 billion, split evenly between the EU and the rest of the world.[11] As the pace of technological change accelerates, and the capacity to think and act creatively increases in importance, our creative industries are promoting capabilities that will be crucial in the twenty-first century.[12]

The broader picture

These successes speak to the UK's continuing economic strengths. But despite them, it is hard to disguise the fact that the overall performance of the UK economy over the last decade has not been good.

This period starts with the financial crash of 2007–8. The crash revealed that the previous decade of apparently strong growth had been built on weaker foundations than had been understood at the time. It led to the deepest recession since the Second World War, with output falling by 4.2 per cent in 2009 alone.[13] Since then, the UK has seen its slowest recovery after any recession in the postwar period, with GDP (gross domestic product) taking more than five years to recover its pre-recession peak.[14] In fact, once population growth is taken into account (and subtracting income flowing between the UK and other countries), disposable income per head only returned to its pre-crisis level at the end of 2016, creating almost a 'lost decade' of economic output.[15]

Since 2013, the economy has grown at around 2 per cent a year.[16] But in 2018 the Office for Budget Responsibility (OBR) expects UK growth to be just 1.5 per cent, and in 2019 1.3 per cent.[17] Among developed economies only Japan and Italy are expected to grow more slowly.[18] All this comes after a decade of large and unprecedented policy interventions: fiscal 'austerity' (spending cuts and tax rises), near-zero interest rates, and a £445 billion programme of monetary stimulus, so-called 'quantitative easing' or QE.[19]

Indeed, behind the figures for growth the picture looks even more worrying. Across a whole range of economic indicators, the UK economy exhibits serious underlying weaknesses. On investment, research and development, trade and productivity, we perform worse than most of our European neighbours – and have done so not merely over the last ten years, but for much of the last 40.[20] As we discuss in more detail in chapter 3, it is hard to say the UK economy has been performing well.

The lived economy

The economy that ordinary households experience, however, is not that of national aggregates such as GDP. What most people observe is more direct: they see their own individual and family incomes, the ways in which jobs and job opportunities are changing, and the sense of prosperity or decline in their local community. Looked at from this perspective, for many people the economy does not appear to be working at all.

Earnings and incomes

For most people, the last decade has seen little or no improvement in living standards. In 2018, average (median) earnings remain 2–3 per cent below their level in 2007–8; indeed, they are not much higher than as far back as 2002.[21] And they show little sign of rising significantly in the future. In fact, average (median) earnings are not forecast to recover to their 2008 level until 2025.[22]

If the forecasts up to 2020 are correct, the 2010s will be the weakest decade for average real earnings in 200 years.[23] The UK is one of only five developed countries where earnings are still below their 2007 level.[24]

This has happened *despite* economic growth. Over the last decade, the UK economy has undergone a remarkable change: average weekly earnings have 'decoupled' from GDP growth (see figure 1.1). Whereas in the past, average earnings by and large tracked growth, since 2008 this has no longer been true. The country has been getting richer, but most people in work are no better off.

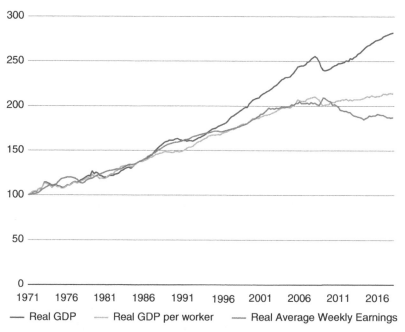

Figure 1.1 Average weekly earnings have decoupled from GDP growth for the first time since comparable data has been available

Real GDP, real GDP per worker and real average weekly earnings Q1 1971 to Q1 2018 (Index: Q1 1971 = 100)

Source: IPPR analysis using ONS (2018)[25]

Note: The official average weekly earnings (AWE) series does not go back before 2000. AWE prior to 2000 has been derived from imputed ONS data on a like-for-like comparison to the modern series. All AWE data has been converted to real terms using an RPI index.

The experience of the last ten years exacerbates a story stretching back over many decades. Over the last 40 years, half of the UK's population has barely shared in the growth of the economy at all (see figure 1.2). Between 1979 and 2012, only 10 per cent of overall income growth went to the bottom 50 per cent of the income distribution, and the bottom third gained almost nothing. Meanwhile, the richest 10 per cent took almost 40 per cent of the total.[26] Under

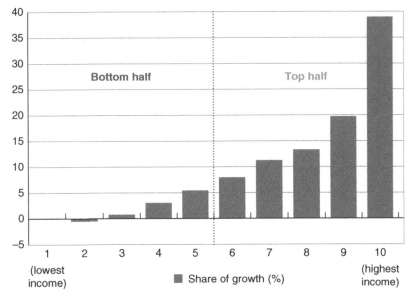

Figure 1.2 **The pre-tax, pre-benefit incomes of the poorest half of the population have barely benefited from overall economic growth**
Share (%) of the growth in real original household incomes among economically active households between 1979 and 2012, by income decile

Source: Reproduced with permission of Oxford University Press from Bailey D, Cowling K and Tomlinson P (2015) *New perspectives on industrial policy for a modern Britain*, figure 4.1, © Oxford University Press.

Note: 'Original incomes' are defined as incomes prior to any taxes or benefits

successive governments, the gains from growth have been very unequally shared.

One of the consequences has been a long-term decline in the share of national income which has gone to wages and salaries. In the mid-1970s the Bank of England calculates that the 'labour share' of national income was almost 70 per cent; today it is around 55 per cent (see figure 1.3).[27] The other side of this coin has been the rising share of income going to the owners of capital, as the returns on financial and real estate assets have consistently outpaced the rate of economic growth.[28]

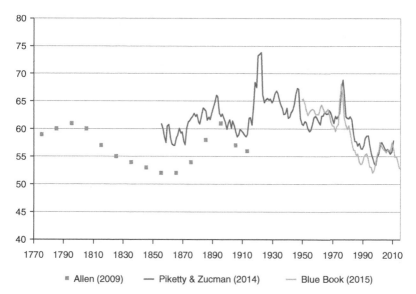

Figure 1.3 The labour share of national income is in long-term decline
The UK labour share of income (%) since 1770

Source: Haldane (2015)[29]

Note: Self-employed labour income is imputed differently in each series due to data availability

Employment

The UK economy has been good at generating jobs. Employment is at its highest rate since records began, with 75.6 per cent of the working-age population now in work. At 4.2 per cent, unemployment is at its lowest level for 40 years.[30] But high employment levels disguise important changes in the nature of work. A proportion of people enjoy high-quality jobs, with good salaries and working conditions. But increasingly large numbers have found themselves in poor and precarious jobs on low pay.

The UK has a much higher level of part-time work than in most other developed economies, and surveys indicate that as much as

8 per cent of the workforce is now under-employed: that is, wanting to work more hours than they do.[31] Self-employment has risen to around 15 per cent of the workforce, or 4.8 million people.[32] For some, this reflects an active choice for improved flexibility or entrepreneurship. But it is clear that many others have been forced into a form of 'bogus self-employment', driven by businesses seeking to take advantage of a more flexible workforce and minimise social security liabilities.[33] Almost a million people are now on 'zero hours contracts', which provide little or no security at all.[34] Many of those working in such casualised conditions experience the kind of exploitation, ill-health and stress which was once thought to have been consigned to the nineteenth century.[35]

Poverty and inequality

Partly as a result of these changed patterns of employment, low-paid work has become more prevalent. Having a job used to be a reliable route out of poverty. But the rise in low-paid work means that this is no longer the case. After taking housing costs into account, more people in poverty now live in working households than in non-working ones.[36] Overall, 14 million people (22 per cent of the population) live on incomes below the poverty line after housing costs; this includes four million children, or nearly one in three, and the number is rising.[37] As the significant growth of homelessness and use of food banks attests, poverty has made life desperately hard for very large numbers of people.[38]

Combined, these trends have left the UK one of the most unequal of western European countries. On some measures, income inequality has declined a little in the last few years, as a result of the reduction in top incomes after the financial crisis, and the rising minimum wage.

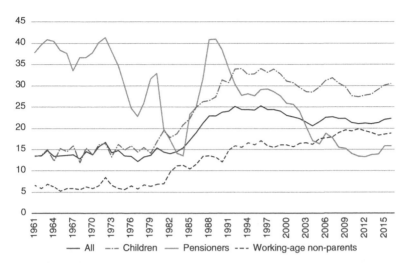

Figure 1.4 Nearly one in three children are living in poverty and the rate is rising

Relative poverty rates (%, after housing costs) since 1961: overall and by demographic group (Great Britain)

Source: Cribb, Norris Keiller and Waters (2018)[39]

Note: The relative poverty line is defined as 60% of median income after housing costs in each year. Years refer to calendar years up to and including 1992 and to financial years from 1993–4 onwards. 'Working-age non-parents' is shorthand for adults of working age who are not living in the same household as any of their dependent children. Calculations using the Family Expenditure Survey and Family Resources Survey, various years.

But there remains a six-fold difference between the incomes of the top 20 per cent of households and those of the bottom 20 per cent. This makes the UK the fifth most unequal country in Europe.[40] Inequality between the richest 1 per cent and the rest of UK society continues to rise.[41]

Inequalities extend beyond income groups. Although falling, the gender pay gap has remained stubbornly higher in the UK than the European average; median hourly pay among women is 18.4 per cent lower than for men.[42] A similar pay gap exists between white and black, Asian and minority ethnic (BAME) workers, while unemployment rates among BAME groups are almost double those for the white population.[43]

Inequalities of wealth

Inequalities of wealth, meanwhile, are even larger than those of income. Forty-four per cent of the UK's wealth is owned by just 10 per cent of the population, five times the total wealth held by the poorest half,[44] while the richest 1 per cent are estimated to own 14 per cent of the nation's wealth.[45] By contrast, 15 per cent of adults have no or negative wealth (that is, they owe more than they own).[46] Inequalities of income and wealth have particular impact on both social mobility and health: in the poorest areas of the UK, people live on average a startling ten years less than those living in the richest areas.[47]

There is a sharply intergenerational aspect to wealth inequality. The huge growth in property values since the early 1990s, coupled with the decline in final salary pensions, have made older generations successively wealthier than younger ones at the same age: young people are now set to be poorer than their parents. The housing divide is stark: millennial families (those born between 1980 and 2000) are only half as likely to own their own home by the age of 30 as were the 'baby boomer' generation born in the 20 years after the Second World War, and four times more likely to be renting privately. On average, a quarter of millennials' income is now spent on housing.[48]

The geographical divide

If the UK has become divided by age, it is also divided by geography. Median incomes in the North West, North East, West Midlands, Wales and the South West are now more than 30 per cent lower than in London and the South East; in Scotland, more than 20 per cent.[49] In London, the UK has the richest region in northern Europe, yet the stark fact is that we also have six of the ten poorest regions, making the UK the continent's most geographically unbalanced economy.[50]

These disparities in income have made the experience of the last decade very different in different parts of the country. Many of the UK's older industrialised and coastal towns have seen a palpable decline in their local economies, with few good jobs available, high rates of unemployment and many people dropping out of economic activity altogether. As once-thriving high streets have emptied of shops and life, it is not hard to see why so many people believe that the economy is not working.

Rethinking the economy

For the Commission, the economy experienced by so many people today does not look just. Too many are struggling to make ends meet, seeing their living standards stagnate or even fall; too few are able to look forward to the future with hope. Most of the trends we have described are not getting better, and in some cases they are getting worse.

Our conclusion is that we need to re-evaluate what our economy is for, and in whose interest it is working. Our economy's thriving sectors are vitally important. But islands of prosperity in a sea of injustice is not good enough. We need to rethink what we consider a successful economy to be.

2

Prosperity and Justice:
A New Vision for the Economy

In the last chapter we saw that, across a range of issues, the economy is no longer working for many people and for many parts of the country. This raises a profound question about what we want our economy to do. What should count as economic success?

From the end of the Second World War to a decade ago, this was not a difficult question to answer. As GDP rose, most people's incomes rose with it. Up to around 1980, it was also true that as GDP rose, inequality declined. As growth created jobs, poverty fell.[1] So the steady growth of national income seemed like a pretty reliable measure of economic success.

But this can't be said any more. As we saw in the last chapter, since the financial crisis GDP growth has not led to higher incomes for a majority of the population, and average living standards have stagnated even as growth has been restored. In a sea of injustice, a rising tide no longer lifts all boats.

In this chapter, we offer a new way to think about what we want and need from the economy, and what that means for economic policymaking.

Redefining prosperity

When we think about what makes us better off, it is natural to focus on income. Many of the things that make our lives better need to be bought, and higher incomes enable us to consume more. Yet such a statement reveals its own limitations. We all know that the things we consume are not enough to make us happy or give us a sense of a fulfilled and flourishing life. Income is very important, particularly for those whose incomes are relatively low. But job security and satisfaction, health, personal and family relationships, and social goods such as the levels of crime and trust in society matter too. Their absence can outweigh increases in income in determining an individual's sense of overall wellbeing.[2] It is widely assumed that if individual incomes are rising, society must be getting better off. But this is not how most people actually think, either about their own lives or what it means for society as a whole to prosper.

Our relationship to the economy is more than simply our income. Though every pound allows the same amount of consumption, it matters how our incomes are acquired. Our place in the economy is important to us. Receiving unemployment benefit is not the same as earning a wage: being unemployed deeply undermines most people's sense of self-worth and happiness.[3] And an income from a job with little or no security – increasingly experienced in today's economy – confers much less wellbeing on most people than the same income from secure work. People whose jobs allow autonomy to make decisions, opportunities to learn and develop, and a say over how work is organised and decisions are made, are consistently happier than those who do not enjoy these things.[4] Mental ill-health derived from work-related stress has been rising inexorably in recent years.[5]

What it means to prosper goes well beyond our income and our work. For most of us, leading a flourishing life means having time to love and care for our children and our parents, to enjoy leisure activities and personal development with our friends and family, and to serve and contribute to our communities. Over recent years, many people's working hours have risen, and many report that they have risen too far.[6] Many women in particular (as well as some, but far fewer, men) face a constant battle to juggle work and family responsibilities, draining their wellbeing. So household incomes alone are not a sufficient measure of 'the good life'. If we are to increase society's prosperity, we need to pay attention to the quality of work and work–life balance too.

At the same time, many of the goods we need to flourish, and by which we judge society's prosperity as a whole, are not consumed individually. They are public goods, which we pay for through our taxes and achieve through public institutions or policies. Some, such as education and healthcare, are experienced as benefits to the individual. But most are 'social goods', which we experience together with others as members of society. Public safety and security, clean air and beautiful natural environments, public parks and spaces, arts and culture, the sense of belonging to a community – these are all important contributors to individual wellbeing, but can only be enjoyed if we pay for and secure them collectively.

A prosperous society values the 'common good' – those features of our collective life that matter for us all.[7] These include the quality of our democracy and public discourse, the trust we have in one another and in institutions, the fairness and social cohesion of communities, our scientific and cultural achievements, and the conservation both of those aspects of the natural environments we directly experience, and those (such as rare species) we may not. We *do* tend to think there is such a thing as society, that it can be in a better or worse condition, and this affects how we feel ourselves. It is a striking fact that countries where these factors are perceived to be better are also those where individuals report themselves to be happier.[8]

Contrary to the assumption of most political debate, disposable household income is therefore not the sole measure of our individual prosperity. If we have a high income, but taxes are low and public goods correspondingly poor, we may be worse off than if higher taxes give us less disposable income, but better public goods. Indeed, there is strong evidence that such a trade-off does indeed raise wellbeing. The countries with the highest tax rates in the world – the Nordic countries of Denmark, Sweden, Norway, Finland and Iceland – consistently top international surveys of subjective wellbeing and life satisfaction.[9] Higher taxes bring better quality public and social goods and greater levels of social cohesion, and the trust which goes with them. Taxation is thus a contributor to our prosperity, not a drain on it. Politicians and commentators frequently argue that we should pay as little tax as possible – not as much as is necessary. We believe we need to shift the public debate on taxation to focus on the common good it can build, rather than solely the burden it imposes.

We must also recognise a deeper source of our prosperity. All economies are dependent on the natural environment. Natural resources and systems provide our materials and energy, absorb our wastes, and provide the critical services on which human society relies, such as ecosystem balance and climatic regulation.[10] Yet this 'natural capital' is now undergoing severe degradation and depletion, on a global and national scale. From climate change to the pollution of the oceans by plastics, from the loss of fish stocks to the extinction of species, from urban air pollution to water scarcity: the impacts of our current forms of economic growth are undermining the foundations of wealth creation, both now and in the future.[11] So it is impossible to understand prosperity today without considering the sustainability of the natural environment on which it rests.

In all these ways we need to change the way we think about, measure and judge economic success so that it reflects what we value as well as what we earn.

Defining economic justice

Prosperity alone is not enough. For an economy to be successful, it must be broadly shared.

The concept of justice provides a moral foundation common to every human society, one that is strongly and intuitively felt.[12] A 'sense of fair play' is an important cultural value in this country and an idea with a significant role in our public discourse. Yet public debate tends to interpret it too narrowly, as the fair application of rules. We believe it needs to be understood more broadly and applied to the economic sphere. We offer our own definition of economic justice – the fairness with which the economy generates prosperity and distributes its rewards.

First, in any advanced economy, economic justice must mean no-one living in absolute poverty. It is not morally acceptable in a country as rich as the UK for people to go without the basic goods and services required for a decent life, including a home. While there are different definitions of absolute poverty in the UK today, and different calculations of the level of income required to escape it, there must be a social minimum below which no-one should be allowed to fall. It is evident that far too many people are currently below it.[13]

Second, economic justice requires that everyone should be treated with dignity in their economic life. Citizenship does not stop when people enter the workplace. Exploitation through very low wages or forced labour, inhuman and unsafe working conditions, degrading treatment – whether at work or (for example) in accessing welfare benefits – are all aspects of injustice, and should never be acceptable.

Third, no group in society should be systematically or institutionally excluded from economic reward. The large gender and race pay gaps which characterise our economy, and the discrimination and exclusion widely experienced by women, ethnic minorities, people with disabilities and others, are evidence of structural injustice – the unfair outcomes of the gendered and discriminatory way in which economic life and institutions are currently organised.[14]

Fourth, economic justice means narrowing inequalities of wealth, income and power over time. In today's highly unequal society, there is little need to ask what level of equality or inequality is the 'right' one. We can be confident that the current distribution of income and wealth has little basis in merit or desert. This means the gains of economic growth should be biased towards the bottom half of the income distribution, leading to a progressive decline in overall income and wealth inequality.

Fifth, economic justice means that no places should be left behind. The inequalities of income and opportunity between the richest areas of the country and the poorest have grown far too wide. Too many places experience widespread deprivation; in those where few school students go to university or even do A-levels, disadvantaged communities are being locked into poverty in the future.[15]

Sixth, economic justice means looking after the future as well as the present. Today, our environmental impacts place the welfare of future generations at risk. So sustainable development – based on the moral principle that those coming after us should have the same opportunity to use and to benefit from natural resources as we do – is central to justice as well as prosperity.[16]

Sustainability is also about justice between different groups of people in society today. Those suffering the worst impacts of environmental degradation are the poorest people and communities in the world.[17] In most cases, they have contributed the least to the environmental degradation they experience. It is *our* consumption, in rich countries such as the UK, which is the primary cause of global climate change, plastics pollution and land degradation. And the richer we are, the more that is true. Reducing our environmental footprint is a moral obligation in the present as well as in the future.

This speaks to a wider truth. Our economy does not end at our borders. We buy goods from across the world, many of them from poor countries where wages are very low and working conditions are sometimes appalling. The use of child and forced labour, shocking working conditions and rampant pollution should force us to take responsibility for the distant impacts of our spending.[18] A just economy upholds fair trade, decent working conditions and human rights wherever it reaches.

On none of these dimensions can the UK economy today be said to be securing economic justice. But these principles are not simply a means to judge the economy we have. They are a guide to building the economy we want.

A fairer economy is a stronger economy

Economic justice is a moral imperative. But it also has important economic implications. For there is now a great deal of evidence that a fairer economy will also generate greater prosperity.

It used to be thought that the opposite was true: that inequality was the inevitable price of economic growth.[19] To generate growth, risk-taking entrepreneurs and owners of capital had to be rewarded sufficiently to incentivise them to invest and innovate. Those with the scarcest skills would command the greatest incomes, commensurate with their contribution to the productive process. As the wealth produced was circulated throughout the economy, it would 'trickle down' through the income distribution, enabling everyone to become better off. But the gap between rich and poor would inevitably be large. Indeed, attempts to reduce it through redistribution of income would almost certainly, it was thought, retard the process of growth. Both taxing the well off and giving welfare benefits to the poor would reduce their incentives to work.

But these arguments are now outdated. Over the last decade, a new body of research, led by both the Organisation for Economic Co-operation and Development (OECD) and the International Monetary Fund (IMF), has found that economies with more equal distributions of income and wealth tend to have stronger and more stable paths of economic growth than those with greater inequality. At the same time, redistribution either helps growth, or has little effect on it.[20]

There are several different reasons for this. First, people on low incomes tend to spend a larger fraction of their income than the wealthy, who are more likely to save. So improving the earnings of those in the bottom half of the income distribution is a much surer way to raise consumption and aggregate demand, and so boost growth. (This is particularly the case in today's conditions of excess global savings, when there is little need to incentivise the rich to save in order to create funds for investment.[21])

Second, inequality of income and opportunity prevent some people from achieving their full potential, including their potential to contribute to the economy. Low educational achievement and skills, discrimination in the labour market and the difficulties of working in the absence of adequate child and social care all tend to hold the economy back.[22]

Third, low wages damage productivity. This relationship is often thought to be the other way around: that only higher productivity allows for higher pay. But the reverse is the case too. When employers can get extra output by taking on a 'flexible' low-paid worker by the hour, they have little incentive to invest in the equipment or skills which will raise productivity. When wages rise, for example through a higher minimum wage, firms are forced to find new and more productive ways of organising work and training employees in order to afford the higher pay.[23]

Fourth, inequality tends to make economies more unstable, as the higher savings of the rich are channelled into financial and real estate assets prone to volatility. More unequal economies tend statistically to have shorter periods of growth.[24]

Fifth, more equal societies tend to have higher taxes, which if spent on public goods – such as education, health, transport and other infrastructure – help boost the economy's productive potential. At the same time, inequality generates a variety of social ills, including poor health outcomes, which drive up public spending costs.[25]

There is now, in fact, a great deal of evidence on the social effects of inequality.[26] It is not just that it slows growth. It also makes people unhappier. In cross-country studies, high levels of inequality are correlated with higher rates of mental and physical ill-health, obesity and crime, and lower recorded social trust, educational attainment and social mobility – and this is true not just for those on low incomes, but across the population as a whole. More equal societies are happier societies.

It is not difficult to see why this should be. We are social beings: our happiness is less a function of absolute income than of our income relative to those to whom we relate in our society.[27] Inequality therefore fuels dissatisfaction; and in turn it drives rising levels of household debt, as consumption becomes a means to belong in a society where material riches are on constant and competitive display. And high debt levels make individuals and households – and the economy as a whole – less resilient to shocks.

The empirical evidence does not show that unequal societies are poorer than equal ones. Some countries have high GDP levels with high levels of inequality, such as the UK or the US; others are prosperous with low levels of inequality, such as Denmark or Sweden.[28] But it does show that unequal economies do less well than they would if they were more equal. It is in this sense that justice is a strategy for prosperity too. A fairer economy will be a stronger one.

Hard-wiring for economic justice

The belief that high levels of inequality were inevitable did not mean that they could not be reduced. It has been widely accepted that society should seek a measure of redistribution from those at the top to households at the lower end of the income scale, accomplished through the tax and benefit system.

Yet redistribution is no longer sufficient to ameliorate the deep inequalities that now characterise our economy. While redistribution will always be essential, it is also, in one sense, a measure of failure. The more it is needed, the more unfair the economy must be in the first place.

If the core processes of income and wealth distribution within the economy are generating widening inequalities, taxes and benefits can only ever play catch-up. Inequality today results from the structure of the labour market, the system of executive pay, the ownership of assets and the increasing returns which accrue to the owners of capital. So it is on these issues that policy has to focus, not just on tax and welfare measures 'after the fact'. If we are to make the economy fairer, we need to stop regarding inequality as an afterthought, and focus on its causes in the structures of the economy.[29] Economic justice needs to be 'hard-wired' into the processes of production and consumption. In this report we seek to show how this can be done.

Sustainable and inclusive growth

Our argument, then, is that the purpose of the economy – and of economic policymaking – should be to achieve prosperity and justice together, and to ground them both in environmental sustainability. We are not the first to argue this. The concepts of 'sustainable development' and 'sustainable and inclusive growth' speak to similar ideals and have been widely adopted by governments and leading economic international institutions such as the OECD and World Bank.[30] But it has been harder to get them adopted in practice.

Some have argued against growth as a goal. The green movement has offered a powerful critique of growth, arguing both that it is the primary source of environmental degradation and that it does not contribute to human wellbeing.[31] Some have argued for a 'post-growth' economy, which would meet environmental limits while still allowing poor countries to become richer.[32]

There is no question that current patterns of economic growth are not environmentally sustainable. And, as we have argued, for rich countries, rising material consumption in itself is not an automatic source of either individual or social wellbeing. But we do not believe this means that economic growth is itself undesirable. It depends on the form it takes.

Growth is measured by an increase in GDP. It is a measure of economic value and income, not of the flows of resources and energy through the economy. Through changes to technologies, outputs and lifestyles, it is possible to generate higher income while reducing material flows and environmental impacts.[33] No-one should underestimate the efforts that will be required to achieve such 'green growth', and it will ultimately be an empirical question as to how far it is possible on a global scale. But the constraints of environmental limits do not make the aim of rising incomes redundant, particularly for those who currently have least. Our goal is a different pattern of production and consumption, which can achieve prosperity and justice in a sustainable form.

Measuring what matters

If we are to achieve this, we need to change the way that the economy is measured. It is now a commonplace argument that GDP alone is not a good measure of economic progress.[34] It does not take environmental damage into account; nor does it recognise unpaid work, such as caring, housework and volunteering. It does not measure wellbeing. It does not now even correlate with earnings. Yet GDP growth continues to be used as the primary measure of how well our economy is doing.

GDP growth will always be important. It is a measure of national output and income; it was never intended to be a measure of either wellbeing or progress.[35] So it needs to be complemented with other measures (and updated), not discarded.[36]

Over recent years there have in fact been many attempts to develop new indicators which can measure economic performance in a broader way. In the UK, the Office for National Statistics (ONS) publishes a collection of indicators of 'national wellbeing', including a variety of economic, social and environmental factors and subjective wellbeing surveys.[37] The OECD'S Better Life Index offers a way of comparing such indicators between countries.[38] But it is striking how little these get used in national economic debate. So we can see great merit in developing a more focused set of indicators that speak more closely to people's experience of the economy as well as its overall performance.[39]

A new vision for the economy

The economy should give expression to our values, not be the place that we leave them behind. Although now largely overlooked, Adam Smith's 'Theory of Moral Sentiments' was the ethical foundation upon which he built 'The Wealth of Nations'.[40] Putting the economy back on a moral footing is not just a matter of morality. It will create a stronger economy too.

We believe that broadly-defined prosperity and economic justice can and should be the basis for a new economic consensus. Successful change demands a destination to guide its direction. So we have written down our vision of the kind of economy we believe our society should be aiming for. Critics will no doubt say that such a vision is utopian. But there is no reason why we cannot build an economy like this if we have the will. And the first step is to have the ambition to do so.

The good economy[41]

Our vision is of a good economy, where prosperity is joined with justice. The good economy works for all by achieving sustainable growth and broadly shared prosperity. In the good economy, everyone – in all parts of the country – has an equally good chance of leading a good life. It allows each of us to flourish: to fulfil our economic and human potential, no matter our starting point, and to meet our needs at each stage of life. This means opportunities for good and fulfilling work; a decent income providing good living standards; and time for love, leisure, creativity and care and service to others. The good economy values people for who they are as much as what they do. It is judged not only by its results but also by the conduct of those within it, and is concerned with reciprocity, generosity and kindness. It offers hope for the future by fulfilling the promise that successive generations will have the opportunity to lead better lives.

The good economy is concerned with building the common good as well as with improving individual living standards. It meets our human and economic needs for education throughout life; for high-quality health and social care; for affordable housing and transport; for a diverse culture and vibrant democracy; and for beauty and safety in our shared spaces as well as in our private ones. The good economy ensures that our commons are well tended: valuing our natural inheritance and being good stewards for future generations by diminishing the impact of economic activity on the earth's climate and resources.

3

Reshaping the Economy

It is evident that today's economy is delivering neither prosperity nor justice, as we illustrated in chapter 1. In chapter 2 we described the kind of economy we wish to see. In this chapter we look at some of the underlying causes of the UK's poor economic performance, many of which are longstanding weaknesses. We propose five shifts that we believe now need to be made, both to the way that the economy is structured, and in the approach that governments take to economic policy, to set it on a different path. In the Commission's interim report, we argued that the UK has an 'economic muddle', rather than a coherent economic model.[1] Here, we describe the way in which the economy needs to be reshaped to achieve both prosperity and justice.

From short-term finance to investment-led growth

The UK has an unbalanced model of growth. The Office for Budget Responsibility (OBR) estimates that, in 2017, household consumption drove nine-tenths of the entire (2 per cent) growth of the economy.[2] But it is investment, rather than consumption, that is the real economic engine, driving both productivity and long-term income growth.

Consumption-led growth has been financed by increasing household debt, which has been rising since 2016 and is forecast to reach 146 per cent of disposable income by 2023 (see figure 3.1).[3] Savings are at record lows.[4] The Bank of England has already warned of the risk this poses to financial stability.[5] At the same time, consumption has become heavily reliant on rising property values, which have allowed households to borrow and spend more.[6] As a result, house price inflation has come to be regarded in the UK as a positive economic good rather than a problem. Given its impact on inequality, not least the way it has forced young people to spend increasing proportions of their income on rent (and therefore less in the rest of the economy), this is not a healthy basis for economic growth.

In fact, the UK has a serious investment problem. At around 17 per cent of GDP, the rate of public and private investment in the UK

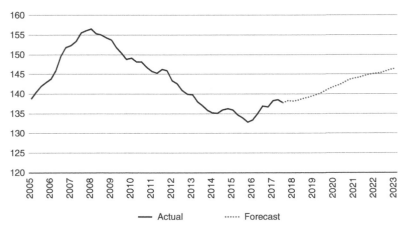

Figure 3.1 Household debt is lower than its pre-crisis peak but is rising once again
Household gross debt as a percentage of disposable income (%), actual and forecast
Source: Office for Budget Responsibility (2018)[7]

economy is around 4 per cent below the OECD average.[8] This gap has widened over the last 50 years; indeed, the UK investment rate has been falling for most of the last 30 (see figure 3.2).[9] A similar gap exists for private sector investment alone: business investment fell from 10 per cent of GDP in 1997 to 9 per cent in 2017 – below the rate of capital depreciation, meaning that the stock of business capital is actually falling.[10] The comparable rate of corporate investment in the US in 2016 was 20 per cent.[11]

The UK's record of investment in research and development (R&D) is an area of particular concern. R&D is the engine of innovation: it drives long-run productivity improvement and keeps the economy at the frontier of globally competitive sectors. Over the last 20 years, as a proportion of GDP, UK spending on public and private R&D has

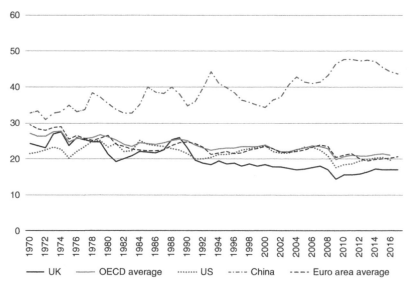

Figure 3.2 Investment is lower in the UK than in most other comparable economies, and has been declining for the last 30 years
Gross fixed capital formation as a percentage of GDP (%), UK, China, US, and euro area and OECD averages, 1970–2017
Source: World Bank (2018)[12]

remained more or less flat, while those of our major competitors has risen.[13] In 2016 the UK invested 1.7 per cent of GDP in R&D, compared to 2.9 per cent in Germany, 2.7 per cent in the US, and 3.1 per cent in Japan.[14] Some of the gap can be accounted for by the UK's proportionately larger service sector, but not all – and, given the importance of R&D and innovation to overall economic performance, that is little consolation.[15]

The causes of under-investment

What explains this poor investment record? Three key causes have become apparent.

The first is the reduction in the time horizons of corporate shareholders, the phenomenon known as 'short-termism'. Over the past 20 years or so, the UK's capital markets have increasingly prioritised short-term over long-term returns.[16] As the Bank of England has shown, this has had a measurable cost in terms of profitable long-term investments which have not been undertaken.[17]

A major reason for this change lies in the structure of shareholdings. Between 2000 and 2016, the percentage of the market value of UK shares held by individuals, insurance funds and pension funds – those with a direct interest in long-term investment – fell from 55 to 20 per cent.[18] They have largely been replaced by overseas investors and various kinds of intermediary funds, whose managers tend to be rewarded on the basis of short-term stock market performance relative to one another, rather than on long-term value creation by the companies in which they trade.[19]

Companies have responded by focusing on short-term investment returns and guaranteed dividend payments. Executives are incentivised by their remuneration packages to keep share prices high.

The result is that the distribution of dividends to shareholders by UK companies over the last decade has remained largely constant even as profits have fluctuated.[20] The rise of 'share buybacks' reflects the priority given to sustaining share prices.[21] As the proportion of profit distributed to shareholders has risen (from 39 to 55 per cent between 1990 and 2016), the level of long-term corporate investment has inevitably declined.[22]

At the same time, while the UK has succeeded in attracting foreign investment, our permissive takeover rules have allowed shareholders to sell a string of long-established UK businesses to overseas buyers over recent decades – in some cases primarily to extract their value for short-term gain rather than add to it through long-term investment.[23]

A second cause of low investment is that banks in the UK have a poor record of providing finance for businesses. Business loans account for only around 5 per cent of total UK bank assets, around a third of the proportion typical in the eurozone.[24] In contrast, UK banks are much more focused on lending for land and property, the bulk of which does not increase the productive capacity of the economy or contribute to growth, but simply raises asset prices.[25] Their business models – highly centralised operating models in a heavily consolidated sector – tend them towards secured rather than relationship-based lending, a trend compounded by recent regulatory pressure to reduce risk.[26] UK banks are unusually focused on real estate as collateral, which limits the ability of many firms to grow and ignores the potential to value other, more intangible assets.[27]

Third, demand has been too weak. Companies invest when they believe it will be profitable. But this requires demand for the additional goods and services that it generates. Since the financial crisis, the UK has suffered from chronically deficient demand, as businesses have held back on investment, and exports have been weak.[28] Yet during this period, government has cut back not just on current but also invest-ment spending, reducing the current budget deficit by around 6.5 per cent of GDP between 2010 and 2018.[29] This pro-cyclical approach has exacerbated weakness in private sector demand, thus further under-mining investment. Since all saving and borrowing in the economy must balance, it is no surprise that household debt has risen. Public investment – notably in infrastructure and R&D – has continued to be lower than in other advanced economies.[30]

Breaking the cycle

This unbalanced pattern of demand – too little private and public investment, too few exports, too much debt-fuelled consumption – is one of the reasons why the UK has not yet escaped the abnormal policy conditions set in train by the financial crisis. The Bank of England has signalled its desire to raise interest rates from their current historic lows, but has so far been unable to do so significantly; quantitative easing remains in place.[31] The economy is too weak to remove these sources of life-support. This is the condition sometimes described as 'secular stagnation': persistently deficient demand and excessive cor-porate saving mean that normal rates of economic growth can only be sustained at very low or negative interest rates.[32]

Breaking out of this cycle will require a new focus on 'investment-led growth'.[33] In turn, this will involve three sets of reforms, which we set out in more detail in part II. First, we need to change the way large companies are governed and their executives are paid. We need more purposeful companies focused on long-term value creation, not short-term returns, and executive pay incentivised to achieve it. Second, we need a finance sector geared more towards the long term. This will require reforms to the regulation of banks, to focus them less on lending for real estate and more for business growth; changes to the fiduciary duties of intermediary investment funds; and reform of the takeover rules to reduce the risk of acquisitions aimed at value extraction. Third, we will need to raise the level of public investment, particularly in research and development and in infrastructure, where there is a shortage of 'patient capital' willing to take long-term risks.

This will not be an easy transition to make. It means a slower rate of household consumption growth, and a higher rate of savings, not least for pensions (though in the long term, higher savings are good for people as well as for business). But there are other countries that have built their economies on investment-led growth and achieve more of the goals that we aspire to, such as Germany, Switzerland, Denmark and Sweden. We will need to do likewise.

From trade deficits to 'new industrialisation'

As we described in chapter 1, we have a handful of sectors where the UK is world-leading. These include financial and professional services, life sciences, aerospace and automotive manufacturing. These sectors are successful at exporting around the world.

By definition, our most successful sectors have flourished under the status quo. As a result, they are particularly exposed to the consequences of the change in our economic relationships as a result of the decision to leave the European Union. A good Brexit deal will therefore be essential if we are to secure our existing economic strengths. At the time of writing, the UK's future trading arrangements with the EU – and indeed the rest of the world – remain unclear. But it is evident that we will need to secure trade deals that enable us to access European and global markets as widely and freely as possible.

Future trade agreements

As a member of the European Union (EU) for more than 40 years, the UK has incorporated the EU's regulatory framework covering labour, consumer and environmental standards into its trading relationships.

At the time of writing it is not clear whether the UK will still be in a customs union with the EU after Brexit, and therefore whether we will be making new free trade agreements (FTAs) with other countries. But if we do, it is important that the negotiation of FTAs, particularly with larger, more powerful trading partners, does not lead to an undesirable reduction in standards. Any new trade agreements must also ensure that the UK can maintain control of public services and public enterprises as decided by democratically elected governments.

Transparency around trade negotiations is key to addressing these concerns. Greater public transparency would allow citizens to engage with trade negotiations, and to debate their implications.[34] Greater scrutiny via parliamentary processes would serve to bring any potential welfare loss through signing up to a trade deal into the light.[35] Both forms of transparency should be actively promoted by the government in the event that the UK directs its own trade policy following Brexit.

Not paying our way in the world

While we have some high productivity sectors that successfully export goods and services, we do not have nearly enough of them. Overall, the UK buys far more from the rest of the world than we sell to it. Our trade deficit in goods is around 7 per cent of GDP, outweighing the surplus of around 5 per cent of GDP in services. Our overall trade deficit has been negative for 20 years, and in 15 of those years has exceeded 1.5 per cent of GDP (see figure 3.3). In 2017, the UK recorded the largest current account deficit as a percentage of GDP of all G7 countries.[36] This indicates a serious problem of competitiveness relative to other developed economies.

The UK is able to finance the deficit on its current account (which comprises trade in goods and services and other forms of international income) with a surplus on its financial account. This is made up of capital flows (including both long-term foreign direct investment and short-term purchases of shares and bonds) to and from

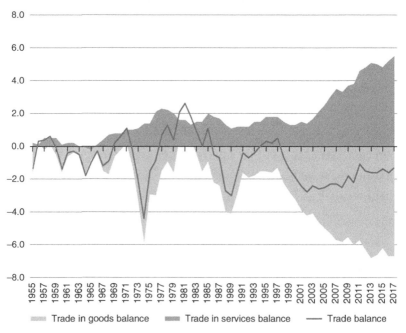

Trade in goods balance   Trade in services balance   —— Trade balance

Figure 3.3 The UK trade deficit has grown significantly since the late 1990s
Trade balance, trade in goods balance and trade in services balance (% GDP), 1955–2017
Source: ONS (2017)[37]

the UK. So long as there is demand for UK assets, the current account can continue to be financed in this way.[38] However, if the value of UK businesses and their perceived future growth prospects were to decline – with foreign lenders demanding higher returns to hold UK assets – the value of sterling would fall and the current account would have to adjust, at least in the short term, with a reduction in imports and a decline in consumption and living standards. This would pose real recessionary risks. The large current account deficit therefore makes the UK especially vulnerable to a weakening in domestic economic conditions.

The depreciation of sterling since the EU referendum is a reflection of such concerns. Yet although it has raised import prices, it can in many ways be seen as a welcome correction of a currency that had become overvalued. Throughout the past three decades the pound has been sustained at levels that have both reflected and supported the success of the UK's financial sector. The effect on the rest of the economy has arguably constituted a kind of 'financial Dutch disease', with UK exports made too expensive compared with those of our competitors, and imports too cheap.[39]

In turn, this has both driven, and exacerbated, the decline of manufacturing, which has gone much further in the UK than in most other developed countries. Manufacturing now makes up just 10 per cent of the economy's gross value added (GVA), compared with 23 per cent in Germany, 21 per cent in Japan and 12 per cent in the US.[40] Manufacturing has often been dismissed as part of Britain's industrial heritage but not an important part of our future. The UK, it is said, should focus on our existing strengths in services, our 'comparative advantage'. Yet the most successful trading countries, such as Germany and Japan, are also the most diversified in their export base. The UK's exports, by contrast, have become systematically less diversified over the last 20 years, and are now disproportionately dependent on a small number of industries, particularly financial services.[41]

Diversifying our exports

Improving our competitive position with the rest of the world will therefore be crucial to sustaining the UK's prosperity over the coming years. This will require a new approach to industrial strategy.

Until recently, the UK's industrial strategy was largely implicit rather than explicit. Each of the UK's most successful sectors enjoyed considerable government assistance. Government and NHS spending supported our defence industries and life sciences; the BBC underpinned many of our creative industries. The financial sector benefited from new regulatory rules and was then bailed out in the financial crisis. As a result, industrial policy reinforced existing strengths in already successful sectors able to make their voices heard in government.[42] Many of these sectors are predominantly located in London and the South East.

Over the last ten years, industrial strategy has become an explicit focus of government, which we strongly welcome. But if we are to succeed in a globally competitive economy, it needs to have a much clearer emphasis on diversification of our innovation-frontier and export sectors, which are closely linked. We can no longer rely only on existing strengths.

The key characteristic on which to focus is tradability, rather than on manufacturing or services. That distinction is increasingly breaking down – as any modern car reveals, advanced manufacturing is now as much about sophisticated software as hardware. Yet this will still entail a greater focus on manufacturing in the future than in the recent past, because more manufactured goods are tradable than services.[43]

And it is possible to be both strong in services and in manufacturing. Switzerland, for example, has a successful financial sector while manufacturing accounts for 18 per cent of GDP, almost double that of the UK.[44] And the breadth of its manufacturing sector is striking: from high-quality chocolate through precision engineering to advanced pharmaceuticals.

Building industrial clusters across the country

The crucial question is how to achieve this improvement in our exports. We propose a strategy we call 'new industrialisation'. By this we mean the development of innovation-based industrial clusters across the UK, anchored around our universities.

It has been known for some time now that the clustering of industry in specific places is associated with higher levels of competitiveness and growth. Proximity spreads know-how and fosters innovation.[45] Yet the UK has relatively few large-scale industrial clusters. We have major strengths in software, electronics and biotechnology in Cambridge, health and life sciences in London and Manchester, the automotive industry in the West Midlands, advanced manufacturing in Sheffield, oil and gas in Aberdeen, among others. But the potential of university research departments to catalyse industrial growth in general has been under-utilised. International experience – in the US, Japan, EU and elsewhere – shows that proactive policies to develop and support industrial clusters can significantly increase the collaboration between firms, and lead to stronger regional growth.[46] Since our universities are not only internationally competitive but geographically dispersed, this can be a strategy for justice as well as prosperity, with the potential to create more, and better-paying, jobs right across the country.

The development of clusters means focusing on domestic supply chains as well as innovation-based exporters. Today, UK exports across a whole range of sectors have a much higher proportion of imported components than our major international competitors.[47] By strengthening the 'value chains' which link firms both within and across sectors, a greater proportion of value added can be retained in the UK and in local economies.

Building on the strengths of our universities also means focusing on the commercialisation of research and the scaling of companies. We are unusually good at discovery and invention, but poor at building large firms. While the UK has among the highest proportion of start-up firms in the OECD, comparatively few survive to maturity, and many are sold before becoming major businesses.[48] Many fail because they cannot bridge the commercialisation funding gap often known as the 'valley of death'.[49] Productivity is closely related to scale: larger firms tend to be more productive than smaller ones, as they are able to capture more scale economies.[50] But the greatest differential in productivity is between domestically focused firms and those that export.[51] We therefore need a much sharper focus on scaling up businesses to succeed as exporters, and making sure that these are distributed across the whole country. It is for this reason that we propose the establishment of a National Investment Bank, with strong regional divisions: the private financial system is not providing the patient capital needed to create new world-leading firms.[52]

From flexible labour markets to raising productivity in the 'everyday economy'

The productivity of the UK economy is much lower than that of our major competitors. Measured by output per hour, productivity in the

UK is fully 13 per cent below the G7 average.[53] This gap is sometimes stated in the form that 'it takes the average British worker five days to produce what a worker in Germany, France or the US produces in four'. But this is misleading: it is not to do with how hard people work, but rather is a result of a much lower level of investment – in physical and human capital, in management and production systems, and in the creation and diffusion of technology across sectors – compared with other leading economies.[54] Since the financial crisis, productivity growth in the UK has more or less stalled altogether. This is a stark divergence from the long-running trend (see figure 3.4), and it has occurred across almost all sectors. The UK's poor productivity is a problem for both prosperity and justice. It holds back growth and holds down wages.

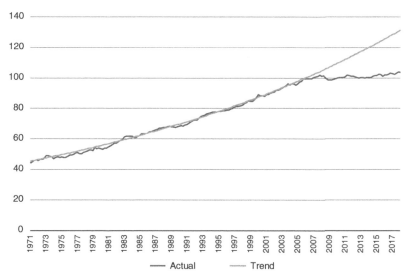

Figure 3.4 UK productivity growth has stalled since the 2007–2008 financial crisis
UK output per hour (actual versus long-term trend), Q1 1971–Q1 2018 (Index: 2013 = 100)
Source: IPPR analysis using Office for National Statistics (2018)[55]

What explains this poor record on productivity? It is not that leading British firms are less productive than their competitors overseas. It is that we have a 'long tail' of low-productivity firms.[56] The UK has a small proportion of businesses with high productivity, of over £100,000 per worker; and a very much larger number earning under £50,000 per worker.[57] This dispersion is considerably greater in the UK than in other OECD countries.[58] The 'long tail' of low-productivity businesses is particularly marked geographically. There are high- and low-productivity firms in every area of the country; but on average productivity is much higher in London and the South East than elsewhere.[59] This is partly because of the different sectors that predominate in different regional economies, but that is not the whole explanation: there is wide geographical divergence in productivity even between firms in the same sectors.[60]

The problem within firms

The UK's productivity problem has a number of causes. Some relate to general economic conditions such as the level of demand in the economy, competition and planning policy, the education and skills systems, and infrastructure. It is clear, for example, that the extraordinary skewing of infrastructure spending towards London – which over the next five years is due to get more transport spending than the rest of England put together – contributes to the UK's unbalanced regional productivity performance.[61]

A key causal factor also appears to lie at the level of individual firms. Here the UK suffers from three interrelated problems.

The first is persistently poor management capability. Many British businesses appear to be less well managed than those in other advanced economies, and there is a clear correlation between poor management and low productivity.[62] While the UK has a small number of top-tier business schools, we do not offer business education or management training at anything like the scale of many comparable countries. The problem is particularly acute in middle management tiers, where there are few qualifications that command the respect of employers.

Second, the UK lags behind European leaders on the uptake of digital technology, from basic websites to internet trading and cloud computing.[63] Whereas frontier firms are innovation makers, the vast majority of firms are 'innovation takers'. It is the adoption of innovations by ordinary firms – capital equipment, software and production techniques created by frontier firms – that raises productivity in most of the economy, and the pace of innovation diffusion which therefore determines the overall productivity rate. In turn the UK's problems come from the stalling of diffusion, not the stifling of innovation.[64] The CBI estimates that adopting existing good practice more widely across the economy could be worth £100 billion to UK GVA.[65]

Third, businesses fail to make use of the skills that people already have. It is often remarked that the UK has a skills problem, but this is generally thought to be one of insufficient supply of appropriately skilled workers. In fact, the deficiency lies as much in the *demand* for skills.[66] Many British businesses are not organising their workforces in a way that maximises the productivity of the workers they currently have, and they do not seek to employ enough workers with higher skills. A recent cross-European study estimates that one-third of adult employees in the UK, over five million people, are over-qualified for their job, the highest proportion in the EU.[67]

The low-wage, low-productivity equilibrium

Another key cause of low productivity lies in our labour market. The World Economic Forum ranks the UK eighth of 140 countries in terms of labour market flexibility.[68] It is now possible for an employer to take on a worker with almost no attached responsibilities on the employer's part, or rights for the worker, at all. It is notable that the development of the 'gig economy' and other forms of casualised work has occurred much faster and further in the UK than in many other developed countries.[69]

It is this flexibility that largely explains the simultaneous occurrence of high employment levels and largely stagnant wages.[70] Most economists would expect low unemployment rates to lead to rising earnings, as relatively scarce workers are able to bid up their pay.[71] But workers in flexible labour markets have little bargaining power. This has been made worse by the decline in the membership of trade unions. Only one in four workers is a union member today, compared with half of the workforce in 1979. In the 1970s more than 70 per cent of workers were covered by collective bargaining agreements; today it is just 26 per cent.[72] It is little surprise that working conditions have deteriorated so far.

The result is that too much of the economy has settled into a low-wage, low-productivity equilibrium. Flexible working conditions cut employers' costs. But they also too often reduce productivity. While wage rises will come from higher productivity, the reverse is also true: higher wages prompt improvements in productivity. When workers are cheap, firms have little incentive to invest in new technology or innovate in workplace organisation: it is simpler to meet additional demand with more labour.[73] In this way, low wages have become a cause of our productivity problem as well as a result of it.

Raising productivity in the everyday economy

If we are to raise productivity, therefore, we need to escape from the idea that wage costs must be as low as possible. The low-wage, low-productivity equilibrium is found particularly in sectors such as retail and wholesale, hospitality and tourism, food and drink and social care, where large numbers of people work. Many of them are women, and many work in highly flexible or casualised conditions. It is in these often-neglected sectors – what we call the 'everyday economy' – that productivity policy needs to focus.[74]

Once upon a time, it might have been enough to focus simply on productivity in leading sectors, since this would translate into higher wages everywhere else. Leading firms would set wage levels in the local labour market and, in turn, higher paid workers would boost consumption, recycling the productivity gains to the wider community. But today these transmission mechanisms no longer work. High pay in banks in Canary Wharf does not pull up the wages of shop workers in Tower Hamlets: high productivity firms require a different set of workers, with highly specialised skills. In effect, there are multiple labour markets in a single place, not a single labour market in any given place.[75] Since the propensity to consume falls as income rises, over time a smaller proportion of the gains are recycled in the local economy through consumption. So focusing on the productivity of leading firms is unlikely to raise wages for everyone else. If wages are to be raised, it is imperative to improve the productivity of the everyday economy.

This will require a number of different approaches, which we explore further in part II. First, we need to focus industrial strategy as much on the everyday economy as on the frontier sectors, which has not been done before. This means helping improve management capacity, encouraging the adoption of new technologies, and improving both the demand for and supply of skills. Second, we need to regulate the labour market better, raising the minimum wage, giving workers more rights and strengthening their enforcement, and making it more expensive for employers to use casualised labour. Third, we need to strengthen the bargaining power of workers to enable them to negotiate for higher pay. This means making it easier for unions to gain access to workers and increasing the coverage of collective bargaining agreements. Companies cannot pay wages that are not earned: the ability of unions and management to negotiate productivity improvements must lie at the heart of this process.

From technology laggards to managed automation

Of all the new technologies remaking our world, it is the rapid advance of artificial intelligence (AI) which raises the most profound questions. AI describes a broad range of computing techniques that allow machines to infer appropriate solutions to problems on the basis of external inputs. Traditionally, machines had to be given a fully specified set of commands, describing exactly what actions needed to be performed at every step. With AI, computers are increasingly able to solve problems, and 'learn', independently. This is already leading to software and robots able to perform tasks that were previously reserved for people.[76]

The prospect of AI and other advanced forms of automation has led to apocalyptic predictions that a large number of jobs will soon disappear, leading to mass unemployment.[77] Yet automation is not new: it is a process that has occurred for over 200 years. In that time many jobs have disappeared, but many more have been created. The impact of automation will be more complex than is sometimes suggested.

It is in fact rarely whole jobs that can be automated. Rather, it is specific activities that different jobs involve. Activities that have high potential for automation are those which involve processing or collecting data, performing routine manual work or operating machinery in a predictable environment. By contrast, those involving interfacing with people, applying expertise to decision-making, planning, creative tasks and managing and developing people have low automation potential.[78] In an analysis of more than 2,000 work activities across more than 800 occupations, the McKinsey Global Institute estimates that fewer than 5 per cent of all occupations could be automated entirely. But about 60 per cent of occupations have at least 30 per cent of constituent activities that could be automated with currently available technologies.[79] In general, lower-waged and lower-skilled occupations have higher automation potential, but all occupations have some activities that could be automated.[80]

The application of automating technologies is consequently likely to change the character of most jobs rather than destroying them, in the same way it has done in the past. Routine and data-processing activities will increasingly be carried out by machines and software, while the non-machine-replicable 'human' aspects of work – caring, cognitive, decision-making, creative and managerial roles – will become more important. As human labour and machines increasingly complement one another, this could raise the skill level (and likely satisfaction) of jobs that are partially automated. Conversely, these trends could increase the number of low-quality jobs, particularly if labour costs remain low; as long as many low-skilled jobs continue to be paid very low wages, automation will remain unattractive for many firms. Though automating technologies will offer significant performance benefits for many businesses, many will remain underutilised by those which are not sufficiently capitalised or innovative to adopt them.

The number of people employed in occupations that undergo some degree of automation may still decline, in some cases steeply. But the impact of automation on jobs in the economy as a whole is not certain. The historical experience is that a whole series of effects occur simultaneously.[81] In some sectors, the number of jobs will undergo drastic reduction, as the demand for the things they produce does not keep pace with productivity improvement, as was the case with the decline in agricultural employment in the twentieth century. In others, technological advances will combine with rising demand to increase employment, notably in the health and care sector. In general, rising productivity from automation raises incomes and makes goods cheaper, leading to higher demand for goods and services throughout the economy – and therefore raising employment in the sectors producing them.

At the same time, technological advances generate new products altogether, while employment is also raised in the sectors producing the automation technologies themselves – as the huge growth of jobs in software and information technologies over recent decades demonstrates. Historically, the net effect of these various dynamics has tended to be positive rather than negative, with the overall level of demand in the economy a crucial determinant. The way in which automation plays out over the next few decades cannot be known, but it will not simply mean a loss of jobs.

Automation and inequality

In fact, the greater risk from automation is of rising inequality. The effects of automation are likely to be uneven across the skills distribution. In the last wave of automation, the substitution of routine tasks with computers predominantly replaced middle-skill and middle-wage jobs. By contrast, high-skilled workers were complemented by computers rather than substituted, helping to increase their productivity and driving up their wages. This led to a form of 'wage polarisation', in which the highly skilled pulled away from low-skilled workers whose wages were held down by technological change.[82]

Analyses to date suggest that jobs at the low-skill end of the labour market have the greatest potential to be replaced by automation. It is estimated that, in the UK, jobs paying less than £30,000 are five times more susceptible to being automated than jobs paid over £100,000.[83] This also means wages for high-skill jobs are likely to increase relative to lower-skill ones. Moreover, higher-skilled individuals are better equipped to adapt their skills to changing circumstances, and thus to find ways to complement the capabilities of AI. Individuals lower down the skills distribution often have skill-sets and qualifications that are less adaptable. They will therefore find it harder to find new work.[84] This means there is a risk of increasing wage inequality, and exacerbating geographic, gender and ethnic inequalities, as high-skill roles are concentrated in London and other cities, and dominated by men and particular ethnic groups.[85]

Automation is also likely to drive a falling share of national income going to labour relative to capital. Technological change is estimated to have caused at least half the decline in the labour share in advanced economies in the last four decades.[86] This has been driven by a combination of rapid progress in information and telecommunication technologies, and a high share of occupations that could easily be automated; and the trend is expected to accelerate.[87] In the UK, IPPR analysis suggests that the value of earnings associated with occupations that could feasibly be automated is £290 billion – a third of all wages and earnings from labour.[88] Automation would see a proportion of this flowing to capital instead. Unless capital ownership can come to be more broadly distributed than now, this will heighten inequality and bear down on the living standards of the large majority who rely on work as their main source of income.

In this way the major challenge presented by automation will be the need to redress the distribution of the dividends from technological change, not the redundancy of human labour. And this is more than a matter of equity alone: for the economy to continue to function well, it will be vital to ensure the proceeds are recirculated to sustain demand. Managed poorly, automation could create a 'paradox of plenty': society would be far richer in aggregate, but, for many individuals and communities, technological change could reinforce inequalities of power and reward.[89]

Managed automation

For the UK, the prospects of automation present something of a paradox. We are the world's fourth leading nation for artificial intelligence start-ups, behind only the US, China and Israel.[90] We have world-leading research in robotics and other digital technologies. And yet we lag behind most other advanced economies in the uptake of these technologies. The problem is not that we are being taken over by robots; it is that we do not have enough of them. The UK currently has 71 installed robots per 10,000 manufacturing sector employees, below the world average of 74, and far behind other European countries, including Germany, France, Italy, Spain, Sweden and Denmark.[91] Our international competitors are accelerating their investment in robotics, and we risk falling further behind from a weak starting position.

If we are to promote prosperity and justice together, we need to boost productivity, and that means accelerating the diffusion and adoption of automating technologies. But at the same time, we have to ensure that the benefits are fairly shared.

We therefore propose an approach of 'managed automation'. Four policy directions will be required, which we discuss further in part II. First, industrial strategy needs to promote faster diffusion of automating technologies across sectors and regions, encouraging and supporting firms in their take-up. Second, this must be joined with measures to protect workers (rather than currently defined jobs) by ensuring people are re-skilled, re-trained and re-employed in the new economy. This will require the establishment of new social partnerships at both firm and sector levels to manage automation, as Sweden has done.[92] Automation agreements between businesses and unions can ensure, not just that new technologies are adopted, but that the workforce shares in the rewards of the productivity improvements that result. Third, where workers are displaced, we propose the creation of a new fund to provide training and employment support. Fourth, to ensure that the economic gains do not flow simply to a narrow group of capital owners, but are recirculated in the economy, we propose new measures to broaden capital ownership in the economy, and for appropriate levels of business taxation.

From market power to open markets

Open and competitive markets drive businesses to innovate, to become more productive and to serve their customers better. They are good for the economy, and many British companies operate successfully in competitive global markets. Yet over recent decades policymakers in the UK and globally have become complacent about the degree of market concentration and the consequences of rising market power.

New research from the IMF shows that mark-ups – the amount added to the price of goods and services to cover overheads and profits – have increased by an average of 39 per cent since 1980 across advanced countries (see figure 3.5). High mark-ups are a signal of market power, and they are correlated with other indicators of market power such as profits or industry concentration.[93] At first, both investment and innovation increase as mark-ups rise. But over time, as markets become more concentrated, the rates of both begin to fall. Firms have lower incentives for both capital investment and for R&D

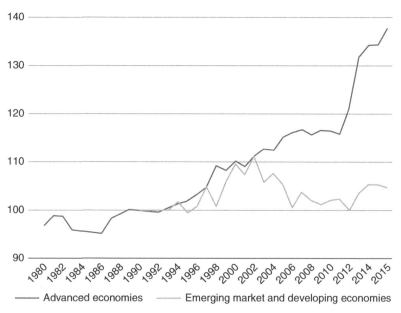

Advanced economies   Emerging market and developing economies

Figure 3.5 Mark-ups – a proxy for market power – have been rising in advanced economies since the 1980s
Average mark-ups of listed firms in each country income group
(Index: 1990 = 100)
Source: Díez, Leigh and Tambunlertchai (2018)[94]

as their market position strengthens.[95] And falling capital investment and innovation have a negative impact on productivity.[96] At the same time, as market power increases, the share of revenues that go to their employees' wages falls.[97] Market concentration is therefore a clear problem for both prosperity and justice.

In the UK today, eight out of ten of the major consumer markets are highly concentrated.[98] Six energy companies share 82 per cent of the retail energy market.[99] Four supermarkets have 69 per cent of the grocery trade.[100] Five banks have 85 per cent of retail bank accounts.[101] Four mobile phone providers have 89 per cent of customers.[102] Elsewhere, the 'big four' accountancy firms audit 96 per cent of the top 250 UK companies,[103] while the collapse of construction company Carillion in early 2018 highlighted market concentration in public outsourcing. A very small number of companies deliver a very high proportion of all central and local government contracts to deliver public services.

The emergence of a small number of dominant firms within a sector can effectively close that sector to entrepreneurs, since new entrants by definition cannot capture scale economies in the same way as incumbents. This does not mean that no competition exists at all. Independent suppliers have gained a rapidly growing share of the energy market, and supermarkets have engaged in fierce price wars. But it does mean less innovation and choice, well illustrated in retail where UK high streets are amongst the most homogeneous in the world and surveys consistently report consumer dissatisfaction.[104] There is also widespread dissatisfaction with the major utilities, driven by their complex pricing structures and persistently poor customer service.[105]

Market concentration is a problem for suppliers too. Where there are not enough competing buyers, dominant firms can use their purchasing power to squeeze suppliers' prices. This has been a frequent cause of complaint among agricultural and other suppliers to the major supermarkets.[106] Though this can result in cheaper prices for consumers, it typically comes at the expense of the profit margins and viability of supplier firms, and the pay and conditions of their workers. Recent research in the United States has highlighted the problem of growing concentration in labour markets[107] and the threat to wages and job quality from 'monopsony' power.[108] These seem likely to be problems in the UK too, and merit further investigation.[109]

The digital economy

The most concentrated markets of all are in the digital sector. Google has approximately 70 per cent of the global search engine market;[110] Amazon has a market share across a number of product categories of 80 per cent;[111] Facebook has over 2 billion active users globally.[112] Between them, Google and Facebook now take more than 60 per cent of global advertising revenue.[113] While these companies are particularly dominant, the tendency towards monopoly exists across all the digital 'platforms' that connect online consumers and producers. This is due to the significant 'network effects', which benefit the early market leaders: a large network of users and their data is much more valuable than a smaller one.[114]

While dominant digital companies raise the usual problems of oligopoly in relation to their consumers and suppliers, they also pose more profound challenges. The data that is generated by dominant firms gives them access to market information that is not available to other market participants.[115] They are able to track and analyse both prices and volumes in ways that have not been possible before. In some cases, they can control who is able to access the market altogether. The digital economy has seen the emergence of firms that participate in the market, set its rules, and monitor the activities of other market participants. This is an unprecedented degree of power for a small number of firms.

Data in the twenty-first century is playing a similar role to electrical power in the late nineteenth and early twentieth century: it is driving radical changes in business models and step-change improvements in productivity. It is the creation of large datasets that generates value, not individual elements of data. The concentration of data collection is therefore giving the digital market leaders a vital advantage in the development of new technologies which depend on it, notably in artificial intelligence. A wave of corporate acquisitions by Google, Apple, Facebook and Amazon has not only increased their market dominance but positioned them at the leading edge of many new technologies.[116]

Excessively powerful firms can both invest in innovation and at the same time erect barriers to innovation by others. This has raised fears about over-concentration of innovation in the global economy: as data becomes an increasingly critical source of technological advance, it is almost certainly a constraint on innovation, and therefore growth, that so much of it is held in so few hands.[117]

The market valuations of some major technology firms cannot be justified by their present earnings.[118] The gap between current earnings and present valuation implies that the market expects such firms to be able to achieve 'supernormal' profits in the future, expectations that are encouraged by the leadership of the firms themselves. If financial markets and management teams both anticipate the establishment of dominant positions that enable rent extraction, it seems reasonable that regulators should be able to pre-empt this eventuality, rather than to wait until after the fact.

In all these cases the argument we make is not that dominant companies have failed to bring innovation, dynamism and growth to the economy. The evidence shows that they have. It is that as market power continues to rise, it reaches a tipping point where rates of both investment and innovation begin to fall.

A new approach to competition and data

For these reasons we argue for a new emphasis on 'open markets': those where new entrants can gain market share and incumbents can be challenged; where competition drives innovation and dominant market power is limited. We make proposals in two principal fields.

The first is competition policy. Today, the purpose of the Competition and Markets Authority – 'to promote competition ... for the benefit of consumers'[119] – emphasises outcomes of prices, quality and choice. It is agnostic about the structure and concentration of markets unless they can be proven to have detrimental effects on consumers. But few of the emerging issues we have identified can be addressed through the consumer welfare perspective.[120] Where internet search and social media, for example, operate on zero price models, such a framing provides few useful insights into their structure or functioning. It is questionable whether the interests of innovation or entrepreneurship, or the interests of suppliers or the labour market, can be adequately understood through the consumer lens. So it is time to design new regulatory frameworks that anticipate future challenges and are able to meet them.

We therefore need a new approach to competition policy with the objective of creating open markets that better promote investment, innovation and entrepreneurship. This should include a revival in the traditional tools for confronting excessive market power: rules proscribing price discrimination, so that all market participants have access to digital marketplaces on equal terms, and the prohibition of vertical integration, so that those who control the digital market do not also provide the goods and services sold within it. Given the emerging evidence on the impact of market power, there appears to be a good case for competition policy to seek to limit market concentration as an end in itself.

At the same time, we need a new approach to data that enables innovation to flourish. Given that data is created by us all, we believe that it should be thought of as a 'digital commonwealth', a common resource for entrepreneurs, citizens and government to draw on to create valuable services and products. We propose new measures to rethink the governance of data and the digital economy.

Conclusion

In each of these five ways, the UK economy needs to be reshaped if we are to achieve prosperity and justice together. And change must happen on a sufficient scale to achieve 'escape velocity' from the economy we have today to the one we need. In part II, we set out the specific sets of reforms that are required to implement this programme.

4

Partnership and Power

If we are to reshape the economy, we will need to make major changes to the way in which it is governed and managed. In this chapter, we describe the need to reimagine the role, function and structure of the state. We make the case for more effective partnerships at all levels in the economy to boost our economic performance. And we set out the common thread which runs through all our proposals – the rebalancing of economic power across the economy and society.

Reimagining the state

One of the most powerful economic ideas of recent decades has been that the state's role in the economy should be as limited as possible. It is widely agreed that governments should improve overall economic conditions: improving the 'supply side' by investing in infrastructure and skills, controlling inflation, and managing government deficits and debt. But until very recently, the dominant thinking was that the state should leave it to the private sector to generate growth. In the past 40 years, active fiscal policy to maintain aggregate demand and investment has been largely eschewed; and until recent years, successive governments have resisted the idea of industrial policy to guide and support business investment. 'Free markets' were said to generate the best outcomes for society as a whole, and governments' attempts to 'intervene' in them would result in inefficiency and failure.

If this view were ever tenable, we believe it is no longer. It misunderstands how markets work in modern economies, and the vital roles which only states can play. All markets today operate within a myriad of laws and regulations which constrain what firms and consumers can do. Company law, labour market law, consumer protections, environmental regulations, taxes, public services: all these help shape the behaviour of firms and consumers. It is misleading to talk about governments 'intervening' in markets, as if markets could somehow exist without them. The real question is always what policies governments should adopt, and how active or passive they should be. If we are to deal with the problems we face, we need now a much more active and purposeful state.

Market failure and systemic failure

In the dominant view, the rationale for government action is said to be when there is 'market failure'. Markets fail in well-established ways: for example, when there are environmental 'externalities' such as pollution; or in the under-supply of public goods such as scientific research or transport infrastructure. It is widely accepted in these circumstances that government should 'correct' these failures, for example by adopting environmental regulations or taxes, and investing in universities and roads. The concept of market failure generates important microeconomic policy solutions, focused on specific market problems.[1]

But this is too limited an understanding of market failure, and therefore of the role of the state. Modern economies also generate *systemic* failures, when the interaction of multiple markets has an adverse effect at the aggregate level of the macroeconomy.[2] The 2008 financial crisis was a particularly dramatic example. But many other systemic failures are also evident. It is clear today that private sector investment and demand are insufficient to sustain employment and output at normal interest rates. This is not simply the failure of individual markets, but of the aggregate impact of corporate and financial sector behaviour across the economy as a whole. The same is true of inequality, which is a function of the way income and wealth are distributed throughout the economy, not just in particular parts of it. Climate change and other forms of global environmental degradation provide another example – consequences of the core structures of modern economies dependent on fossil fuels, plastics and intensive agriculture.

These systemic failures require more than microeconomic policies in individual markets. They require governments to be concerned with the direction and outcomes of the economy as a whole. Governments need to take responsibility for the way the economy behaves in aggregate: for its overall financial stability, the aggregate level of demand and investment, its overall levels of inequality and environmental impact. If the state fails to do this, these systemic outcomes will effectively be determined by the unintended consequences of market forces, under no-one's control. That is neither democratic nor just, and it risks a badly under-performing economy. This is why we argue that the state needs to 'hard-wire' economic justice into the economy through policies on labour markets, wealth and corporate governance, among others. It is also why we argue for the introduction of a Sustainable Economy Act to define the environmental limits within which the economy must operate.

The co-creation of wealth

The crucial recognition here is that a more active role for the state – if intelligently performed – creates *better* outcomes for the private sector. Business investment and innovation depend on the expectation of demand and the management of risk and uncertainty. The state has played a central role in the success of each of our leading sectors. Financial services, aerospace, automotive, life sciences and the creative industries have benefited from an active state.[3] Whether through regulation, financial support, tax breaks, investment in universities, and even leading marketing efforts overseas, the state has been intimately involved in their success.

When private sector demand is insufficient, active fiscal policy – particularly public investment – needs to fill the gap. Far from 'crowding out' private investment (as proponents of the limited state suggest), public investment can 'crowd it in', taking on risks which the private sector may not.[4] This is why a more explicit and active form of industrial strategy has been revived by governments over recent years: it is an acknowledgement that the private sector alone may not invest sufficiently, or may not direct investment into the most advantageous fields or locations for the economy as a whole. We believe there are particular opportunities from the establishment of industrial strategy 'missions' to meet some of the great challenges society faces, such as environmental degradation and an ageing society.[5] Such public purposes offer a triple benefit: a focused driver for innovation, the creation of a stronger industrial base and a means of addressing crucial societal issues.

The state can provide stabilisation and stimulus in the economy, not only through the demand it generates directly and indirectly through government expenditure (its 'size'), but also through the predictability and coordination provided through its institutions (its 'scope'). In both cases, the state can help to give assurance against risk for the private sector, either through the predictability of (public) demand in the economy or through the predictability of the private investment environment.[6]

Private sector profitability relies on public goods. These are things which businesses cannot provide for themselves, such as infrastructure, education and skills, healthcare, childcare, social order and environmental protection. Wealth is not just created by the private sector and spent by the public sector. It is 'co-produced' by the activities of the private and public sectors together. Good businesses recognise the need to contribute through taxes, and value fair and sensible regulation. Some will always object to any taxes or regulation; it is easy to prefer others to pay. But it is in the nature of public goods that the benefits we all enjoy require us all to contribute.

Our argument, therefore, is that we need to move from the idea of a limited state to an 'active state'. This does not mean 'central planning' or 'state control'. Market forces will remain key determinants of overall economic outcomes. But the state needs to become more active in shaping and guiding the way in which the economy generates the systemic outcomes that affect us all.

We are not complacent about the ability of the state to do this. We need much smarter and more agile public institutions, which understand the dynamism of markets and the motivations of the private sector, and which are innovative and entrepreneurial. In general, we favour bodies at arm's-length or devolved from central government, which can develop expertise and cultures in their own fields: hence our support for a National Investment Bank, for example, and for English regional authorities or 'economic executives'. We are well aware that public institutions, like markets, can fail. But there is plenty of evidence from around the world that they can also succeed, if given renewed purpose. Government can and does attract talented and ambitious people: they need to be energised by seeing their potential to co-create public value, not merely manage and mitigate risk.

Decentralising the state

We noted in chapter 1 that the UK is the most geographically unbalanced economy in Europe. It is also one of the most centralised states in the developed world, and these things are connected.[7] Economic policymaking is simply too remote from many of the places where businesses are located and where people live and work. National government departments in Whitehall cannot possibly understand the assets and capabilities, nor the challenges and issues, of a country as large and diverse as the UK. Although Scotland, Wales and Northern Ireland have achieved a measure of devolution, only in Scotland does this encompass significant economic powers. And it is no coincidence that in the last decade Scotland has outperformed all regions except for London and the South East in terms of GVA per head.[8]

In economic terms England is ruled almost entirely from London: it has no regional tier of governance, as almost all other successful developed economies do, while the new programme of devolution to city-region mayors is as yet embryonic. The unfair distribution of infrastructure spending described in chapter 3 is a good example of how an unbalanced governance system generates unbalanced outcomes.[9]

In other countries, regional and local tiers of government, many with strong powers and independent fiscal resources, have played an important role in promoting economic development and more diversified economies.[10] The evidence strongly suggests that this is required in the UK too if we are to build a more geographically balanced and resilient economy. In chapter 3 we argued for the development of regionally dispersed industrial clusters as part of our proposal for a new industrialisation, and for higher public investment in both innovation and infrastructure. It is precisely because these key economic activities must be distributed right across the UK that we will need to devolve greater economic powers.

So we call for a new tier of regional economic executives in England, able to deploy significant assets and capabilities, alongside regional divisions of our proposed National Investment Bank. And we argue, too, for stronger economic powers in Scotland, Wales and Northern Ireland. Devolution is the necessary precondition for the state to be an effective partner to the private sector in the co-creation of wealth.

The partnership economy

Just as the state needs reform to be an effective partner for the private sector, greater partnership between different actors has the capacity to create value at every level of the economy. Change of the magnitude that we propose cannot be delivered by government alone, nor by business, trade unions or civil society acting in isolation either. It must come from each part of the economy working in partnership with others.

Businesses as partnerships

The most successful businesses know that their workers are not simply a resource to be hired and fired, but key partners in the productive process.[11] It is now widely recognised that employee engagement in decision-making is a major contributor to improved productivity and innovation, particularly as a more knowledge-based economy has placed a higher premium on human capital and skill.[12] For the Commission, companies are therefore best understood as 'communities of common interest', in a shared endeavour of long-term value creation and distribution. This means management and workers seeking to work with one another to raise productivity and ensure that the gains are fairly shared between profits and wages.

For the group that has the greatest long-term interest in the success of companies is the workforce. In the modern economy, employees typically have a longer-term relationship with their companies than either senior management or shareholders. Yet unlike in other European countries, most UK employees are excluded from representation on company boards and afforded almost no formal rights to information or involvement in decision-making.[13] We therefore propose the reform of corporate governance to include workers on company boards, as well as reforms to directors' duties to make the long-term success of a business their primary objective.

We also propose new measures to strengthen trade unions. Trade union membership in the UK is at a historic low, and significantly lower than many comparable economies.[14] Trade unions are vital both to secure better pay and conditions for workers, through greater collective bargaining (both at firm and sectoral level), and as a means to engage employees in productivity improvement. Crucially, these are mutually reinforcing: when employees are beneficiaries of the productivity gains, they are more likely to help deliver them. Moreover, engaged employees can themselves be the originators of workplace innovation – they are, after all, experts by experience. So unions can be a way to harness the energy and creativity of the workforce for improving their firms. Trade unions are also vital social institutions that help bring belonging to communities and purpose to work. As experience in Germany, Sweden and elsewhere amply demonstrates, businesses are made stronger by unions that work in partnership with them.[15]

Partnership between businesses

The UK has a peculiarly 'disorganised' economy, with lower membership of business organisations than comparable countries. For instance, whereas 50 per cent of US businesses are members of chambers of commerce, and 24 per cent of Japanese businesses, in the UK just 3.5 per cent of firms are members.[16] This is likely to be one of the explanations for the UK's lower productivity. Business associations have three important functions. They represent the interests of their members to the state, enabling sectors to make coherent requests of government for particular policy interventions. They act as mechanisms for the diffusion of innovation from one business to the other through the exchange of good practice and by creating greater fluidity between firms. And by building relationships, they create direct commercial opportunities for business-to-business commerce, and as a gateway for international trade. We need businesses that compete on price, quality and customer service, but collaborate to secure wider economic objectives, especially productivity improvement.

Partnership across the economy

The same logic applies to the economy as a whole. To reshape the economy in the ways we have set out, significant change will be required. It is only through partnership that such change can be successfully managed. This is particularly true of the challenge of automation, which risks significant social costs even as it benefits the economy in aggregate. The concept of 'social partnership' – familiar across Europe – expresses the idea that the economy does better when businesses, trade unions, the state and civil society work together for a common purpose.[17] It is a means for reconciling different interests – an arena for negotiation and compromise. The UK has some examples of social partnership institutions, such as the Low Pay Commission, and the Scottish Fair Work Convention. But there are no longer very many. We propose a social partnership model in each of the institutions we seek to create in this report, at both national and devolved levels.

The scale and scope of the changes we propose in this report will require a great national effort. If we conceive of the economy as a zero-sum game – where the sharp-elbowed get ahead and the rest get left behind – we will never achieve prosperity and justice together. We therefore argue for the creation of a national economic plan, drawn up by a new National Economic Council. Based on the principles of partnership and consultation, we argue that the Council should be the key mechanism to secure greater coordination between central government and the devolved nations and regions, and between government and business, trade unions and civil society. Partnership of this kind has sometimes been scorned in this country. We believe it to be essential if we are to transform our economy on the scale required.

Rebalancing power

A deeper thread runs through our proposals. If we are to build the economy we need, we have to rebalance the relationships of power which currently exist between different actors in the economy.

A major part of the sense of injustice that is so widely experienced across the UK today is the lack of control people feel they have, over both their own economic circumstances and those of the country as a whole. That sense of powerlessness reflects something real. Today the economy is characterised by concentrations and imbalances of power that are both a cause of some of our economy's problems and a barrier to their solution.

By power we mean the capacity to determine or shape the economic outcomes that affect people's lives, and that together define the character and direction of the economy as a whole. Power can be held by individual actors and institutions, or can emerge in the way economic arrangements and relationships generate particular outcomes.

In the UK economy today, we believe that power has in many areas swung too far towards some interests and institutions, and too far away from others. If we are to achieve prosperity and justice, these imbalances need to be redressed. While the precise nature of power varies in different areas of the economy, it is a helpful lens through which to understand both why the economy is now performing poorly and what kinds of changes are needed to help it perform better.

Within firms, too much power is concentrated in the hands of management, and too little is held by workers. Hierarchical governance models hold back productivity improvement and the spread of workplace innovation, and hold down wages and working conditions.[18] Across the economy, workers hold too little bargaining power in the labour market, as a result of weak rights and low trade union membership. This is clear from the simultaneous occurrence of stagnant wages and high employment. If both productivity and pay are to be increased, power will need to be rebalanced in significant ways from employers to workers. This will require stronger labour market regulation and strengthened trade unions.

In particular markets, too much power is held by a small number of dominant firms. This is true for large parts of the economy, from consumer markets and professional services firms to the new digital economy. The excessive power of dominant firms will need to be curbed if we are to have open and competitive markets that work in the interests of innovation, and for entrepreneurs, suppliers and workers as well as consumers.

In the finance sector, there is an imbalance of power between those with a long-term interest in long-term value creation, and those that benefit from short-term returns. As we discuss in chapter 11, the finance sector now charges more to the rest of the economy than it did half a century ago, despite extraordinary productivity improvements through innovation. There must be a rebalancing so that more of the productivity gains are passed on rather than retained. The interests of productive investment must be better served.

In policymaking, there is a major imbalance of power between Westminster and the devolved governments of Scotland, Wales and Northern Ireland, and the regions of England. Power must be rebalanced through the devolution of economic decision-making and investment, and economic policymaking at the national level must become more open, participative and inclusive.

For individuals and households, there is an imbalance of economic power between those that have the financial security and social and economic opportunity that comes with wealth, and those that do not. This must be redressed through new measures to give more people a share in the nation's wealth. In particular, the acute wealth inequality afflicting the younger generation must be addressed through a new approach to housing.

And across the economy as a whole, there is an imbalance of power between market forces and society. We need an economy in which markets serve society, not the other way around. So we need a more active and democratic state able to represent the community as a whole in shaping and guiding the economy towards better outcomes for all.

Power is not just the means to a better performing and fairer economy. It is as much about the purpose of the economy and what we mean by economic justice. Powerlessness is an affront to human dignity, which is why 'taking back control' has become such a potent political idea. We are citizens in the economy as well as in society.

5

Time for Change

To achieve prosperity and justice, the economy we have must be profoundly reshaped. Making that change happen will involve new ways of making economic policy and a rebalancing of economic power. In this chapter, we show why this is not just necessary but possible. Fundamental economic reform has been achieved before, and with sufficient political imagination it can happen again now.

The decade of disruption

In the past, in moments of economic and political upheaval, this country has often made a virtue of 'muddling through'. But that is not an option today. For in an era of profound change, doing nothing will not maintain the status quo: to attempt to stand still will be to fall back. The 2020s are set to be a 'decade of disruption', in which at least five major trends will reconfigure the economy in profound ways.[1]

The first is plainly Brexit. Leaving the EU represents a momentous change to the UK's economic governance and trading relationships, and few parts of the economy will be unaffected. Forty years of EU membership have left many UK businesses deeply embedded in the complex supply chains of the single market. Changes to these, and to the regulatory frameworks which underpin them, will inevitably lead to uncertainty and disruption. Whatever happens, the UK economy will need to be as strong and resilient as possible if it is to thrive. Our structural weaknesses made change necessary before Brexit; they will make it all the more important afterwards.

Second, globalisation continues to shift the weight of international production and consumption east and south.[2] As the urban middle class in Asia and Africa expands, a third of all global trade in 2030 is likely to be between emerging markets, more than double their share today.[3] China and other emerging economies are moving up the value chain, capturing a larger share of global trade in high-end goods and services at the expense of the traditionally advanced countries.[4] Where once sophisticated R&D would be carried out in the developed world and simpler manufacturing assembly in developing countries, this will no longer hold true. These trends emphasise the need for the new industrialisation we call for. If we do not improve our international competitiveness, we risk only further deterioration in our trade position.

Third, we are living through a major demographic change. By 2030, the UK population is projected to reach around 70 million, exceeding that of France.[5] We will be more diverse, and we will be older: over a fifth of the population – more than 15 million people – will be aged over 65. While the working-age population (aged 16–64) will increase by just 1.4 per cent, the number over 75 will increase by more than a third.[6] The ratio of the working to non-working population will therefore decline.[7] As society ages, pressures on health and social care, the state pension and other old-age benefits will rise. Unless the overall level of taxation is raised, revenues will not keep pace, leaving a growing 'fiscal gap'.[8]

This demographic shift is likely to lead to continuing high levels of demand for immigration; it will maintain pressures to raise the pension age still further; and widen the shortfall in private pension provision.[9] If we do not raise productivity – and ensure the fruits of automation are shared – we will be unable to pay for the public services on which society depends. At the same time, we need a new framework for immigration to secure economic success.

Fourth, as we discuss in chapter 3, the new wave of technological change we are now experiencing has significant implications for patterns of work and the ways in which wealth is produced. We need to manage the process of automation to ensure that its impacts on employment are mitigated and its propensity to increase inequality is addressed. Given the importance of data in the new economy, the concentration of market power among the major platform companies has serious implications for future innovation and growth.[10] So we must urgently update our regulatory frameworks to keep markets open.

Finally, as we have noted, environmental degradation is reaching critical global and local thresholds across a number of fields, including climate change, air and ocean pollution and global biodiversity loss. We can no longer treat environmental protection as a luxury or policy afterthought. Without urgent action both nationally and globally, we risk a wave of catastrophic change.[11] So we must find ways to bring economic activity within environmental limits and to embed sustainability into the way the economy works.

In an era of extraordinary change, our economy cannot stay the same.

Fundamental reform has happened before

Any call for 'fundamental reform' may sound unrealistic: perhaps desirable, but not achievable. But it has happened before. Twice in the last century, a major economic crisis led to a significant reappraisal of how the economy works, and to a subsequent large-scale change in economic policy. There are considerable parallels with the conditions we face today.[12]

The first of these 'paradigm shifts' occurred in the 1940s. Prior to the Wall Street Crash of 1929, economic policy was largely built on classical ideas of 'laissez faire'. Markets operated efficiently without government intervention; unemployment was the consequence of wages being too high; and currency devaluation could restore competitiveness. The Crash and the Great Depression that followed it discredited this approach. John Maynard Keynes showed that cutting wages in a slump merely exacerbated it; that government spending was needed to restore aggregate demand and to give investors confidence in future growth; and that devaluation simply led to 'beggar-thy-neighbour' responses by other countries.

After the Second World War, Keynesian ideas formed the basis for a new economic settlement, focused on maintaining full employment, directing investment through nationalised industries, and building a welfare state of collective social provision in housing, health, education and social security. Internationally, a new system of international coordination was established through the 'Bretton Woods' institutions. Different countries (and different political parties) took different approaches to this programme, but the broad contours of what became known as the 'postwar consensus' were largely accepted across the developed world, and across the political spectrum, for around 30 years.[13]

The postwar settlement eventually broke down too. In the early 1970s, the US ended the Bretton Woods system of fixed exchange rates, the oil exporting countries dramatically raised oil prices, and the subsequent phenomenon of 'stagflation' (simultaneous unemployment and inflation) appeared to undermine the Keynesian economic ortho-doxy. The UK economy of the 1970s struggled with a series of structural weaknesses, including the sclerotic state of much of British industry and poor industrial relations. The Thatcher Government in the UK and the Reagan Administration in the US created a new economic settle-ment drawing on the free market ideas of Friedrich Hayek and Milton Friedman.[14]

Governments withdrew from fiscal demand management, nation-alised industries and public services were privatised, the finance sector was deregulated and trade union rights rolled back. While most European countries did not adopt this programme in full, ele-ments of what became known as the 'neoliberal' approach were widely influential, on both right and left, and have shaped much of economic policy in the developed world for the last 30 years.[15] With some important variations, the main tenets of this new consensus were accepted by successive governments until the financial crisis hit in 2008–9.[16]

So major 'paradigm shifts' in economic thinking and policy have happened in the past, and they have led to transformative changes in the shape and structure of the UK economy. Of course, no era is the same as another. But it is striking that the new economic settlements of the 1940s and 1980s were established around ten years after the preceding settlements broke down. Today, a decade on from the financial crisis of 2007–8, there are good grounds for arguing that we are at a comparable moment. It is not just that the economy is failing in the multiple ways we have outlined. It is that the ideas and policies that governments have been using to get us out of the crisis have not been working. It is precisely because we have achieved change of this magnitude before that we believe it is possible to do so again.

Other countries show change is possible

One of the characteristics of public debate about the economy in recent years has been a remarkable degree of fatalism. People have come to believe that 'there is no alternative'. But we know this is not so. Other countries have economies with very different characteristics from ours, and many of them perform considerably better.

Germany has a much larger manufacturing sector than the UK; it also has a state investment bank, mandatory workers on company boards, and a 'social partnership' approach to economic management. The Scandinavian countries have high-income economies with far greater shares of public spending and taxation, and much lower levels of inequality. In Sweden this comes with high levels of trade union membership and collective bargaining; Denmark has pioneered green economic policy; Finland combines a focus on high-tech exports with improving the quality of work and work–life balance. France and Japan have both moved to stronger regional government. The United States has a large and sophisticated government machinery for supporting technological innovation.

The UK is not the same as any of these countries, and we start from a different place, both economically and politically. So we cannot simply copy other economies. But we can learn from them; and most of all we can recognise that there is nothing inevitable about the kind of economy which we have today. It can be different.

We are by no means the only ones attempting to rethink how advanced economies best function. Indeed, we have been struck by the extent to which mainstream economic institutions are reassessing previous orthodoxies and arguing for a new approach. In different forms, and to different degrees, the OECD, the World Bank, the World Economic Forum and even the IMF have acknowledged that the economic policies of the past have led to unjust outcomes and poor economic performance, and are seeking new solutions.[17] There is not yet universal agreement on what these are, but the need for a new economic model of inclusive and sustainable growth is widely recognised.[18]

Making the change

In the second part of this report we describe our plan. In ten separate areas of policy, we set out our analysis of the challenges we face, and our specific recommendations for reform. We believe our proposals could be adopted by the present government or a future one. There is no silver bullet: a new economic settlement will require a systematic and integrated programme of economic reform across many areas. It will require vision, determination and patience.

For many of us, our country feels more divided than at any time we can remember. We are split along old dividing lines – such as gender, class, income, geography or ethnicity – and new ones that have come to prominence, such as the generational divide, attitudes to immigration, and whether we voted to leave or remain in the EU – or indeed, to leave or remain within the UK. Most people recognise that these divisions are not good for us: they corrode the social cohesion on which a flourishing society is based.

Yet no matter the problems we have in the present and the challenges of the future, we have a great endowment on which to build. We have vast ingenuity and creativity among our people and an extraordinary cultural heritage. We have long-established and globally respected institutions, from our courts and civil service to the BBC. The UK is home to some of the world's leading industries and we are a scientific superpower, defining new frontiers of technological possibility.

We are therefore unapologetically bold and ambitious in our proposals. People and governments commonly overestimate what they can do in two years and underestimate what they can achieve in ten. We believe that prosperity and justice can and must be achieved hand-in-hand – and that these principles can be the foundation for a new consensus that brings a divided country back together. The economy we have is a matter of choice, and changing it is a matter of democracy. We have no doubt this can be achieved, if we have the will to do so.

PART II

OUR 10-PART PLAN

6

Reshaping the Economy through Industrial Strategy

The UK economy suffers from deep and longstanding weaknesses. Our productivity growth, rate of investment, and research and development activity are all too low, contributing to poor export performance and a widening gap in living standards between the South East and the rest of the country. Over recent years, a growing understanding of these weaknesses has sparked a revival of interest in the idea of 'industrial strategy'. The UK government renamed the business department in 2016 as the Department for Business, Energy and Industrial Strategy (BEIS); it has published a White Paper setting out its industrial strategy plans and committed £4.7 billion in new funding.[1] The Scottish government has developed an industrial strategy for Scotland; and the Northern Ireland Executive published a draft industrial strategy before the breakdown of the power-sharing agreement.

The change in departmental name – effectively incorporating 'industrial strategy' into the core goals of the machinery of government – and the development of industrial strategies by the devolved governments marks an important moment. They signal a welcome, and long overdue, recognition that the UK's problems are structural, not temporary, and that a more active role for government to drive investment in the economy is needed. But there is much more that still needs to be done. In this chapter we argue that only by coordinating the full range of supply-side interventions available to government, and integrating them with demand-side management, can the structure and direction of the UK economy be fundamentally reshaped; and we set out some of the ways in which this can be achieved.

The objectives of industrial strategy

In most developed countries, industrial strategy has been a familiar and longstanding feature of economic policy.[2] But after the 1970s, in the UK it was largely abandoned as an explicit approach. Since the 2007–8 financial crisis, successive governments have taken a renewed interest. But there is still considerable argument about what it should do and how far it should go.[3]

We define industrial strategy as the purpose-driven coordination by the state of its supply-side economic policies.[4] The 'supply side' refers to the economy's productive capacity and the market conditions in which investment and production occur. Industrial strategy therefore encompasses a number of familiar policy areas, such as infrastructure, skills, R&D spending, land use planning, competition, business taxation, regional economic development and export promotion. All of these policy areas provide means by which the state seeks to raise business productivity and output by improving the conditions in which the private sector invests (many of these policy areas are devolved to the nations of the UK). But industrial strategy implies more than just the sum, or listing, of these policies. It must mean their overall *coordination*, aimed at a clear set of objectives or purposes, and in a particular direction.

It is clear that in the UK today, the overarching objective should be to change the structure of the economy to address its major weaknesses. Industrial strategy should be aimed at strengthening and expanding the UK's innovative and exporting sectors, raising productivity across the economy as a whole and rebalancing its uneven economic geography. It can also play a vital role in reducing the economy's environmental impacts.

Up to now, industrial strategy has tended to focus on just the first of these, targeted almost exclusively on sectors at the frontier of technological innovation and global markets, such as life sciences, the automotive sector and aerospace. There is a logic to this narrow approach: these are the firms that undertake the majority of the country's research and development and provide many of its exports. They are also the easiest constituency to target, as they are relatively few in number, and well organised to take up offers of government support. But while nurturing innovation in such sectors is one essential objective of industrial strategy – we need a greater number of world-leading firms – the UK's structural problems require it to do more than this.

First, as noted in chapter 3, the *diversity*, as well as the quantity, of what we produce has declined.[5] The UK has a revealed 'comparative advantage' in a number of service sectors, including insurance, finance and communications, but in few manufacturing industries, and our export diversity has reduced significantly since 2007.[6] One consequence of this is that the UK's domestic supply chains are weak, making us more reliant on imported inputs than otherwise comparable countries. So a key goal of industrial strategy should be to diversify the number and range of the UK's exporting sectors, as well as to support our existing strengths. To achieve this, there should be a sharp focus on tradability as the key characteristic, which in turn will lead to a greater emphasis on manufacturing. This is the strategy we have called 'new industrialisation'.

As we argued in chapter 3, building regionally distinctive high-tech clusters across the country will be key to this. The UK already has strong clusters in areas such as health and life sciences in Manchester, the automotive industry in the West Midlands, advanced manufacturing in Sheffield, and the major Cambridge cluster focused on software, electronics and biotechnology.[7] A key aim of industrial strategy should be to drive the development and expansion of the smaller and nascent clusters which exist around many of the UK's research-based universities.[8] As we also noted in chapter 3, the UK's productivity problem is not primarily among its leading companies and sectors. Among the top 5 per cent of firms (measured by GVA per worker), productivity has been rising since 2011.[9] It is the quantity, diversity and scale of these firms, rather than their productivity, which is the problem for the UK economy. We do not have a sufficient number or variety of them, and they need to be supported to scale up and better access world markets.

Second, the UK's productivity problem can only be addressed by improving the way that the majority of firms operate. It is among firms in what we characterise as the 'everyday economy' that productivity is lower than most of our European neighbours and where productivity growth has stalled. These are the firms that produce the unexceptional goods and services that make up a large proportion of the routine transactions of economic life. Lifting productivity in these sectors (such as retail and wholesale, hospitality and tourism, social care, food and drink and light manufacturing) will require the faster diffusion of new technologies, including automation: letting machines and software take on an ever-greater share of tasks, allowing the redeployment of workers to progressively more productive activities.

Third, focusing on innovation without acknowledging the spatial distribution of activity risks perpetuating the UK's considerable geographical imbalances. As we note in chapter 15, earnings and living standards vary substantively by region and nation of the UK. To reduce these imbalances, industrial strategy must have a strong spatial dimension.

Integrating demand and supply

If the objective is to change the structure of the economy, focusing on supply-side policies alone will not be sufficient. Supply-side interventions must be integrated with demand. There are three ways this needs to be done.

First, fiscal policy needs to work with, not against, industrial strategy. It makes little sense to enact supply-side policies to encourage businesses to invest while at the same time taking demand out of the economy through contractionary fiscal policy. Business investment is driven by demand – without it, no amount of supply-side policy will work. So, as we argue in chapter 10, the government should now significantly increase the level of public investment over and above current plans in order to drive up private sector investment. We propose that around £7.5 billion of this increase should be directed into industrial strategy itself by 2022. In doing so, the government can improve the economy's demand and supply side simultaneously.

Second, public procurement should work in support of industrial strategy. Procurement by public sector organisations represents a significant source of demand: in 2015 it totalled £268 billion, or 14 per cent of GDP.[10] For many years the orthodoxy in UK public procurement policy was that it did not matter where goods and services were produced: they should be purchased simply at lowest cost. Value for money (as opposed to cost minimisation) is a key objective of government in making procurement choices, and UK-based businesses should not simply be favoured over international competitors.

However, a key role for industrial strategy should be to help domestic businesses put themselves in the best possible position to supply the goods and services required to meet the demand created by public spending and policy. There is every reason that the criteria by which suppliers are judged should include the potential social impacts, such as increased domestic employment, that would result from awarding the contract to a firm that would deliver it in the UK. Strengthening the Social Value Act is one means to do this and is discussed in chapter 8.

Third, government has a vital role to play in driving the *direction* as well as the rate of investment. Some of the world's most successful government innovation strategies have been 'mission-oriented', focused on solving major societal and technological challenges.[11] Governments can not only increase investment and stimulate GDP growth; they can do so in fields which will generate specific forms of public value.

The government has already accepted this approach, announcing four 'grand challenges' which it wishes to use to drive its innovation strategy.[12] These aim to put the UK at the forefront of the artificial intelligence and data revolution; harness the power of innovation to meet the needs of an ageing society; maximise the advantages for UK industry from the global shift to clean growth; and to become a world leader in shaping the future of mobility. We strongly support this approach; the task now is to turn these broad goals into more specific and targeted innovation strategies.

This is partly about providing greater support for R&D and its commercialisation. But it is also about creating demand for innovation through wider public policy. It is the demand of the NHS for new health solutions that helps drive advances in healthcare technologies; it is environmental targets that incentivise innovations in renewable energy and low-carbon transport. So, through industrial strategy 'missions', the government has a vital opportunity to integrate innovation into its wider policy agenda, achieving public value objectives while simultaneously strengthening the economy. We give some more detail on how this can be done by 'green industrial strategy' in chapter 14.

Scaling up industrial strategy

The government has made an important start in developing a more active industrial strategy. But we believe that this now needs to be scaled up. *Our proposal is therefore for an expanded and mission-oriented industrial strategy, focused on achieving investment-led growth, with the aims of diversifying our industrial base, driving up exports, raising productivity and addressing regional imbalances.*

Since the objective of industrial strategy is to reshape the economy – with the deployment of significant public investment – it is essential that it is developed in an open and transparent way. Clear rules are required to ensure that government institutions are not captured by vested interests. In chapter 4, we describe the need for a partnership approach to economic policymaking. This means that industrial strategy must be developed collaboratively, involving both business and trade unions in sector councils, and at subnational level the devolved nations and English regions and combined local authorities. *To establish a lasting structure for the organisation of industrial strategy, we propose that it is governed by a new Industrial Strategy Act.* This would, among other things, set out clear goals and criteria for state support for industry, and create an independent Industrial Strategy Committee to provide oversight and guidance.

A National Investment Bank

The UK economy needs greater investment in key fields, especially infrastructure, innovation and business development, and it needs the money to be spread across the country, rather than concentrated in the South East. But it is clear that this is not going to happen on its own. As we discuss in chapter 11, the financial sector is not investing sufficiently, particularly in areas that need long-term, 'patient' capital: partly due to a lack of demand, partly due to its orientation towards short-term returns, and partly because infrastructure and innovation projects often come with an unacceptable level of investment risk.

Co-investment – the private and public sector investing in projects together – is a familiar approach in infrastructure. Both the European Investment Bank (EIB) and the UK's own Green Investment Bank (GIB) have pioneered co-investment, using specialist subject expertise and risk-sharing to leverage additional private capital where it would otherwise not have invested.[13] The British Business Bank and Innovate UK similarly use public funds to leverage private capital for small and medium-sized enterprises (SMEs). With the UK about to leave the EIB, and the GIB having been sold, there is a strong case now for establishing a public investment bank, on the model of the highly successful KfW in Germany and comparable models in other countries.[14]

Public investment banks have three key advantages. With restricted investment mandates, they can develop the specialist expertise in their chosen fields, which most private investors do not possess.[15] They can therefore discover, help to develop and conduct due diligence on projects which the private sector would not, and in turn can 'crowd in' private finance which would not otherwise flow. Second, the backing of government gives a public investment bank in normal circumstances a strong credit rating, allowing it to borrow more cheaply – and in turn lend on at lower cost – than other investors. Third, a public investment bank can cover some of the project risks which private investors are reluctant to cover, particularly policy risk. Where projects are dependent on stable government policy, notably in infrastructure, it is highly attractive to private investors to know that the government effectively has some financial 'skin in the game' which will make policy change less likely.[16]

Operating in these ways, the KfW has played a major role in Germany's economic development since the Second World War, and the EIB has played a comparable role across the EU as a whole since its foundation in 1958.[17] The UK's own GIB was a notable success before its sale, lending £3.4 billion over four years into over 100 renewable energy and related projects, collectively worth £12 billion.[18] In the last three years, the GIB reported a forecast project-level rate of return of around 10 per cent over the lifetime of its investments.

We therefore propose that the government establishes a National Investment Bank (NIB). This new institution should be given a mandate to invest in infrastructure, innovation and business growth, and over time should become the main mechanism through which government spends on industrial strategy. It should have the objective of 'crowding in' private investment into projects that help to diversify our innovation-based and export sectors, that enhance productivity and competitiveness in the economy as a whole, and that rebalance the economy geographically. It should prioritise investment in companies and sectors that are focused on exports, particularly those located in the industrial clusters that we propose.

The Scottish government has already decided to establish a separate Scottish National Investment Bank, which it plans to capitalise with £2 billion over the next ten years, and there is a Development Bank of Wales.[19] To address regional imbalances in the availability and allocation of finance, we believe the NIB should have specific divisions in Northern Ireland and the regions of England, with specialised mandates to invest in these economies, and accountability to the devolved government and to the regional executives we propose in chapter 15. There is good evidence of the value of regional and local investment banks;[20] our view is that regional divisions backed by a national balance sheet able to pool risk will (at least initially) be the most effective approach.

The NIB should be capitalised by both direct funding from government and borrowing from the capital markets. In terms of scale, most state investment banks around the world are capitalised at a size equivalent to between 0.9 per cent and 1.6 per cent of GDP.[21] We would propose, therefore, that the NIB should initially be capitalised at around £20 billion (equivalent to around 1 per cent of GDP) in 2017 terms. With a leverage ratio (based on international experience) of between 2.5 and ten times its capital, this would mean total NIB lending of between £50 billion and £200 billion.

Alongside its core lending activities, the National Investment Bank should have a range of other funding instruments.

First, *we propose that the NIB should be able to provide equity financing, particularly for innovation.* Over the last 30 years, a number of public investment banks across the world – including in Finland, Israel and Brazil – have turned towards a 'venture capital' model, in which they finance firms through equity as well as debt. This allows them to share in the success of the companies they support, and has yielded significant financial returns.[22] Adopting this approach in the UK would enable the taxpayer to share in the rewards as well as the risks of innovation.

Second, the NIB may need to offer incentives to encourage start-ups to take up an offer of equity finance rather than a loan, as it effectively means selling a stake in their business.[23] It could do this by tackling one of the biggest barriers that business-to-business start-ups face in getting off the ground: the lack of a track record, which makes it risky for early customers to work with them as a supplier.[24] *We therefore recommend that the NIB offer innovative start-ups a 'first customer' guarantee which can de-risk for other businesses the decision to become one of their early customers.*

Third, prompt payment is essential for SMEs, as many firms struggle to survive the cashflow problems that late payments create. Yet despite concerted government action, 12 per cent of SMEs still have to wait 90 days or more to get paid under their customer's payment terms.[25] Commercial factoring is costly for firms: it typically ranges from 0.5–5 per cent of the invoice value for each 30-day period it is required (a rate of 3 per cent is equivalent to 38 per cent APR).[26] *We therefore recommend the NIB creates a National Factoring Agency to help SMEs improve their cashflow at low cost.* By doing this at a national level, and thereby pooling the risk, it should be possible to lower the price substantially. Moreover, it would enable late-paying firms to be identified and remedies sought.

From indirect to direct support for innovation

In financial terms, present innovation policy is dominated by fiscal incentives through the tax system. Direct financial support through government grants or loans comes largely through the budget for Innovate UK, the specialist agency (under the UK Research and Innovation umbrella) responsible for delivering the government's innovation strategy. In total, Innovate UK's annual budget comes to around £0.5 billion per year.[27] Yet this compares to an expected outlay in 2017–18 of more than £3.9 billion in reliefs on corporation tax, through R&D tax credits and the 'patent box' system.[28]

The evidence suggests that neither of these indirect support mechanisms through the tax system are effective at expanding and diversifying the UK's base of innovative businesses. Both policies predominantly channel funds to large, established companies – which are the least likely to develop new areas of innovation[29] – rather than new and smaller firms. In 2014–15, more than 800 firms made use of the patent box system, but 95 per cent of all relief claimed went to the 305 largest companies.[30] At the same time, a review by Her Majesty's Revenue and Customs (HMRC) of R&D tax credits found that, in 2012–13, 80 per cent of all spending eligible for relief came from large firms, rather than SMEs, with a particular concentration in the pharmaceuticals sector.[31]

The R&D tax credit system has a particular problem of deadweight – subsidising investments that would have occurred anyway. Using the econometric methods applied by a recent review by the Irish Department of Finance of their own R&D relief scheme,[32] research conducted for the Commission estimated deadweight loss in the UK R&D tax credit system. The findings suggest that between 71 and 74 per cent of R&D tax credits are deadweight, at an annual cost of £1.8–1.9 billion.[33]

The patent box is a tax relief enabling companies to apply a lower rate of corporation tax to profits earned from patented inventions. Widely adopted across Europe, patent box schemes are generally regarded as a poorly targeted way to stimulate innovation.[34] Patent royalties are a form of passive income which can easily be moved from one country to another. So, in practice, patent box schemes have been introduced largely as a form of tax competition – or as a defence against it where they have been introduced in neighbouring countries. There are currently 14 EU countries with patent box schemes, effectively eliminating their value to any country.

In contrast, the government's targeted direct expenditure on innovation through Innovate UK appears to represent far better value for money. Through its various challenge funds, competitive grant programmes and support for 'Catapults' and other research and innovation centres, Innovate UK has been developing a strong array of innovation strategies that can improve the number and scale of exporting companies.[35] *We therefore propose that government shift the bulk of its spending from indirect to targeted direct interventions to support innovation in exporting companies and sectors. This should involve the phasing down and eventual abolition of R&D tax credits other than for SME firms younger than seven years old, and the phasing down and abolition of the patent box.* The money released should be channelled into funding for innovation through Innovate UK and the National Investment Bank. The phasing down of the schemes should be gradual, with the pace of change responsive to trends in the economy, in order to give firms time to adjust in a way that does not jeopardise jobs and output. The winding down of the patent box scheme would ideally be done in collaboration with other European countries which have adopted similar schemes.

Raising productivity across the economy

Raising productivity across the UK economy as a whole will require a sustained focus on the principal causes of low productivity at the level of the firm. These include poor management levels and practices; the slow adoption of new technologies, including digital technologies; and the poor design of jobs and use of workforce skills.[36] Many SMEs are not aware that they are less productive than they could be, and do not take up traditional sources of business advice and support.[37] We thus believe that industrial strategy needs to take a new approach.

We therefore propose the establishment of a new social partnership body, Productivity UK, to focus on raising productivity in the everyday economy. This would be governed by a council including representatives of government, businesses, trade unions, public sector enterprises, the further education sector and academic business schools. Its remit would be to drive higher firm-level productivity across the economy, by providing advisory and support services, and where appropriate direct grants and loans to businesses to enable them to invest in technological, organisational and marketing innovation, improved job design and both management and workforce training.

Such services would need to be delivered both geographically and sectorally. So in practice we would see Productivity UK operating as separate devolved institutions in Scotland, Wales and Northern Ireland; and in England working through combined authorities (see chapter 15). In key sectors Productivity UK would work with accredited sectoral bodies, which we discuss below. Given the centrality of skills to this agenda, it could incorporate current programmes aimed at coordinating skills development and vocational training, including the Institute for Apprenticeships. We envisage initially Productivity UK having an annual budget of around £100 million.

Some of the work the new body would undertake has been pioneered by a new business-led organisation, Be the Business.[38] Through a variety of outreach methods it is helping increase business awareness of the potential for productivity improvement; has created a digital platform that firms can use to measure and benchmark their productivity against other firms in their sectors; and is piloting new methods of getting businesses to adopt new management practices, technologies and skills. Though still on a small scale, its early results are encouraging. We would therefore envisage Be the Business becoming a core private sector partner of Productivity UK, and a key source of innovation and good practice in the field.

Managed automation

The adoption of existing technologies is vital to lifting the productivity of the everyday economy. Yet, as we discuss in chapter 3, despite the rhetoric about 'the rise of the robots', the reality is that the UK is adopting automating technologies at a relatively slow pace, lagging behind most advanced European economies.[39] The UK has just 71 robot units for every 10,000 manufacturing sector employees, compared with 303 in Japan, 309 in Germany and 631 in South Korea.[40]

Three-quarters of potential productivity improvements related to automation come from the broader adoption of best practices and technologies, as companies catch up with sector leaders. Only a quarter is from technological, operational and business innovations that go beyond best practices and push the frontier of the world's GDP potential.[41] This means that speeding up the adoption of technologies could prove transformative. If productivity growth of firms in the second, third and fourth quartiles could be boosted to match the productivity growth of the quartile above, it would deliver a boost to aggregate UK productivity of around 13 per cent, taking the UK to within 90–95 per cent of German and French levels.[42]

We therefore propose that Productivity UK should have a core objective of accelerating 'managed automation' and the diffusion of digital technologies across the economy. Its goal would be to help SMEs in particular to understand the productivity-raising potential of new technologies and to accelerate their introduction, through information and advisory services, and grants and loans for investment. This would be done alongside its wider management education and consultancy services, and support for skills training. It would be done in close cooperation with trade unions, alongside the processes of collective bargaining we discuss in chapter 7.

This is important, because accelerating automation will speed up the rate at which demand for skills changes. Some tasks will require far less human input, while new tasks and jobs will be created. It is therefore essential that the workforce is able to adapt to these changing demands for labour – and this is not something the market will deliver on its own. The process of managed automation should therefore include a commitment to support those workers displaced by digital technologies. *We therefore propose that the government introduce a 'Technology Displacement Fund' to support workers displaced by technology to be retrained and supported back into the labour market.* Under the aegis of Productivity UK, such a fund would provide businesses, trade unions, sector councils and devolved and local governments with resources to identify jobs at risk and skills training packages for affected workers.

Creating a skilled workforce

The skills systems across the UK have not responded well to the changing nature of the economy, a policy failure that has helped to create sectoral imbalances, structural unemployment, and large geographical variations in the quality and quantity of jobs available.[43] The problem is one of both demand and supply. On the demand side, employers do not invest enough in training, and many do not use the skills of their workforces effectively. Fully one-third of adult employees in the UK are estimated to be over-qualified for their job, the highest proportion in the EU.[44] On the supply side, skills training, particularly in England, is often of low quality and does not provide the workforce or business with the specialist skills most needed.[45]

In order to help raise skills levels, particularly among young people, the UK government has introduced an apprenticeship levy, a charge on large employers (those with a wage bill of over £3 million), which goes into a fund from which they can draw to pay for apprenticeships in England, with funding used by the devolved governments in Northern Ireland, Scotland and Wales to fund existing skills provision. But the early indications are that it has not worked well. Companies complain that it is overly bureaucratic and inflexible. In England, it appears to have resulted in the inverse of its objective, with more than a 70 per cent decline in apprenticeship starts in the first quarter after the levy's introduction.[46] So far only £108 million of the £1.39 billion paid into the fund has been drawn down by businesses.[47]

We believe that focusing skills funding on apprenticeships alone will not be sufficient to bring about the step-change in skills investment the workforce needs. Apprenticeships are important, but firms need to be able to deploy funds for a broader range of approaches to develop the skills of their workforces. *We therefore propose that the current apprenticeship levy is abolished, and replaced by a 'productivity and skills levy'.* This would be redeemable by participating companies for a wider range of initiatives aimed at raising productivity through skills training and workplace organisation, including, but not limited to, apprenticeships. If levied at 1 per cent for employers with 250 employees or more, it would raise £5 billion. As now, funding should continue to be devolved to Scotland, Wales and Northern Ireland. In England, a quarter of levy funds should go towards devolved regional skills funds for combined authorities to invest in high-quality training, in association with sector councils.

Such councils can help to drive up standards and spread best practice, and in so doing, increase demand for skills. Currently, a network of 21 sector skills councils cover 550,000 employers, 90 per cent of employees and a range of sectors, from retail and care to land management and nuclear power.[48] But their funding is limited, and many lack the capacity to fulfil their role effectively, with limited participation from SMEs.[49] They are also employer-led, limiting their ability to engage with workforces. With more resources with which to engage with businesses, and an expanded mandate, we believe these organisations could assume a central role in driving up skills levels and productivity across the country. *We therefore recommend that a portion of the current apprenticeship levy underspend goes to expanding and resourcing enhanced sector councils.* Councils receiving government funds should be required to adopt a partnership model, involving trade unions in their governance and policymaking.

At the same time, there is an important opportunity to give workers a better means of increasing take-up of skills training by giving them more autonomy. *We therefore recommend the introduction of Personal Training Credits, to provide low-paid workers and unemployed adults with up to £700 a year to invest in their own skills.*

A 'good jobs standard'

There is now a lot of evidence that changing the way in which jobs are configured can help improve productivity, earnings and job satisfaction.[50] A number of countries have initiatives specifically aiming to help employers improve the quality of jobs through better job design and workplace innovation. These include Scotland, which has pioneered such work through its Fair Work Convention, a voluntary partnership between government, business and unions.[51] We see great potential in the wider diffusion of this idea.

We therefore propose that the UK government establishes a 'good jobs standard' for England (with the potential for devolved equivalents in Wales and Northern Ireland), aimed at encouraging better job design. This would be a set of guidelines for employers – and for employees and trade unions – on the design of high-quality jobs. As in Scotland, this could be an entirely voluntary initiative. But there is also potential to use public procurement policy to encourage take-up by employers, making accreditation under a good jobs standard a requirement for firms delivering certain public contracts.

Rethinking the immigration system

In the Commission's view, the UK's immigration system should be designed to promote human dignity, prosperity and justice, rather than using reductions in net migration as the definition of success. *We therefore propose the adoption of a new immigration framework aimed at supporting the UK's economic strategy as well as the vitality and cohesion of our communities and the dignity of migrants.*

We put forward six specific proposals for reform:[52]

- Replace the net migration target with an Annual Immigration Framework composed of separate targets for different types of migration. This would ensure that the UK remains open to types of immigration which help promote growth and productivity, such as that of the highly skilled workers.
- Give the devolved nations more control over their own immigration rules. This would deliver a fairer system, allowing the

level and type of immigration to be tailored to geographical need, and potentially help to close geographical economic imbalances. In due course, this could be extended to the regional economic executives we have proposed for England.

- Launch a Global Talent Visa. This would enable the UK to actively recruit top global talent in sectors critical to driving forward innovation.

- Introduce a Trusted Sponsor Scheme for employers who seek to sponsor skilled migrants. Employers who qualify because they can demonstrate that they are responsible employers and invest in the UK workforce should enjoy significant advantages in the visa system.

- Introduce a new scheme, similar to the previous Postgraduates for International Business scheme, to harness the opportunity for trade promotion offered by diasporas and international students in the UK.

- Redouble investment into integration in order to ensure migrants can make a full economic contribution and use the route to settlement as a way of incentivising integration and contribution.

In these ways we believe industrial strategy has the potential to reshape the economy so that it achieves greater prosperity and justice across all parts of the country.

7

Securing Good Pay, Good Jobs and Good Lives

Work shapes our lives. It influences how individuals see themselves in society and whether they believe the economic system to be working. The nature of work – its hours, pay and quality – is therefore central to a just and prosperous economy. Good work provides people with a decent income and standard of living, creates personal dignity by enabling people to provide for themselves and their families, and gives people a sense of purpose and contribution to society.

On the surface, the UK labour market appears to be performing strongly: there are almost 2.7 million more people in employment today than ten years ago.[1] But headline figures mask multiple problems: too many people experience low wages and stagnant incomes, poor conditions, insecurity, unequal access, and too little time for commitments to family and community. In this chapter we examine the nature and causes of these problems and propose a series of measures through which they can be addressed.

A divided labour market

Many people have stable, secure jobs offering autonomy and flexibility, decent pay and fulfilling work. People at the top continue to do well. The UK has some of the highest skilled people in the world doing some of the most interesting and stimulating work. In leading sectors such as life sciences, financial services, the creative industries and advanced manufacturing, and in thriving professions such as medicine, law, accountancy and public service, the UK economy generates good jobs on good pay.

But for too many others, the labour market is not working well. Real median employee earnings are still 2–3 per cent below their 2007–8 level,[2] and are only forecast to recover to their pre-crisis peak in the middle of the next decade.[3] The decline in UK real wages between 2007 and 2016 was the largest of all developed countries apart from Greece, Mexico and Portugal.[4] The introduction of higher minimum wages has had a welcome impact on the lowest paid workers, but growing insecurity and use of non-standard contracts mean earnings can still be low even when people are paid above the minimum wage.

Almost a fifth of all employees are on low pay, defined as below two-thirds of the median hourly rate.[5] Of these, the majority (61 per cent) are women. In the East Midlands, West Midlands and Yorkshire and Humber, 27 per cent of employees are paid below the voluntary living wage, compared to 19 per cent in the South East and 20 per cent in London and Scotland.[6] Low wages mean that work is no longer a reliable route out of poverty: two-thirds of people living in poverty are in a household where someone is in work,[7] and between 2004 and 2014, just one in four poorly paid people moved out of low pay.[8]

In early 2018, the UK unemployment rate stood at 4.2 per cent, a 42-year low.[9] But this headline figure conceals large underlying discrepancies. In some former industrial areas, the level of 'real unemployment' is estimated to be as high as 10 per cent, when people who are inactive, but would like to work, are taken into account. This compares to rates of 2–3 per cent in much of southern and eastern England.[10] Around 8 per cent of British workers are 'underemployed', that is, wanting to work more hours than their employer is willing to offer them.[11]

Insecurity in the labour market has risen dramatically over the last decade: 3.2 million people are now estimated to be in insecure work such as temporary work, low-paid self-employment or working on a zero-hours contract.[12] The use of such contracts has grown precipitously in recent years, such that now more than 900,000 people are employed this way – up from just 168,000 in 2010.[13] It is indicative of a labour market that has shifted risk from employers to individuals. Other forms are various kinds of non-standard contracts, 'gig' work, 'bogus self-employment' and agency work. Greater flexibility has enabled employers to create more jobs, but has reversed income gains and protections secured over much of the previous century. As we discuss in chapter 3, this has almost certainly contributed to the UK's stalled productivity growth too.

Looking at how work fits into our lives, a modern-day 'crisis of time' also emerges across the labour market, from top to bottom. Work may provide an income with which to enjoy life and care for family, but long working hours undermine those goals. Our economic and welfare systems are increasingly designed to encourage all adults in a family to work, but this is coinciding with an ageing population in need of more care. Since 2010 there has been a 27 per cent reduction in the number of people receiving state-funded social care, placing more of the burden on family members.[14] In the UK, unpaid work, primarily carried out by women, was calculated in 2014 to have a total value of £1.01 trillion, equivalent to approximately 56 per cent of GDP.[15] Those on lower incomes are also more likely to do unpaid work,[16] and this falls unevenly; Pakistani and Bangladeshi women are more likely to be burdened with it than women of other ethnicities.[17]

Since the end of 2014, more people have wanted to reduce their paid hours than increase them: one in ten in employment would like to work fewer hours.[18] Often this additional work is unpaid: in 2016, the average employee did 7.7 hours of unpaid overtime a week, with the public sector relying on it more than the private sector. This amounts to an estimated £33.6 billion worth of productive but unpaid labour.[19] But it does not translate into better economic outcomes: in the UK, we work longer hours, less productively, and for lower real wage growth than most other advanced economies.[20]

In 2018, whether you can access the best jobs depends to a large extent on where you live, your gender, class, age, ethnicity and whether you have a disability. Job opportunities and the chance to progress through a career are most available in big cities, particularly in London and the South East. Personal contacts and whether you can afford to undertake an unpaid internship still act as gatekeepers to many professions.[21] Women still face an employment gap and pay gap, earning on average 18.4 per cent less per hour than men; part-time jobs which tend to pay less per hour are overwhelmingly held by women.[22] Bangladeshi and Pakistani women are both much less likely to work than white women, and more likely to be unemployed than men from the same ethnic groups.[23] Disability also creates difference in employment outcomes. Fewer than half of working-age people with a disability are in employment, compared to four-fifths for people without disabilities.[24]

In all these ways the UK has come to have a highly divided labour market. While many do well, there is too large a group of people at its sharp end who lack security, voice, time, predictability, progression or good pay. We believe the UK labour market has lost its way – delivering high employment rates, but for too many people not enough of the things that provide a good life.

The change in bargaining power

The structure of the UK labour market has changed dramatically over the past 40 years. This period has witnessed the decline of mass production, the shift to a service economy, and patterns of globalisation that have increased the movement of people, capital and production. These trends have led to huge changes in the types of work available. They have in particular hollowed out many middle-skilled jobs, especially in regions that had previously had strong manufacturing and mining industries.[25]

At the heart of the UK's stagnating wages is our poor record on productivity. Productivity is key to delivering higher earnings, as higher output enables employers to pay workers more. Yet productivity is not the only factor which determines pay and working conditions. These also depend on the bargaining power of workers: the ability of employees to secure a fair share of their companies' success.[26] And this has been in decline.

As the UK's labour market has become more flexible, it has become harder for many workers, particularly in lower-skilled jobs, to seek higher rates of pay and better working conditions. Too many lack the security of employment and voice in the workplace which would give them the ability to bargain with their employers. In normal circumstances, one would expect that the UK's high employment rates over recent years would have led to higher average earnings, as scarce workers were able to bid up their pay. But the prevalence of less secure work has further weakened the relative bargaining power of workers, and increased the power of employers to use available and cheap workers rather than to seek productivity improvements.

This has been exacerbated by the decline of trade unions in the UK economy. There is extensive evidence that the presence of trade unions in workplaces helps improve not just pay, but a variety of aspects of job quality, from training and working time to job security.[27] It is therefore likely that the decline of union membership and collective bargaining in the UK over recent decades has contributed to the worsening conditions experienced by many workers.

In 1979 around half of all employees were trade union members; today it is fewer than one in four.[28] The union movement is now highly concentrated in the public sector. Entire industries have virtually no union presence; just 2.9 per cent of workers in accommodation and food service activities, for example, are union members. It is notable that workers who could most benefit from union membership – those poorly qualified and paid people who have least power in the labour market – are least likely to join.[29] At the same time, the decline of union membership and the fragmentation of many industries have led to a major fall in the number of workplaces where unions bargain collectively on behalf of their members. In the 1970s, the proportion of workers covered by collective bargaining agreements was more than 70 per cent. Today, it is just 26 per cent. The decline in the UK has been the largest in the OECD.[30]

The weaker bargaining power of workers has contributed not just to slower wage growth. It has led to a longer-term decline in the share of national income which goes to wages and earnings, and the rising share which is returned to capital. Different measures produce different estimates of the 'labour share' of national income, but the Bank of England has calculated that it has fallen from almost 70 per cent in the mid-1970s to around 55 per cent today (see Figure 1.3).[31]

The weaker bargaining power of workers has also contributed to higher inequality. This is true within the workforce: while those with higher levels of skills can secure high pay, many workers with lower bargaining power in a fragmented labour market end up stuck in low-pay and poor-quality work. It is also true between workers and those whose incomes are primarily derived from capital. Figure 7.1 gives a striking illustration of this. Over a hundred years the rise and fall of union membership has been mirrored by a parallel fall and rise in the share of income going to the top 1 per cent of the income distribution. Around 40 per cent of the increase in the average income share of the top 10 per cent in advanced economies is estimated to be related to declining union membership.[32]

There are many, interrelated reasons for the decline in union membership. The structure of workplaces has changed: traditionally highly unionised private sectors such as manufacturing and mining have declined, and a greater proportion of the workforce now work in

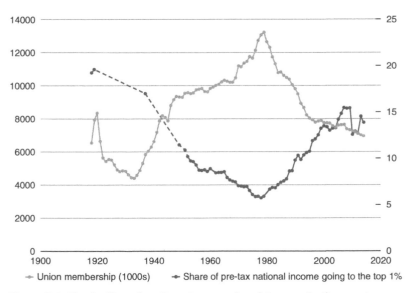

— Union membership (1000s)   — Share of pre-tax national income going to the top 1%

Figure 7.1 The decline of trade union membership over the last century mirrors the rising income share of the top 1 per cent
Union membership (1000s, left-hand side) and share of income (%, right-hand side) going to the top 1 per cent, 1918–2014
Source: World Inequality Database (2018)[33] and BEIS (2017)[34]

service sectors which have typically had lower union representation and are more difficult to organise. The decline has also been a consequence of the policy decisions of successive governments. Whereas in many European countries unions are seen as vital social institutions, in the UK unions have often been viewed as an obstacle to economic success rather than a partner in achieving it. Various policies have therefore aimed to diminish the role of the labour movement in the economy.

At the same time, globalisation, technological change and capital mobility continue to shape the world of work and the relative bargaining power of workers within it.[35] The development of the 'gig' economy has been enabled by new digital platforms which enable workers to be hired on an extremely flexible basis.[36] Growing attention in both the US and UK has also focused on 'monopsony' in the labour market: when there are a small number of employers in a particular area, they have huge power to select staff and set wages, leaving employees less able to bargain.[37] In the UK, there is evidence that low-paid employees are indeed concentrated in a smaller number of firms than higher-paid workers: twenty firms employ one in six of all low-paid employees, but less than one in ten high-paid employees.[38]

As these various trends continue to shape the labour market, the Commission's view is that we need a new policy framework. The framework we have today was largely designed for a time of high employment and rising wages and has not kept up with the impact of new technologies, fragmentation, growing insecurity and geographic concentration. In some cases, policy has exacerbated the effects of these trends. Risk has been transferred to the individual at the same time as social protections have been diminished through changes to the welfare system. We need a new and more modern approach.

In chapter 6 we set out policies to boost productivity through investment and a good jobs standard, recognising the link between job quality and productivity. In the following sections, we set out a list of proposals aimed at rebalancing power within the labour market. We wish to give workers more bargaining power, to enable businesses to do the right thing by their employees and themselves, and to help create jobs that match the economy and working lives of the twenty-first century. We propose five principal areas for policy reform: labour market regulation; trade unions and collective bargaining; widening work opportunities; reorganising working time; and improving work–life balance.

Labour market regulation

Modernisation of labour market regulation has the potential to improve the working lives of millions of people. We propose three areas for improvement: raising the minimum wage; strengthening employment rights; and improving enforcement.

Raising the minimum wage

It seems hard to deny that the UK's lowest paid workers need a pay rise. Higher wages are essential to lift people out of poverty and low earnings. While income and living standards depend partly on family structures, as well as the tax and benefit system, decent wages are the single biggest factor for most families. In 2016 the government introduced a higher minimum wage for workers aged 25 and over which it called the 'national living wage'. Yet despite the name, this is not in fact based on the cost of living. And it excludes young people, who have continued to receive the lower 'national minimum wage'.

The Living Wage Foundation has calculated that the wage required to cover living costs in 2018 – the 'real living wage' – is £10.20 in London and £8.75 in the rest of the UK, compared to the £7.83 national living wage and £7.38 rate for under-25s.[39] We believe that the minimum wage should be based on the cost of living. *We therefore propose that the national living wage should be raised to the level of the 'real living wage'.* These wage levels should be overseen by the Low Pay Commission, so that they continue to rise with living costs. We believe the living wage should apply to everyone aged 21 and over, and the apprenticeship rate should be raised proportionately to it.

The usual argument against raising the minimum wage is that it will lead to unemployment, since, without a rise in productivity, firms will not be able to afford it. But the evidence suggests the reverse is true. Raising the minimum wage will boost productivity, as firms adapt to the change by reconfiguring jobs and working practices to enable them to pay it. This is what largely happened after the introduction of the 'national living wage' in 2016.[40] But we acknowledge that an immediate increase in the minimum wage may be hard for some businesses to pay, which could lead them to seek savings through undesirable reactive measures. So, to ensure that businesses are able to adjust to the new rates, *we propose that there should be a temporary reduction in employer national insurance contributions (ENICs) for employees and workers paid at or just above the new minimum wage.*[41] This would be determined by the Treasury with guidance from the Low Pay Commission; on their advice it could be applied universally or to certain sectors only. It would be phased out after an adjustment period of three years.

As the minimum wage is raised in future, there are good grounds for believing that this will help improve the country's productivity levels.[42]

Chapter 6 sets out how policy could support businesses to become more productive. Increases in minimum wage rates will clearly affect some sectors more than others; social care and childcare are likely to be among those finding it hardest to adapt.[43] As sectors in which government is a major purchaser, we acknowledge that this will need to be addressed through increased funding for key services.

We also believe that a new minimum wage should be applied to uncontracted hours. As zero-hours contracts have become more prevalent, there has been some discussion about whether they should be banned. Recognising that the flexibility they afford is sometimes desirable, we believe that an outright ban would not be appropriate. Instead, *we propose that a new minimum wage set 20 per cent higher than the standard rate should be introduced for hours that are not specified in a contract.*[44] This would mean that employees were compensated for the risk they take on where flexibility is legitimately required, while acting as a strong incentive for employers to improve their workforce planning and change their scheduling practices to avoid the use of such contracts. Many retail firms, for example, have been setting shifts with very little notice, even though doing so could be more efficient.[45] Such a change would level the playing field between good employers who live up to their obligations to their employees and those who seek to shirk those obligations.

Improving employment rights

Employment rights are currently very unclear, with both workers and employers frequently confused about how to identify an individual's employment status and rights. The definition of categories has been constructed through the courts, rather than in legislation. Many people working in the 'gig' economy who are reported as self-employed are actually classified as workers under existing law, and are missing out on rights to which they are legally entitled. Furthermore, incorrect classifications of employment status tend only to be challenged if raised by the individual concerned – often with support of their union – in an employment tribunal; those unaware of their rights are unlikely to do this.

Lack of clarity allows unscrupulous employers to avoid the law and makes it harder for individuals to decide whether to challenge their status. It is therefore important that the law is clarified and better communicated, and that individuals are empowered to exercise their rights. *We therefore propose that:*

- all workers should be entitled to a written statement of their status and conditions from their first day at work
- people working irregular hours should have the right to a two-week notice period of their shifts, and right to compensation if this is not followed
- people on zero-hours contracts should have a right to a regular contract if regular hours are being worked
- ACAS (the Advisory, Conciliation and Arbitration Service) should provide clear guidance on the law in relation to employment categories, including the most recent cases and results
- the burden of proof in tribunals should shift from the individual to the employer, so that workers can have greater confidence in taking employers to court. There should be no return of employment tribunal fees.

One of the biggest features of the labour market since 2010 has been the growth of self-employment. The self-employed receive fewer employment rights than employees.[46] *We therefore believe that work-related benefits and support should be extended to people who are self-employed.* This should include statutory parental pay and contributory Jobseeker's Allowance. We propose that it should be funded by requiring employers that rely on a large proportion of self-employed labour to pay a block national insurance contribution, and by raising the national insurance contributions paid by the self-employed.

Enforcing workplace laws

Current enforcement of employment regulation is weak. Many individuals do not receive the legal minimum wage or rights they are entitled to, such as paid leave. In 2017–18, an estimated 300,000–580,000 people aged 25 and above were paid less than the minimum wage. If unpaid overtime is included in the estimates, that number increases to between 1 and 2 million underpaid workers, or between 4 per cent and 9 per cent of employees aged 25 or above. And these figures do not include self-employed people who earn less than the minimum wage from their business, or from working through a digital platform.[47]

In these circumstances government needs to make it easier for people to raise their concerns without fear of repercussions from their employer, and there should be greater proactive enforcement. This approach has been successful in increasing the identification of minimum wage underpayment: between 2014–15 and 2016–17, the number of workers identified as not being paid the minimum wage each year increased more than 13 times to over 68,000. At the same time the launch of an online complaints service increased the number of complaints over minimum wage underpayment and helped HMRC to identify a record number of cases in 2017–18.[48]

We therefore believe that enforcement agencies should be given the power and resources to proactively investigate employers, not just over minimum wage payment, but on wider employment status and rights. The enforcement agencies should be supported by a well-advertised one-stop helpline for employees to raise complaints. It should also enable people to report cases where the law has been flouted, even if they were not directly affected. Alongside making it harder for employers to avoid the law, the penalties for doing so should be tougher – involving both increases in fines, and greater use of 'naming and shaming' of transgressing companies.

Trade unions and collective bargaining

We want employers and trade unions to work in partnership to boost productivity and build more successful businesses where the gains are fairly shared.[49] To build that kind of partnership, there needs to be an increase in collective bargaining, especially in the private sector. While minimum wage policies can create a pay floor and reduce the number of people in extreme low pay, they do not have as large an effect for those above the floor, and they risk leading to an increasing number of people stuck on it. In 2017, 7 per cent of workers were on the wage floor, twice as high as ten years earlier.[50] Collective bargaining can achieve wage rises beyond this minimum at both a firm and sectoral level.

We believe that government should actively promote collective bargaining, with the aims of raising productivity, tackling inequality and boosting pay. *We therefore propose a target of doubling collective bargaining coverage to 50 per cent of workers by 2030, with a focus on the lowest paid sectors.* Collective bargaining should be conducted through the establishment of sector councils, with both employer and worker representation, to agree minimum standards of pay and other terms and conditions. The aim should be to ensure that pay is not driven down, responsible employers are not undercut, and that competition between firms is based on job quality and productivity, rather than just wage costs. At the same time, firm-level collective bargaining should be supported by lowering the barrier to achieving statutory recognition and giving unions stronger rights of access to workplaces. Government can also use procurement as a tool to promote collective bargaining by amending the Social Value Act (see chapter 8).

We believe trade unions should be partners in the workplace to boost productivity and improve pay. This means enabling unions to recruit more effectively and to embrace innovation. *We propose that this should be achieved through a new 'right to access'* – based on the recent New Zealand model – that would give unions stronger rights of physical access to workplaces, combined with a 'digital right of access' to reach remote workers. *At the same time, to encourage new workers to join a union, we propose a 'right to join'.*[51] As part of a statement of rights for workers, this would set out the right to join a union and the benefits of joining, and allow workers to 'opt in' to membership on starting employment, with subs deducted from the payroll.

We also want to see technology innovations embraced for twenty-first-century trade unionism. It has become clear that many people working through digital platforms face low pay, exploitation and the denial of their employment rights. Union membership in this group is low, and there are inherent difficulties in organising such an atomised workforce. The same technologies that have been used to atomise workers could be used to collectivise them. *We therefore propose a trial of auto-enrolment into trade unions within the 'gig' economy*, on the model of auto-enrolment into workplace pensions. *We also propose a*

WorkerTech Innovation Fund, building on the Union Modernisation Fund, to support unions to innovate and use digital technology to recruit and organise. This fund should be worth £10 million over five years, and could be paid for through a surcharge on Employment Tribunal compensation payments from employers. The ban on electronic balloting in trade unions should be ended.

Widening work opportunities

Despite progress on many fronts, today's labour market still has inequalities of gender, region, class, disability and ethnicity. We believe many of the recommendations in this report would help solve inequalities by increasing availability of and access to opportunities, generating prosperity and improving pay across the economy, and setting a higher floor for wages and conditions. In addition, we propose greater transparency and reporting to close gaps in employment outcomes and to accelerate the pace of change. In 2018, large employers were required to publish their gender pay gaps. We now need to go further.

We believe that pay and pay gaps should be made transparent across the economy. *We therefore propose that all firms above 250 employees should be required to publish their pay scales (both ranges and averages by role) to employees within their firms.* To help diminish pay gaps, there should be a requirement for all UK job descriptions to include an advertised salary, since unlisted salaries allow for large variations in pay upon joining a company. In addition, it should be stated whether the salary is negotiable or not, as women are more likely to negotiate when they know this is possible.[52]

While the reporting of gender pay gap data has become mandatory for large firms, reporting of ethnicity pay gaps remains voluntary and has not been widely taken up.[53] *We therefore propose that reporting on this should be made mandatory.* We also believe that mandatory reporting on disability employment and pay gaps should be considered, with an assessment of how this could be done while observing important sensitivities. *All pay gap reporting should be accompanied by mandatory action plans.*

But reporting and transparency should not stop with employers. Government decisions and policies can have hugely variable impacts for different groups. While the Public Sector Equality Duty requires all government departments to have 'due regard' to equalities, the main enforcement mechanisms have been weakened.[54] We would like to see government introduce a duty to report on the socio-economic impact of its policies, including their impact on inequalities and social mobility, and for this to be published.

Transforming working time

The organisation of time in the workplace affects everyone's lives: how we combine work with leisure, time with family and caring responsibilities. But it disproportionately affects women, who are much more likely than men to care for children and older people. The availability of flexible work – and the pay, skill level and quality of such roles – strongly shapes whether women participate in the labour market at the same rate as men.[55]

Improving the organisation of time and work should be about enabling meaningful choices about undertaking paid and unpaid work for everybody in the economy. It requires changing societal expectations about who should carry out unpaid work; making sure more jobs are flexible across the labour market (by sector, region and skill level); and providing sufficient state support for care to enable participation in work.

To enable men to take on a greater role in care responsibilities, *we propose that shared parental leave should be changed to include a period of 'use it or lose it' paternity leave.*[56] The current shared parental leave system in principle allows choice over who cares for children, but men's take-up of leave has been as low as 2 per cent, doing little to change society's norms of who takes time away from work to care for their children.[57] A specific, additional paternity leave, paid at a decent rate, is common in Scandinavian countries that also have lower gender pay gaps, and has been proven effective in encouraging fathers to take a period of leave and in reducing the motherhood 'pay penalty'.[58]

The lack of flexible jobs makes it difficult to combine work and family and means that carers – usually women – have less choice about which jobs they can apply for. Flexible working can also benefit people with health conditions and disabilities, and people who may not have a ready form of transport to get to work. *We believe it should be mandatory for all jobs to be available and advertised on a flexible and potential job-share basis, except with good reason.*[59] This would shift the norm over how jobs are designed and would require employers to demonstrate why a job cannot be flexible.

Social infrastructure, in the form of childcare, social care, education services, youth services and the health service, is crucial in determining who can access work and what kind of job. While the specifics of social infrastructure and the welfare state are beyond the scope of this Commission, we recognise their importance and the necessity of reform.

The welfare system

Reform of the welfare state was outside the scope of this Commission. We acknowledge, of course, its vital importance to working life. A comprehensive safety net is vital to ensure that people are properly protected and supported when disruptive life events occur, such as unemployment, insecure work, health problems, ageing and caring responsibilities. Welfare payments will always be essential to redistribute from those with the most to those with the least, even in an economy that is hard-wired for justice. Welfare payments are important for reducing child poverty and equalising living standards between men and women.[60] The welfare system also plays a crucial role in shaping the labour market. It sets a minimum bar (or 'reservation wage') for employers to meet to make work worthwhile. And it can play a crucial role in job-matching and helping people into the right kind of work.

In recent times, changes in the labour market and the rise of automation have triggered a debate about the desirability and feasibility of a 'universal basic income', a system in which all citizens receive an unconditional income payment from the state.[61] Though interesting and important, neither this nor other potential reforms to the welfare system have been within the scope of our work.

Changing the clock

Living standards are determined not only by how much we have to spend but by how we spend our time. In the UK, we work longer hours than many other major advanced economies: in 2017, the average annual hours per worker in the UK was 1,681, compared to 1,514 in France and 1,356 in Germany.[62] Yet though we work longer, we do not work better. Across the 35 OECD nations, there is a strong negative correlation between annual working hours and GDP per hour worked.[63] Those economies with lower hours than the UK are able to compensate with higher productivity.

When productivity rises, we should make a more active choice about whether the gains are realised in higher incomes or more time free of work. While one in three people who would like fewer hours would do so for less pay,[64] the reality of wages for many today is that reducing hours would reduce incomes: so change will need to be earned through higher productivity. New technologies and the potential for automation put this within reach. At the same time, redistributing working hours could also share wage benefits more broadly, given simultaneous over- and under-employment.[65] Reducing men's working hours and redistributing them to women who are more likely to work in part-time roles could help spread caring responsibilities more fairly and reduce the gender pay gap.

There are a number of ways in which reductions in working time can be pursued. These include better enforcement of the minimum wage to stop unpaid overtime, which often pushes earnings below the legal minimum; explicit guidance on the right to request a reduction in working hours as part of flexible working; and supporting trade unions to negotiate reduced working hours alongside pay rises.

But a general reduction in working hours is unlikely to come about simply as a result of individual choices. We will instead need to make such decisions collectively, as a society. We believe we need a national conversation about how we work, and at least the same protections in the future as we have at present. Societal expectations matter. Though it is possible to voluntarily opt out, it is notable that the European

Working Time Directive helped to reduce the number of UK employees working 48 or more hours per week by 700,000 over a ten-year period.[66] To ensure that everyone – not just specific sectors, firms and individuals – can benefit from productivity increases through reductions in working time, *we propose that the number of bank holidays is increased, with new bank holidays linked to national productivity rises and added to existing statutory leave entitlements.* The UK currently has only eight public holidays a year – the fewest of any country in the entire G20 or European Union.

Good work is at the centre of an economy of prosperity and justice, where everyone is valued and able to make their fullest contribution. We believe our proposals can improve the lives of individuals, families and communities while also raising productivity and growth throughout the economy.

8

Turning Business towards Long-Term Success

Successful private sector businesses stand at the heart of the UK economy. The vast majority of them are small and medium-sized firms and companies – those with under 50 or under 250 employees. The best are world class. They do what society needs them to do: create long-term wealth; provide good jobs and sustainable livelihoods for workers; build both physical and human capital; and drive innovation. Many seek to behave as good 'corporate citizens', taking their responsibilities to wider society seriously. There are many good businesses – we want them to flourish, and we want more of them. A successful economy requires businesses that succeed at home and abroad.

If the UK is to thrive and prosper, we need to keep working to improve corporate governance. For the UK's poor performance on investment, productivity and inequality stem in part from how – and in whose interest – our companies are governed. In this chapter we make proposals to achieve more purposeful companies, focused on doing the right things to achieve long-term success.

The problems of the UK corporate governance model

Our current system of corporate governance – the rules and structures by which a company is directed and controlled – gives overwhelming primacy to the rights and interests of a company's shareholders. Shareholders have voting rights to appoint the board of directors and to make other strategic decisions, and the legal duties of directors are explicitly focused on promoting their interests.

This approach contrasts with governance systems common in the rest of Europe, which enshrine the rights of other stakeholders in the firm. This is particularly true of employees, whose representatives sit on company boards in many other countries. In the UK, the interests of employees, and of suppliers and the wider community, remain secondary considerations.

This narrow model of corporate governance is not serving UK companies or the wider economy well. As we describe, it is one of the factors that explains our low rates of investment and productivity, high rates of pay inequality and low levels of public trust in large businesses.[1]

Short-termism and investment

In common with trends in other advanced economies, many UK businesses are too focused on the short term and not sufficiently focused on long-term success. There is some welcome progress; many FTSE 100 companies have already ceased the practice of quarterly reporting. But the result of short-termism has been a rising proportion of earnings distributed to shareholders, rather than being reinvested in long-term growth. Between 1990 and 2016 the proportion of discretionary cash flow returned to shareholders from UK non-financial corporations increased from 39 per cent to 55 per cent.[2] With fewer earnings retained, this has inevitably led to a significant decline in investment (see figure 8.1). The Bank of England estimates that only one in four businesses now prioritise investment as a use of internal funds, with a similar number prioritising the purchase of financial assets.[3]

This trend is unrelated to profit levels. Since the 2007–8 financial crisis, dividend payments have remained relatively constant even as profits have fluctuated (see figure 8.2).[4] It appears that firms have prioritised consistent, guaranteed returns to shareholders. Share buy-backs, another means of distributing earnings to shareholders, have

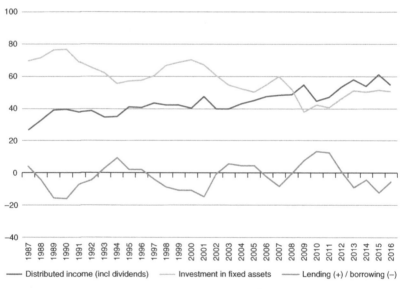

Figure 8.1 Corporate investment has fallen as firms have prioritised shareholder returns

Proportion (%) of UK non-financial corporation cash flow allocated to investment, dividends and saving, 1987–2016

Source: IPPR calculations using ONS (2017)[5] based on Tomorrow's Company (2016)[6]

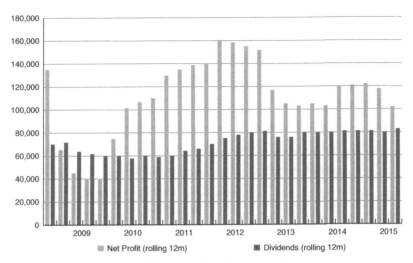

Figure 8.2 Giving shareholders predictable returns has come to dominate dividend payout behaviour, almost irrespective of profitability
Dividends and profits for FTSE 350 firms (£m, rolling 12 month), Q3 2008–Q1 2015
Source: Big Innovation Centre (2016)[7]

also increased markedly over the last quarter of a century.[8] Indeed, in recent years the value of share buybacks among UK companies has consistently exceeded the values of shares issued.[9] This has had the surprising effect of making the equity market less a source of net new financing for UK firms than a means of extracting value from them.

This reorientation from long-term success to short-term financial returns is sometimes described as 'financialisation'.[10] While there are various reasons this has occurred, one of the most significant factors is the shareholder-focused corporate governance model.

Since the 1980s, UK equity markets have become increasingly dominated by short-term trading rather than long-term investment. This is reflected in the length of time for which shares are on average held: this is now less than six months in the UK, down from around six years in 1950.[11] At the same time, the structure of shareholding has changed, with a significant decline in the proportion of quoted shares in UK-domiciled companies held by individuals (down from more than 50 per cent in the 1960s to around 10 per cent today) and by pension funds and insurance companies (from over half of all UK equities in 1990 to less than 15 per cent today).[12] They have been replaced by various kinds of investment funds whose asset managers are generally rewarded on the basis of short-term financial performance relative to one another, rather than on the long-term value of the companies in which they trade.[13] At the same time, UK companies are much less likely than European companies to have 'blockholders', shareholders with significant or controlling numbers of shares, whose interests tend to lie in long-term growth.[14] The result is that companies face increasing pressure for consistent short-term returns, rather than for long-term investment.

The shareholder-focused character of our corporate governance model also helps explain why takeovers in the UK are more common and more likely to succeed than in other advanced economies.[15] Takeovers can drive stronger corporate performance, generating scale efficiencies and reducing operating costs. But it is now widely recognised that many takeovers (particularly large ones) often destroy value, rather than creating it and, in the UK's case, have contributed to long-term industrial decline.[16]

Workers' voice

If Britain is to rise to its productivity challenge, then a stronger relationship must be forged between management, workers and shareholders. It is now widely recognised that employee engagement in decision-making is a key contributor to improved productivity and innovation in modern companies, particularly as a more knowledge-based economy has placed a higher premium on human capital and skill.[17] Having a voice, both individually and collectively, is also crucial to the experience of good work.[18] Yet despite some exceptions, the UK performs badly in promoting meaningful employee engagement and voice. In the European Participation Index, which ranks employee representation and involvement, Britain comes 23rd out of 28 European countries.[19]

The British model of corporate governance is likely to be a factor in this poor performance. Employees are excluded from representation on company boards and afforded almost no formal rights to information or involvement in decision-making. Hierarchical governance models in turn contribute to weak levels of engagement and worker voice, undermining the experience of work for many and reducing productivity levels.

Executive pay

The inexorable rise of executive pay has been a significant factor in making Britain one of Europe's most unequal societies over recent decades.[20] In the 1980s, a typical top chief executive (CEO) in the UK was paid approximately 20 times as much as the average worker; in 2016 the average pay ratio between FTSE 100 CEOs and their employees was 129 to one.[21] Executive pay has significantly outpaced returns from equities over the past 20 years. This contributes to the deep sense of unfairness which many people perceive at the heart of our economic system. Executive pay appears to be more a reflection of who decides it – the corporate governance arrangements – than of company performance.

The corporate governance code recommends that company remuneration committees should consist exclusively of independent non-executive directors, many of whom, in practice, are executive directors of other companies. This has led to a self-referential system of pay awards, with very few structural incentives to hold pay to performance, and many to keep it rising. It has led, for example, to the increasing and widespread use of so-called 'long-term incentive plans' and annual bonuses based almost entirely around short-term metrics which do not in fact properly measure long-term value creation.[22]

The failure of the current governance system to control executive pay has been particularly damaging for public trust in British businesses, which has seen a considerable fall in recent years. Large disparities in pay between senior executives and employees is also one of the sources of employee disengagement, and is negatively correlated with productivity.[23]

Challenging shareholder primacy

A number of arguments are generally made to justify the privileged position held by shareholders in the UK's corporate governance system.

First, it is said that shareholders are the beneficial owners of businesses, and companies should therefore be run in their interest, with the directors acting as their agents to maximise returns on shareholders' investments.

Second, it is claimed that the duty to promote shareholder interests helps solve the 'agency problem' arising from the separation of ownership and control in a modern corporation. Obliging directors to act in the interest of shareholders, not their own interests, prevents them from excessive risk-taking, and helps align risks and rights within the firm.

Third, it is said that shareholders – as the 'residual claimants' on a company's earnings after others (such as employees and creditors) – bear the most risk. To minimise their potential for loss, they should thus have control rights over management.

Last, it is argued that the maximisation of shareholder value is the best means to promote the efficient allocation of capital. Within neoclassical economic theory, shareholder value can be taken as a proxy for the general economic interest – since the price of equities reflects the profitability of companies, and welfare is maximised when resources flow to their most profitable uses.

When each is examined, these arguments do not stand up to scrutiny.[24]

First, it is legally not the case that shareholders are the owners of the company in which they have shares. They own part of the company's capital – as constituted by their shareholdings – but in law this does not make them owners of the company itself. Rather than conferring ownership, shares constitute a package of rights and liabilities; whether they also carry voting rights depends on the company's constitution. There is therefore no reason in law why they alone should have control rights over the company, or for the promotion of their interests alone to govern the duties of directors.

Second, the transformation in the character of share ownership in recent years has greatly weakened the claim that shareholders are best placed to have exclusive oversight of companies. The rise of the 'ownerless company' with few significant shareholdings means shareholders have neither the power nor incentive to exercise control over management.

Third, liability means shareholders are protected from personal bankruptcy if the company goes bankrupt, and most have diversified risks (they own shares in many companies). Employees, on the other hand, bear much greater risk in relation to the company (which will generally be their only employer); they therefore have a much stronger incentive to oversee management and to exercise any control rights. Since the duration of shareholding has reduced over time, and senior management tenure is also in decline, it is often the employees who have the longest relationship to businesses.

Fourth, such a system fails to recognise the critical role played by labour within a firm. Employees are not just another group of 'stakeholders' on a par with, say, customers or suppliers; they are core constituents of the process of production, with long-term and largely exclusive contractual commitments to the company.

Ultimately, we believe that the narrow shareholder model misunderstands the collaborative nature of modern companies. Companies are communities of interests, who share a common purpose and mutual obligations. They are incorporated bodies which bring together a range of stakeholders – owners and suppliers of capital, labour, suppliers and customers – for the purpose of enterprise. In turn, we believe this should be reflected in how they are governed and in whose interests they operate.

It is notable that, while shareholder primacy is widely considered the normal form of corporate governance in the UK, US and other English-speaking nations, it is by no means the universal model in developed countries. The most successful European economies have 'stakeholder-based' corporate governance models. In such models, whether governed by law or social norms, companies must balance the interests of shareholders with those of employees and other stakeholders.

In particular, a majority of European countries give workers some rights of decision-making. In 13 countries, including Germany, France, the Netherlands and Ireland, workers have significant rights of representation across much of the private sector.[25] This includes representation at the board level and on remuneration committees, formally recognising the role of the workforce in shaping the strategic direction of the firm.

Research conducted for the Commission shows that countries which adopt stakeholder models of corporate governance with formal means of employee representation have stronger R&D investment performance, higher productivity and lower inequality than shareholder-centric models.[26] We therefore believe that reforming corporate governance is not only necessary to reflect the true structure of a company. It is also an important means of building a more productive and prosperous economy.

Reforming corporate governance

Our view is that corporate governance reform should be aimed at re-orientating businesses towards more purposeful, inclusive and long-term behaviours, founded on a new partnership between shareholders, management, workers and society. Our proposals are designed to apply to large companies – those with more than 250 employees – whether publicly listed or private. We recognise that different arrangements are needed for wholly owned subsidiaries of overseas companies.

Redefining directors' duties

At present, section 172(1) of the 2006 Companies Act makes clear that the interests of shareholders should take primacy in determining what constitutes the 'success' of a company. Although directors must 'have regard' to 'the likely consequences of any decisions in the long term' and to the interests of employees and other stakeholders, it is widely acknowledged that these secondary factors have little impact in practice.

Some of our best company boards already pay attention to a broader range of stakeholders – workers, customers, suppliers and so on – rather than focusing solely on shareholders. We need to encourage more to do the same. We believe that short-term returns to shareholders should never be placed ahead of the long-term interests of the company. Companies that look to their stakeholders rather than only upwards to shareholders will be more successful, and by doing so will in fact serve the long-term interests of their investors too.

In order to provide directors with clearer guidance on their need to serve a wider range of corporate interests and activities, *we therefore recommend that Section 172 is amended*. It should be made explicit that the primary duty of directors is 'the promotion of the long-term success of the company'. In exercising this duty, directors should have regard for the interests of the company's shareholders; but also, and equally, for the interests of the company's employees; the need to foster business relationships with suppliers, customers and others; the impact of company operations on the environment, community and human rights; and the desirability of maintaining a reputation for high standards of business conduct.[27]

Reformulating directors' duties on these lines would help ensure that company boards did not see their responsibilities simply in terms of the short-term interests of shareholders, but were able instead to focus on long-term performance. To reinforce this change, *companies should be required to report on this in an integrated financial and strategic report*. This should explain their definition of purpose and long-term success, and account for the use not just of financial capital, but of human resources and for environmental impact as well.

Shareholder voting rights

To help ensure that shareholders are more likely to act in the long-term interests of companies, there is also a good case for restricting the voting rights of those who own shares only temporarily. In France, long-term shareholders have since 2014 been given greater voting rights in corporate governance. Companies can opt out and re-introduce the traditional one-vote, one-share principle, but they must take positive action to do so. We believe that such a system would be appropriate in the UK too. *We therefore propose that under normal circumstances automatic voting rights should only be awarded to shares held for more than a year.* Companies could decide to change this, but the default should be reset to favour those committed to companies for the long term.

Bringing workers onto boards and making boards more diverse

Companies are institutions through which capital and labour come together to produce goods and services. We believe it is therefore appropriate for a company's workers to be represented in the governance of the company, alongside the providers of capital, its shareholders. As we have argued, there are both ethical and economic justifications for this, and it works successfully in many European countries.

We believe that worker directors would contribute to creating better governed, more effective companies. They are likely to enhance the quality of strategic decision-making, increase the diversity of opinion and experience on the board, represent employees' interests, and strengthen employee engagement.[28] Instituting this change would help us move towards a different type of economy, one in which a partnership between labour and capital is embedded in how British companies operate. *We therefore propose that large companies of more than 250 employees should have at least two workers, elected by the workforce, on both their main board and the remuneration committee.* They would act as full, independent directors, with the same responsibilities as other board members.

One option to include workers on boards would be through voluntary action, through a new provision to the corporate governance code. However, there is a substantial risk that too many companies would simply fail to comply. So we believe that legislation is likely to be necessary. This is a reform which has long been debated in the UK; we believe it is time it was implemented.

The boards of our companies need more women and more people from diverse communities as well as the inclusion of workers. Increasing diversity improves the quality of decision-making, enriching strategic discussions and sharpening the challenge to management. Today, despite progress made since Lord Davies' review in 2011, too many boards remain 'male, pale and stale'.[29] We therefore support the proposal that companies should be required to establish measurable objectives and policies for achieving gender and ethnic diversity at their upper levels. In particular, *companies should be required to set out their plans to move towards gender-balanced boards – with fully transparent board nomination and appointment processes.*

The introduction of worker directors and more diverse boards will not of itself solve the problems of poor employee voice and engagement in many companies, or remove the obstacles to advancement widely experienced by women, people from black, Asian and minority ethnic (BAME) groups and other minorities. A variety of other institutions and practices in companies are also needed, including formal employee councils, other forums for worker representation and consultation, trade union representation, profit-sharing schemes and specific policies to promote inclusion.

Reforming remuneration

To ensure that the incentives of senior executives are properly aligned with the long-term success of their companies, the structures and systems of executive pay need to be reformed.

More diversity on boards and board remuneration committees should strengthen their resolve to tackle excessive executive pay. *We propose that a third of the membership of remuneration committees should be made up of elected worker representatives, and that the committee's remit should be widened to take account of the pay, incentives and conditions of all company staff.* These two changes would help ensure that the setting of executive pay was properly related to the performance of the company and to pay levels in the organisation as a whole. We support the government's proposals that companies should be required to publish the pay ratio between company directors and the median pay of the company's workforce. Mandatory gender pay-gap reporting has clearly shone a valuable light on institutionalised discrimination;[30] *we propose that this is now extended to ethnic minority pay gaps, with companies required to have equality plans to close both gaps* (see chapter 7).

Second, *executive pay packages should be simplified and linked to the key drivers of long-term value, such as innovation and productivity, not just share prices.* New guidance on appropriate forms of remuneration package should be included in the corporate governance code. And to ensure proper oversight, shareholders should be given an annual binding vote on pay policies and executive packages.

A Companies Commission

Rebuilding trust between business and the public – so badly eroded by scandals at BHS, Sports Direct and other firms – is vital to our future prosperity. Corporate governance in the UK is weakly regulated and enforced. The voluntary code is overseen by the Financial Reporting Council (FRC), a body whose primary function is the regulation of accountants and actuaries. The FRC only has powers to monitor a company's strategic report and financial statements, and can only take action against directors in breach of the corporate governance code if they happen to be accountants, auditors or actuaries.

At the same time, shareholders are the only constituency within a company that can take legal action against the directors if they are in breach of their duties under Section 172 of the Companies Act. Routes of redress are therefore narrow in terms of who is able to take action and weak in what can be done to enforce good governance. This undermines both the effectiveness of corporate governance itself and public trust in the system. We need a stronger, better resourced regulator.

We therefore propose the creation of a new statutory Companies Commission to oversee and enforce both a reformed corporate governance code and the Companies Act. The Commission should take over the corporate governance functions of the FRC, acting as an independent regulator with investigative and enforcement powers into both publicly listed and large private companies. The Commission should publish information on the state of companies' corporate governance; have the power to investigate possible breaches of corporate governance; propose remedies against board directors in breach of governance; and be empowered to take companies to court as a public interest litigator. Where breaches are likely to have occurred, the Commission would be expected initially to engage privately with a company board and ask for its proposed remedies to be implemented. If it were not satisfied this had been done, it would have the power to publish its findings, and in the last resort could initiate litigation under Section 172 of the Companies Act. We believe that such a regulator would help to improve corporate governance and restore public trust in business behaviour.

Reforming takeover rules

Corporate takeovers in the UK are more common, more likely to be hostile and more likely to succeed than in any other advanced economy.[31] This reflects the UK's liberal regulatory regime, prioritising the interests of shareholders, with UK company boards having a fiduciary duty to maximise shareholder interest when considering acquisition and merger offers. This contrasts with many other advanced economies, where governments have the power to consider the wider public interest.

At present, the 2002 Enterprise Act allows government ministers to prevent takeovers and mergers on grounds of national security, financial stability and media plurality. *To ensure the UK's takeover regime supports long-term value creation, we propose that a new statutory public interest test be introduced for bids above a certain size.* This could include consideration of issues such as the likely consequences for innovation, employment, the UK's industrial base and regional development.

Implementation of these measures would, we believe, improve the UK's model of corporate governance. They reflect a more appropriate way of thinking about the purpose and structure of companies and would help to promote long-term investment and success.

Using public procurement to drive company behaviour

As well as reform of corporate governance, government can support and encourage better businesses through its procurement decisions.

Public spending creates large markets for goods and services: total UK public procurement amounted to £268 billion in 2015, around 14 per cent of GDP.[32] Standards driving procurement decisions can therefore have a powerful effect in supporting and encouraging good business behaviours.

We believe the government can do more to implement the principles of 'open contracting', in which all public sector contracts are publicly disclosed, using open, accessible and timely information.[33] Open contracting can broaden the number of firms able to bid for contracts, provide better governance of the procurement process, and reduce the opportunities for corruption and for vested interests to benefit from contracts.

The 2012 Public Services (Social Value) Act takes this idea further. The Act requires all public bodies in England and Wales to consider the economic, social and environmental implications of the services they commission or procure.[34] The Act therefore requires public bodies to look beyond a simple 'value for money' metric, and to consider the wider value that could be delivered by it. This might include, for example, local employment and development of supply chains, standards of working practices, or environmental impacts.

The Act has been widely welcomed as a significant channel through which public spending can support wider public policy objectives.[35] At the same time, it is clear that the Act is not being used as widely as it might be across the public sector. There remains a lack of awareness of its requirements and potential, and confusion over where it can be applied and how social value can be measured and accounted.[36]

We therefore recommend a number of measures to strengthen and widen the application of the Social Value Act. These include requiring that all public procurement decisions above a certain size 'account for' social value, instead of simply having a duty to 'consider' it; codifying standards and expected practices; supporting SMEs and social enterprises to win a greater number of contracts; and lowering the threshold value of eligible contracts.

These measures would, we believe, help capture more of the social value that can be gained from government spending, and would support and encourage businesses which engage in positive activities that provide wider social, economic and environmental benefits.

9

Promoting Open Markets in the New Economy

Open and competitive markets are good for the economy. They force businesses to innovate, to become more productive and to serve their customers better by raising quality and lowering prices. But over recent decades competition policy has not caught up with the changing nature of market concentration.

As we describe in chapter 3, too many sectors in the UK economy are highly concentrated, resulting in excessive market power accruing to a small number of firms. Eight out of ten of the major consumer markets in the UK are highly concentrated, leading to poor outcomes for consumers.[1] Excessive market power creates problems of 'monopsony' too, where a small number of firms have excessive buying power in supply chains (and sometimes in the labour market as well). The most concentrated markets of all are in the digital economy. As chapter 3 argues, this presents fundamental challenges to innovation and entrepreneurship, since dominant firms both invest in innovation and erect barriers to others participating in it.

This chapter looks at competition policy in general, and how we should respond to the growth of digital 'platform' companies and the new role of data in the economy in particular. We explore the underlying theoretical problems with competition policy, describe a new approach to regulation of the digital economy, and set out fresh thinking for creating a 'digital commonwealth' of benefit to all.

Reforming competition policy

The UK's current competition policy was established by the 1998 Competition Act and the 2002 Enterprise Act, subsequently supplemented by the 2013 Enterprise and Regulatory Reform Act, which created the Competition and Markets Authority (CMA). The main elements of UK competition policy include market studies and market investigations to examine whether markets are working in the interests of consumers; merger control to prevent or mitigate the adverse effects of anti-competitive mergers; and anti-trust policy to prevent collusion or the abuse of a dominant market position.[2]

The 2013 Act transferred decision-making on competition from elected government ministers to independent, technocratic public bodies.[3] The Competition Commission and the Office for Fair Trading (OFT), which had previously each been responsible for one of the two phases of a competition investigation process, were replaced by the CMA, which gained responsibility for both initial and more in-depth inquiries. In its examination of the CMA in 2016, the National Audit Office found that the establishment of the new body had helped to improve both coordination within and the robustness of the competition regime, though it noted a continuing problem of 'low case flow'.[4] Between 2010 and 2016 only 24 decisions were made by the OFT and the CMA, with a further eight by their associated regulators. The UK competition authorities issued only £65 million of competition enforcement fines between 2012 and 2014 (in 2015 prices), compared to almost £1.4 billion of fines imposed by their German counterparts.[5]

The main challenge of the existing competition regime is not its institutional structure, but the principles of the regime itself. The 2002 Act changed the basis of decision-making to focus on the promotion of competition for the benefit of consumers. Before 2002, decisions about potentially 'anti-competitive' company behaviour, and acquisitions and mergers, had been made on the basis of a wide notion of the 'public interest'. The public interest has now been narrowed to questions only of national security, media plurality and the stability of the financial system.

The CMA focuses on promotion of consumer welfare, understood in terms of price, quality and choice. In common with other countries, the UK adopted this sharp focus on consumer welfare following academic developments in the 1970s and 1980s, notably led by the 'Chicago School' of economics in the United States. This argued for competition policy to focus on the single goal of allocative efficiency based on quantifiable, short-term welfare effects.[6] Regulators were to be agnostic about industry structures, so long as detrimental effects were not experienced by consumers. Rather than a mechanism to prevent market power from being concentrated in the hands of a small number of large firms, competition policy now tends to be used in a relatively small number of cases, and only where harm to consumers can be proven.

Few of the emerging issues we identified in chapter 3 can be addressed through the consumer welfare perspective. In cases such as internet search and social media, for example, consumer prices cannot be used to judge the state of competition, since zero-price business models are often used. As we describe in chapter 3, recent research by the IMF shows that, over the last four decades, price mark-ups – a proxy for market power – have increased by nearly 40 per cent across a whole range of sectors in many advanced countries.[7] Moreover, it demonstrates that with rising market power comes falling corporate investment, lower rates of innovation, and declining labour shares of firm revenues. This suggests that the current consensus on competition policy has failed to serve the public interest when that is conceived more broadly. The consumer welfare lens appears to be inadequate to meet the challenges of the new economy.

We therefore believe it is time to design new regulatory frameworks that anticipate market developments and are able to address them in the wider public interest. We believe we need a new approach to competition policy, aimed at creating open markets that promote innovation and enable entrepreneurs to enter. This should include a revival in the traditional tools for confronting excessive market power: rules proscribing price discrimination, so that all market participants have access to digital marketplaces on equal terms, and the prohibition of vertical integration, so that those who control the digital market do not also provide the goods and services sold within it.

We therefore propose that the remit of the CMA should be broadened to include a focus on market power that damages the public interest, alongside existing commitments to promote consumer welfare and economic efficiency. In determining the public interest, the CMA should consider the interests of consumers, suppliers and entrepreneurs, alongside taxpayers, workers and the wider public value of innovation. A review of the CMA's powers and decision-making principles could determine whether market share thresholds for regulatory action should be set, whether regulatory tools to address vertical integration and price discrimination should be strengthened, and whether competition policy should have an *a priori* objective to limit market power by limiting market concentration.

The role of digital platforms

In the digital economy, a new kind of company has come to dominate the landscape.[8] 'Platform' companies, such as Facebook, Google and Amazon – and smaller ones such as Uber and Airbnb – provide a new set of digital arrangements that organise and structure economic activity. These are sometimes described as 'multi-sided markets', where the platform functions as an intermediary between the provider of a service and its users.[9] Central to the platform business model is the extraction and analysis of data to generate insights that are sold or used to improve the platform's capabilities.

Platforms provide flexible, on-demand services, for which there is huge consumer demand. The major platform companies have a number of common features.[10] They generate or organise the work of others, outsourcing production and transferring capital cost to others. The marginal costs of scaling this model are almost negligible, meaning platforms tend towards rapid growth. As a result, platforms typically operate with powerful network effects: the bigger the network, the more valuable it becomes to its users, and the more profitable for the company that owns it. This in turn creates a premium for first-movers to attract the most users, rewarding companies that can scale rapidly in 'winner-takes-all' markets.[11]

The combination of these factors mean that platforms tend towards monopoly, with the major universal platforms all dominating their markets, and increasingly also new markets as they expand.[12] In the UK, for example, Facebook now has 74 per cent of the social network market share, Amazon is responsible for around 80 per cent of online physical book sales, and Google enjoys approximately 90 per cent share of the search engine market.[13] This tendency towards monopoly drives a risk of aggravating inequality (as we discuss in chapter 3) and harming innovation.

The biggest platforms are buying a large number of innovative start-up firms, with Google's parent company Alphabet acquiring over 200 companies since 2001, and Facebook over 65 since 2005.[14] These acquisitions serve both to expand the data extraction and analysis capabilities of large platforms, and potentially limit the ability of competitor firms to emerge. By limiting access to their large datasets – crucial for the creation of artificial intelligence (AI) systems of the future – platforms may now be limiting the innovation potential of the economy and the emergence of other start-ups.[15]

Regulating the digital economy

We propose that the CMA should put greater weight on the impact of mergers and acquisitions on innovation, with the power to limit or block those that are likely to reduce it. This may require the CMA to block horizontal market entry or require platforms to open up their data as a condition of expansion. Given that the major platform companies are primarily either American or Chinese, and the toughest regulator to date has been the EU, greater international cooperation will undoubtedly be required.

A small number of firms now provide services that have become essential features of modern life in the digital age. These include searching the internet, making social connections, matching consumers and third-party suppliers, and the cloud-based infrastructure of the digital economy. Provided by a few dominant firms, these services are akin to public goods provided by traditional utilities such as water, electricity, telecommunications and broadcasting. Traditional utilities and modern digital platforms share other similar characteristics: the services they provide cannot be efficiently or easily replicated and they are provided by monopoly or near-monopoly firms. There is therefore a good case for a comparable system of regulation.

We therefore propose that a new regulator, the Office of Digital Platforms (OfDigi), is established to regulate the major platforms in a model comparable to that for utilities. It would regulate those platforms providing one or more of the four services (searching, connecting, matching, infrastructure) once a market share determined by the CMA had been reached. OfDigi would conform to the institutional arrangements of the other regulatory offices, working closely with a reformed CMA. There are a number of roles OfDigi could perform to ensure that digital infrastructure is regulated for the public good. These might include:

- protecting 'network neutrality' – the anti-monopolistic principle that internet service providers should enable access to all content and applications regardless of the source
- enforcing greater transparency and enforcement over the collection and use of data, and stronger public information requirements about the use of personal data
- imposing open standards, including inter-operable digital standards, to reduce barriers to entry for competitors
- enabling more data 'portability', which would increase both individual and collective consumer power and better enable competition between platforms
- requiring companies and public institutions to keep audit logs of the data they feed into their algorithms and be prepared to explain their algorithms to the public on request
- establishing a duty of care for social media platforms for their users, ensuring minimum standards around published content.[16]

A digital commonwealth

Today, most online data is a resource that is captured, analysed and stored to be monetised for private gain, with the digital infrastructure owned by a relatively small number of platform companies.[17] By capturing a large proportion of the data generated by the new forms of digital consumption, these companies have achieved almost unprecedented growth and wealth. The data, and insights gained from it, are jealously guarded. Transparency is minimal. The potential of data is limited to the development of new commercial products rather than to address collective problems.

Public policy should respond to this new era by seeking to make data a common resource, open and available to be used for a wider variety of ends, and shared according to rules set by a common and enforceable governance regime. This would enable more innovation in both the public and private sectors. From start-up businesses to city-level tools for better democratic decision-making and collaborative problem-solving, there is huge untapped potential.[18] Making data more available is essential for a thriving and open digital economy. We call this vision a 'digital commonwealth', an economy where data and digital technologies serve the common good and innovation flourishes. Some steps have been taken in this direction already: for example, Transport for London's 'open data' portal makes all public TfL data freely accessible for developers to use in their own software and services.[19] Over time, digital utilities might be required to make their data available on a similar basis. It would be essential to maintain privacy of personal information in this process.

There is huge potential for the value of public datasets to be unlocked. There is a wealth of data generated in the public realm, collected by a range of major public institutions. We call this a 'digital commons': one where privacy is respected and data is organised as a collective good, accessible and easy to use to create services, insights and value. *We therefore recommend the creation of a 'digital commons' through the establishment of a Digital UK public service.* Digital

UK would better organise and curate public data, working with local, regional and national public bodies. It should be established by statute, perhaps on a similar model to the BBC, and draw on the expertise of the Government Digital Service.

Digital UK would develop the digital capacity of the public realm. It would ensure stringent privacy and security standards were met, enable the standardisation and inter-operability of data, expand the digital services provided by government and coordinate the management of data infrastructures to make more data open and accessible. Digital UK would develop a network of data banks to curate and store wide-ranging public datasets.[20] It could be a hub of research and experimentation, supporting data scientists to work with public institutions to produce better datasets, use data more effectively, and generate fresh insights and products. A further development might be the creation of a 'Digital Citizen Account' system which would provide each UK citizen with an online profile through which they could manage and aggregate key data about themselves held in the public domain – from tax files through to healthcare information and property rental agreements.

Local digital commonwealth strategies

We believe local authorities should develop their own 'digital commonwealth strategies'. These would seek to reimagine the generation and use of data, and ensure its value is retained and circulated among local communities. This approach would unlock the potential to accelerate innovation in the delivery of local services, encourage greater civic participation in decision-making, and create new start-ups and improve existing local businesses. Our inspirations are innovative cities like Barcelona and Amsterdam, which are democratising data within their cities through rethinking how data is created and who has access to it.[21] Each strategy could be underpinned by four key principles: shifting the legal regime towards the accessibility and accumulation of data; ensuring open-source and inter-operable data wherever possible; reclaiming digital infrastructures; and using public procurement to open up private data for the public good.

Digital inclusion

As the digital economy becomes an increasingly important part of daily life, it is essential that we maximise participation for everyone.[22] This should be accomplished by upgrading digital infrastructure, especially in rural areas, and equipping people with digital skills both through the education system and lifelong learning. The UK should aim to be in the top decile in international rankings of digital connectivity, with new investment in digital infrastructure and skills.

Enabling participation is particularly important for SMEs, whether they are located in towns, cities or rural areas. While SMEs account for more than 50 per cent of GVA and employment in the UK, they are responsible for less than 40 per cent of exports.[23] It can be expensive to engage in international markets, meaning that only the most productive firms can afford to do so. For SMEs in particular, their lack of scale means that trading costs represent a higher share of exports – they are disproportionately affected by tariff and non-tariff barriers to trade.[24] Digital platforms represent an opportunity to lower the cost and reduce the complexity for SMEs to access global markets.

By moving towards a 'digital commonwealth', where the ownership and governance of data and supporting digital systems are organised for the common good, we can serve both prosperity and justice.

Raising Public Investment in a Reformed Macroeconomic Framework

Since the global financial crisis of 2008, economic growth in the UK has averaged just 1.1 per cent – and if population growth is excluded, only 0.4 per cent.[1] As we note in chapter 1, the UK's recovery from the crisis has been among the slowest of all developed countries.[2] This is in spite of nearly a decade of unprecedented monetary activism by the Bank of England, combining near-zero interest rates with the unconventional policy of 'quantitative easing' (QE). And after nearly a decade of fiscal austerity, the deadline for achieving a 'balanced budget' continues to be pushed back.

In this chapter we examine why macroeconomic policy has not worked over recent years, and how we believe its fiscal and monetary elements can be combined more successfully in the future.

The tug of war: fiscal and monetary policy over the last decade

Since the Bank of England was made independent in 1997, the two principal levers of macroeconomic policy aimed at managing the aggregate level of demand in the economy have been under the control of different institutions: fiscal policy by the Treasury, monetary policy by the Bank. This has been widely regarded as an appropriate division of responsibility.[3] But since the financial crisis, the two sets of policymakers have essentially been engaged in a tug of war, pulling in opposite directions.

On the one hand, fiscal policy has been drawing demand and spending out of the economy. The policy of 'austerity' (discretionary fiscal contraction) has seen public spending cut from around 45.1 per cent of GDP in 2009–10 – the high it reached in the wake of the financial crisis – to an estimated 38.8 per cent in 2017–18.[4] On current government plans, it will be reduced further, to 37.6 per cent, by 2022–3. Total government borrowing has been cut from 9.9 per cent of GDP in 2009–10 to an estimated 2.2 per cent in 2017–18.[5]

On the other hand, and to counteract this, the Bank of England has been experimenting with ultra-loose monetary policy to increase consumption and investment in the economy. Interest rates were held at record lows of 0.5 per cent or less for more than eight years up to August 2018, reducing the cost of borrowing with the aim of encouraging higher spending. At the same time, a total of £445 billion has been injected into the economy through the unconventional policy of QE – the purchase of government and corporate bonds by the Bank using money electronically created ('printed') for the purpose. By providing banks and other financial institutions with new money, the aim of QE has been to encourage them to lend more to firms and households in the rest of the economy, and thereby to raise overall spending and investment. QE has become a form of 'life support' for the economy when interest rates could fall no further.

This tug of war between monetary and fiscal policy has not generated sustained growth, and it has therefore not enabled the UK economy to escape the emergency monetary conditions that were introduced nearly a decade ago. And as a result, the economy is now very badly placed to deal with the next recession.

As the government pursued its objective of eliminating the budget deficit through reductions in public expenditure, no differentiation was made between day-to-day spending and investment that might help drive long-term growth. As well as having a short-term direct impact on economic output, reductions in public investment have reduced the economy's long-run productive potential. This in turn makes it more difficult to raise the tax revenues which can reduce the deficit. The result is not just that the deficit is not expected to be cleared until at least 2027–8 – 12 years after the government planned.[6] It is that the rate at which the economy can grow without generating inflation has now almost certainly fallen. This makes it likely that the country's 'lost decade' of growth will become permanent, and that GDP will never catch up with its pre-financial crisis trend.[7]

At the same time, we have had near-zero interest rates for the longest period in the Bank of England's history.[8] This has stimulated households to borrow rather than save, but as a result, the economy is more reliant than ever on household debt for economic growth. The OBR estimates that, in 2017, household consumption accounted for nine-tenths of the estimated 2 per cent GDP growth.[9] With wage growth stagnant, household debt has been rising since 2016 and is forecast to reach 146 per cent of disposable income by 2023.[10]

We believe a new approach is now needed. The current reliance on monetary policy to manage demand is no longer sustainable. This is partly because QE is not a satisfactory long-term policy instrument. QE had a crucial impact in the immediate aftermath of the financial crisis. But even the Bank of England is uncertain how exactly the money created is used, and whether or where it will stimulate the economy.[11] It is also highly inequitable. By suppressing the yields on long-term debt, QE has encouraged investors to move into land and equities instead. It has thus substantially boosted the value of some assets, while reducing others. Property and other asset owners have benefited; pensioners and renters have been penalised.[12] Yet the creation of such economic winners and losers has occurred with almost no public discussion or accountability.[13]

But the main reason we need to rethink the role of monetary policy is that interest rates are simply not now in a position to respond to a future recession.

Over the last 40 years, the UK has experienced a gradual, long-term decline in interest rates. A pattern has emerged in which, when economic growth slows, interest rates are lowered in order to stimulate consumer demand and business investment; but each time rates have tended not to recover to their pre-recession levels before being cut again (see figure 10.1). This suggests that the UK economy has adjusted to cheaper credit, with each subsequent downturn requiring increasingly loose monetary policy to pull the economy out of it, while starting from an ever lower base.

This pattern of progressively declining demand requiring ever-higher doses of monetary stimulus is not unique to the UK. It is one symptom of the phenomenon in a number of Western economies sometimes described as 'secular stagnation', in which persistently deficient demand and excessive saving mean that normal rates of economic growth can only be sustained at very low or even negative interest rates.[14] Economists dispute the causes of low demand, citing demographic shifts, overhanging debt, a slowing of the rate of technological innovation, and increased 'financialisation' of the private sector as possibilities.[15] But the surprising persistence of these

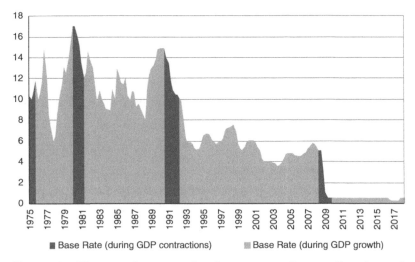

Figure 10.1 The scope for conventional monetary policy to reflate demand is currently limited

Bank of England base rate (%), quarterly average, Q1 1975–Q2 2018

Source: Bank of England (2018)[16] and ONS (2018)[17]

conditions creates a serious problem, with the extraordinary glut of corporate saving across the developed world both a cause and consequence of the phenomenon.[18]

With interest rates still so low at this point in the economic cycle, monetary policy has effectively 'run out of road'. Postwar history suggests that recessions in the UK economy occur on average once every 10–15 years. So we are likely to be nearer to the next one than the last. In the last three recessions, interest rates have been reduced by around 5 percentage points or more. But interest rates are unlikely to be anywhere near 5 per cent when the next recession hits. So, with QE also almost certainly still in place, the Bank of England will have very little capacity to act at all.

A new macroeconomic framework is therefore needed. We propose three sets of reforms: to fiscal policy, to the Bank of England's monetary policy mandate, and to the way in which monetary policy should respond to recessionary conditions.

Reforming fiscal policy

Fiscal sustainability is about ensuring sufficient aggregate demand. Without demand, there can be no growth, and without growth, it is much more difficult – and painful – to reduce the deficit and debt. This requires a much more active role for fiscal policy in the overall macroeconomic framework.

New accounting rules

One of the biggest misconceptions in public debate has been the comparison of the country's finances to those of a household, and the public debt to a credit card bill. A country is not a household: its spending can generate income growth. Investment in education results in a more highly qualified workforce, which earns more and pays more tax; spending on transport and broadband infrastructure makes businesses more productive. Moreover, investment benefits future generations, so there is good reason to share its costs over time through borrowing. It is therefore highly misleading to talk of 'burdening future generations' with debt: they are likely to benefit from the long-term investments it finances.

Two important conclusions follow. The first is that public borrowing should not be combined into a single 'deficit' figure. Borrowing for current spending should be clearly defined as one category; borrowing for investment as another. We support the principle that in normal circumstances, averaged out over the economic cycle or a period of, say, five years, governments should not borrow to pay for current spending (the so-called 'golden rule'). Such spending should be paid for by tax receipts. But this is not true for investment spending. For this, borrowing levels should be determined by an assessment of how far the outlay will contribute to growth, and therefore whether the cost of servicing the debt in the future will be outweighed by increased tax revenues. These two types of borrowing and deficit should be clearly accounted for separately.

Second, this in turn means that the national debt should also be differentiated. The cost–benefit assessment of borrowing will depend in large part on how much it costs to borrow – the interest rate on government bonds. When the interest rate is very low, as at present, borrowing for investment is likely to be attractive; when it is much higher, it will be less so. Without the cost of borrowing, the total level of public debt is not a meaningful figure. It depends on how much the different tranches of borrowing cost in interest payments. In practice, this means that the sustainability of a country's debt depends on two metrics: its 'maturity structure', which determines when the government has to pay or renew its debts; and the difference between the rate of interest it pays on its debt versus the rate at which tax revenues are growing. As the IMF has now acknowledged, as long as the latter is higher than the former, debt is sustainable.[19]

There is therefore no definitive single figure for the 'sustainable level of debt' as a percentage of GDP, and governments should not set arbitrary targets for it. It depends on when it needs to be serviced and how much it costs, relative to the growth of the taxes that must pay for it. At the end of 2017, the average maturity of UK government debt was just under 16 years, while in the first quarter of 2018, it could borrow for a 20-year period at an interest rate of just over 2 per cent.[20] When examined from this perspective, the UK has considerably more space to borrow on a sustainable basis.

It is also important to get the right definition of 'investment'. The current definition of capital expenditure used in the public accounts is almost certainly too narrow for the purposes of setting fiscal rules, excluding some forms of intangible and social expenditure which can contribute to long-run growth. This includes what is sometimes now called 'social infrastructure', such as education, healthcare and childcare, some proportion of which can be classified as a form of investment.[21] *We therefore propose that the OBR and ONS conduct an independent review of public sector accountancy practices, to ensure that investment and debt are better defined, measured and presented.* As part of this process, we believe the definition of public and government debt should be aligned with that used by most other European countries, so that, for instance, borrowing by independent public corporations is not scored as government debt or borrowing.[22]

Increasing public investment

As we argue in chapter 3, achieving long-term prosperity requires the overall structure of demand in the UK economy to shift away from debt-driven consumption towards investment. There needs to be a particular focus on investment in infrastructure, innovation and housing, alongside general business growth. Yet it is clear that private sector investment, which has been largely stagnating in recent years, is not going to be sufficient.

With interest rates still extremely low, and the growth benefits of investment likely to be considerable, there is therefore a very strong case for raising the level of public investment spending. *We therefore propose that annual public investment spending should be increased by at least £15 billion over and above the current forecast by 2022.* That would double the currently planned increase in public investment, equating to an additional 0.8 per cent of 2017 GDP.[23] In turn, this would take gross fixed capital formation in the public sector to approximately 3.5 per cent of GDP, which is the average level over the period 1997–2017 for G7 economies.[24] We propose that around half of this amount, £7.5 billion, should be spent on industrial strategy, as we discuss in chapter 6, with the remainder on other fields of public investment.

New fiscal rules

It is a good idea for governments to adopt fiscal rules. These help prevent short-term political pressures undermining long-run stability, and give businesses and financial markets a degree of certainty about the path of public spending, taxes and borrowing. Correctly designed, they should enable governments to make better macroeconomic decisions. This means the rules must recognise the difference between investment that is expected to generate long-run economic or social benefits, and spending on day-to-day costs. They should formalise the metrics of debt sustainability and provide a framework for undertaking sustainable spending and investment. And they should allow room for manoeuvre in crisis situations, where monetary policy is constrained.

We therefore propose the following three fiscal rules to guide government decisions on spending and investment:

- **Current spending rule** – to balance overall day-to-day government spending with revenues over a rolling five-year period in normal economic circumstances (we define this further below).
- **Investment spending target** – a minimum level of annual public net investment, allowing governments to borrow to produce future revenues and spread the cost of long-term assets over

multiple generations. All new investments should be subject to an independent and transparent assessment of expected economic and social returns, to rule out bad investment choices being made simply to meet the target.

- **Sustainable debt metric** – a rolling five-year target for government debt as a proportion of GDP, set according to an independent assessment of the UK's sustainable debt level, conducted by the OBR on the basis of interest rates, debt maturity and expected tax revenues. As this rule involves greater uncertainty of assessment, it should be applied flexibly in circumstances where it conflicts with the first two.

These rules would, we believe, set a sensible framework for fiscal policy in normal economic conditions. In times of serious recession, when monetary policy is constrained by very low interest rates, governments will be required to engage in more active fiscal policy, sustaining or stimulating demand through higher current expenditure or tax cuts. Indeed, in these circumstances it would be prudent for the Bank of England to clearly state that monetary policy can no longer provide an effective stimulus, and that fiscal policy is required. This could involve, for example, the Monetary Policy Committee (MPC) calculating the value of a 'missing' stimulus, in terms of the size of an interest rate cut they would have wished to make.[25]

A revised mandate for the Bank of England

Since being made operationally independent in 1997, the Bank of England has operated with a simple mandate from the government: to keep inflation at 2 per cent at a two-year horizon. The MPC may consider its impact on growth and employment, subject to meeting its primary price stability objective; it also has scope to allow inflation to depart from the target in the event of an economic shock.[26]

Monetary policy is generally believed to be the nimblest tool for macroeconomic stabilisation in the short term.[27] This is because macroeconomic theory suggests that inflation and output are good proxies for one another; targeting one effectively targets both.[28] But the UK's experience in the period following the financial crisis should serve as a reminder that this theory does not always hold in practice: inflation and output can behave in different ways. Between 2008 and 2014, inflation remained almost exclusively at or above the 2 per cent target, implying that the economy was running 'hot'. Yet output was, in fact, significantly below potential for the entire period. 'Cost-push' inflation can be driven by factors independent of domestic production costs, such as a rise in the oil price, despite economic underperformance.

The MPC has the freedom to 'look through' short-term inflation and informally consider wider economic indicators in setting monetary policy, particularly following an economic shock. That is why it did not raise interest rates between 2008 and 2014. Nonetheless, it came close to doing so: in 2011, the MPC was two votes short of raising interest rates on a number of occasions.[29] Given that, even without a rate increase, output took so long to recover after 2011, this would have been a very costly mistake. Indeed, on the continent, the European Central Bank did raise interest rates, and recession followed shortly afterwards. The close vote shows that an informal understanding to consider more than one indicator may not be sufficient.

We would therefore propose that this informal understanding is made more explicit. *The Treasury should formally revise the MPC's mandate to include explicit targets for unemployment (including under-employment) and the level of nominal GDP, either alongside inflation or as intermediate guides to a primary inflation target.* This would ensure that the MPC focuses on the economy's underlying dynamics of output growth and employment, and not simply inflation. In turn, this would make an appropriate expansionary policy more likely during and after recession.

An additional tool to QE when interest rates are near zero

Conventional monetary policy is likely to remain constrained for a number of years yet. Even if the Bank of England succeeds in raising interest rates from their current extremely low level, they are very unlikely to have reached 5 per cent or more by the time the UK next enters recession. Reducing interest rates alone is therefore unlikely to be sufficient as a policy response. Yet neither has QE proved a reliable, accountable or equitable alternative.[30]

We therefore believe that an additional tool to QE is needed, if and when interest rates reach their near-zero 'effective lower bound' (ELB). Our aim is to establish policy mechanisms that can deliver a stimulus in a more targeted, certain and measurable way than QE as currently practised, with a more transparent and democratically accountable process.

There is now some debate around the scope a central bank has to create money electronically and inject it into the economy through various forms of 'money-financed stimulus'.[31] QE is just one form that this can take. Another would be for the Bank to provide funds to the government to introduce tax cuts, such as a cut in VAT, through money financing. An even more direct form would be through the use of so-called 'helicopter money', where the Bank provided cash directly to households to spend in the economy.[32]

We would favour a 'delegated stimulus'. As discussed in chapter 6, we believe that the UK needs a National Investment Bank (NIB) with the power to borrow to finance economically and socially productive lending in areas such as infrastructure, innovation and business development. A new NIB in the UK would act as a key instrument for the more active industrial strategy we propose.

The additional macroeconomic policy innovation we propose is that the Bank of England be given the power to ask the NIB to expand lending in the real economy when interest rates are at their effective lower bound.[33] It could define the volume of lending to equate to all or part of the interest rate cut that the MPC would in normal circumstances have wished to make.

To ensure that the NIB would always be able to finance a delegated stimulus, our proposal is that it should be able to fund this through the creation of new reserves at the Bank of England, in the same way that the Bank currently funds bond purchases under QE. The MPC could then coordinate its request for a delegated stimulus with a programme of NIB corporate bond purchases in secondary markets. This would mean investors would always know there was a demand for NIB bonds, and it would in effect be a means of money-financing the NIB's expanded investment programme.

It would be possible to do this as soon as an NIB was formed. One way to ensure early market confidence in such a new national institution would be for the Bank of England to announce its intention to purchase a level of NIB bonds on secondary markets to coincide with the first round of issuance. This could be done by reinvesting a small portion of the proceeds of bonds bought under QE once they mature. In most quarters, around £10 billion or more of bonds held under the

Bank's QE programme mature and are actively reinvested to keep the overall level of QE constant.[34] We would propose that some or all of the proceeds from maturing bonds could be invested into bonds issued by the National Investment Bank.

It is vital that the economy is maintained at a sufficient level of aggregate demand to generate the growth it needs. Our proposals are aimed at ensuring that the UK's macroeconomic framework has the right tools available at the right times.

11

Strengthening the Financial System

Over recent decades the financial sector has assumed a position of increasing importance and influence in the British economy. It is one of the largest and most successful financial sectors in the world: in 2017 it contributed around 7 per cent of UK GDP, over 3 per cent of total UK employment, and nearly 5 per cent of tax revenues.[1]

The growth of finance has transformed the structure of the UK economy. In 1970, finance made up 5 per cent of total gross value added (GVA), compared with 32 per cent for the manufacturing sector.[2] From the 1970s onwards, the finance sector grew faster than the economy as a whole: by 2008 it accounted for 9 per cent of GVA, next to 11 per cent for manufacturing.[3] Today, finance accounts for 7 per cent of GVA, with manufacturing at 10 per cent.[4]

While the financial sector has been highly successful, its impact has not been wholly benign. Its development over recent decades has generated serious structural challenges for the UK economy which make it hard to achieve the prosperity and justice we wish to see. In this chapter we examine these issues and propose measures to address them.[5]

The role and impact of the financial sector

The UK economy exhibits what at first sight looks like a paradox. The UK is home to one of the world's largest and most successful financial centre. Yet at the same time it has a much lower rate of investment, as a proportion of GDP, than most other developed economies. There has been a consistent problem in particular of 'patient capital' for long-term investment.[6] Yet the reason is relatively straightforward: the UK is a global hub for international finance, providing capital for businesses all over the world, rather than simply domestic investment.

Yet there remain important questions about the role of finance in the UK economy. One of the most striking findings of recent research into the UK financial sector is that the cost which the sector effectively charges the rest of the economy for its services – the 'unit cost of inter-mediation' – has remained more or less constant for the last 60 years.[7] This is despite enormous productivity advances in this period, in information technologies and analytical capacity, including computer chips, the internet, mobile telephony, broadband and data analytics.[8] A truly competitive market would have ensured that the institutions involved in financial intermediation passed on some proportion of the productivity gain from these technological advances as lower costs to companies and savers (and, potentially, into greater levels of investment too). Yet while in the OECD as a whole the average costs of intermediating finance fell by a third between 2000 and 2014, in the UK costs remained almost identical.[9] What appears to have happened is that, in aggregate, the financial sector has appropriated most of its productivity gains for itself.

The purpose of the finance sector should be to intermediate effec-tively between borrowers and savers, efficiently allocating available capital to the most productive investments.[10] There is evidence to suggest, however, that it is not currently meeting this purpose. Four particular issues arise in the relationship between the finance sector and the rest of the economy. One concerns the provision of long-term investment finance for business development, so-called 'patient capital'. Second, there is the question of 'short-termism', the way in which markets in share ownership put pressures on corporate performance. Third, the UK has a long-term problem of asset price inflation, particularly in land and property. Last, the finance sector has played a key role in keeping the value of sterling higher than it would otherwise have been. We examine each of these issues in turn.

Shortage of patient capital

Economic output is dependent upon investment, but the UK has significantly lower investment levels than other advanced nations. Business spending on replacing or expanding capital in the UK stands at around 17 per cent of GVA, against 20 per cent on average across the eurozone.[11] Over time, this has left the stock of capital in the UK far lower than that of other successful economies.[12]

There appears to be a particular gap in the long-term – or 'patient' – finance being made available to smaller, fast-growing and innovative companies.[13] While lending to SMEs has recovered since the financial crisis, it has been driven entirely by lending to medium-sized firms.[14] Small businesses have continued to pay back more to banks than they have been lent.[15] This is not because they do not want credit: the British Business Bank found that the supply of growth loans (up to a value of £2 million) to the fastest-growing small firms fell short of demand in 2014 by between £170 million and £870 million.[16] The report of the government's Patient Capital Review panel concluded that, while the UK remains a good place for start-up businesses, there is insufficient capital available to match the demand for 'scale-up' finance, particularly outside London and the South East. This is a particular problem for companies requiring more than £5 million in equity investment.[17]

Part of the reason for this is that bank lending in the UK is less focused on business investment than in other comparable countries. Loans to UK businesses account for 5 per cent of total UK bank assets, compared to 14 per cent on average across the eurozone.[18] Bank lending is instead disproportionately directed to land and property: real estate loans account for over 78 per cent of all loans to non-financial businesses and individuals in the UK.[19] Once real estate is excluded, loans to UK businesses now account for just 3 per cent of all banking assets.[20]

Short-termism and equity markets

It is now widely acknowledged that UK financial markets have become more 'short-termist' over recent decades, meaning that investors are seeking to make returns over shorter periods than in the past.[21] This has led to a shift in corporate behaviour, and an appreciable reduction in long-term investment.[22]

Over the last quarter of a century, the proportion of company profits distributed to shareholders, rather than being reinvested, has been increasing: as we note in chapter 8, for non-financial companies this rose from 39 to 55 per cent between 1990 and 2016.[23] This trend has occurred in a way largely unrelated to profit levels: since the financial crisis, dividend payments have remained relatively constant even as profits have fluctuated. The result is that the average 'dividend cover' (the multiple by which post-tax company earnings exceed shareholder payouts) has fallen by a quarter in the last decade, and is now at a

20-year low.[24] Share buybacks, another means of distributing profits to shareholders, have also increased markedly.[25]

These trends have arisen partly as a result of changes in the structure of equity markets, which have become increasingly dominated by short-term trading rather than long-term investment. Hedge funds, high-frequency trading and proprietary trading now make up 72 per cent of equity market turnover in the UK,[26] compared with 51 per cent in the US and 39 per cent in the rest of Europe.[27] For such traders, profit and fees are dependent on the volume of trading and performance relative to other traders, rather than long-term value creation by the companies whose shares they trade. This has seen the proliferation of investment funds, many of which perform no better than statistical averages.[28]

The result is a misalignment of incentives between such shareholders and the savers they ultimately represent.[29] In turn, this influences corporate behaviour, as company boards are pressured into generating short-term returns for shareholders rather than long-term investment, as we discuss in chapter 8.[30] The structure of executive pay in many companies, with incentives based around share prices rather than long-term value creation, frequently exacerbates these pressures.

Asset price inflation and financial instability

The extent to which UK banks are focused on lending against property rather than business development has a wider impact on the economy. Rather than increase the productive capacity of the economy, its main effect is to drive up asset prices.

From 1979 to the end of 2017, house prices in the UK rose almost tenfold, while consumer prices increased by just half that amount.[31]

A self-reinforcing cycle was created, in which increased levels of bank lending helped push up property prices, and high house prices in turn allowed consumers to borrow more against their homes' increasing value (see figure 11.1). Between the late 1980s and 2008, household debt increased from around 50 to 100 per cent of GDP while lending to consumers reached over 160 per cent of disposable incomes and savings rates fell to all-time lows.[32] A similar pattern developed in the corporate sector, where property accounted for more than half of the increase in corporate borrowing in the early 2000s.[33]

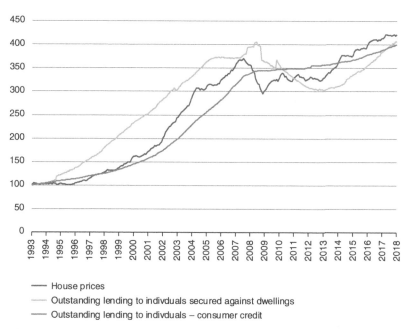

- House prices
- Outstanding lending to indivduals secured against dwellings
- Outstanding lending to indivduals – consumer credit

Figure 11.1 House prices, mortgage debt and consumer credit have increased in lockstep, falling briefly after the global financial crisis before rising again

House prices (Index: Q1 1993 = 100), outstanding lending secured against dwellings (Index: April 1993 = 100) and outstanding consumer credit (Index: April 1993 = 100)

Source: Nationwide (2018)[34] and Bank of England (2018)[35]

The inflation of house prices and other assets as bank lending has increased has created two significant problems. It has increased wealth inequality, as we discuss further in chapter 12. And it has contributed to financial instability. The ratio of UK banks' financial assets and their equity (one way of measuring bank leverage) rose to nearly 12:1 by 2008, one of the highest in the OECD.[36] These high levels of leverage rendered financial institutions vulnerable to fairly small increases in default rates.[37] As banks became more interconnected through the interbank system, problems with single institutions quickly spread to the whole system.[38]

Another important factor was the rise of the 'shadow banking' system.[39] Shadow banks are financial institutions that lend money without taking deposits guaranteed by the state. The scale of shadow banking in the UK grew dramatically in the run-up to the financial crisis, and much of the risk built up in the banking system was concentrated in them, as they were less tightly regulated than deposit-taking institutions.[40] In practice, the two sectors were closely linked through the banks' creation of 'special investment vehicles' and other off-balance sheet entities to hold riskier investments. Driven by regulation, the evolution of fintech (financial technology) and the expansion of the asset management sector, the shadow banking system has continued to evolve since 2009.[41] Non-bank financial institutions are now responsible for nearly 50 per cent of the financial system's total financial assets, an increase of 13 percentage points since 2008.[42]

Sterling and the current account deficit

The UK has run a current account deficit every year since 1984, meaning that we consistently buy more from the rest of the world than we sell to it. In 2017, the UK recorded the largest current account deficit as a percentage of GDP of all G7 countries.[43] As we discuss in chapter 3, this indicates a serious problem of competitiveness.

The outflows of sterling associated with running a current account deficit should, in theory, have led to its depreciation over this period. This would have increased the competitiveness of UK exports and made imports more expensive, in turn reducing the deficit. But the UK has instead managed to cover its current account deficit through large inflows of overseas capital.[44] In effect, the financial sector was able to use very high levels of borrowing in the run-up to the financial crisis to return capital flowing abroad back into the UK economy. Inflows into UK bank deposits and securitised debt instruments together averaged 6.2 per cent of GDP between 1997 and 2008.[45]

When the financial crisis brought this process to an end, the impact on sterling was immediate: between July 2007 and January 2009, the value of sterling declined over 25 per cent.[46] The vote to leave the European Union in June 2016 led to another rapid depreciation.[47] But the core processes by which the financial sector is able to attract foreign capital to cover the current account deficit remain in place. Asset prices have continued to increase since the financial crisis. Households are still able to borrow against the increasing value of their homes, and household debt is now almost at pre-crisis levels.[48] There has also been an increase in foreign direct investment into the UK – mainly in the form of increased foreign holdings in domestic companies – with 2016 marking a record year for foreign mergers and acquisitions of British businesses.[49] Revaluation effects have also increased the value of the UK's foreign investments.[50]

The result is that the UK effectively suffers from a kind of financial 'Dutch disease', the process by which an economy is negatively impacted by the high demand for its currency generated by a major sector. As the financial sector has grown and sustained the value of sterling above what it would otherwise have been, this has had a serious impact on the UK's manufacturing exports.[51] From the point of view of manufacturing and other trading sectors, it has created an overvalued currency. This has contributed both to the decline in our exports and to the high import dependency of many of our remaining manufacturing industries.[52] This means that, even when the value of the pound falls, the UK economy has been unable to respond sufficiently: much of the price gain to exporters has been eroded by the increasing cost of imported components.[53]

For all these reasons, we believe that the financial sector needs reform. We propose a series of measures aimed at retaining a globally successful financial sector while mitigating its negative impacts on the wider UK economy. We want to see a more balanced UK economy achieved by accelerating growth in a more diversified range of sectors, so that we are less dependent on any single sector for our overall economic performance. We should aim to 'level up' rather than to 'level down'. The financial sector is already facing strong headwinds as a result of the decision to leave the European Union and the probable diminished access to the single market.

Increasing investment and patient capital

Increasing the supply of patient capital to the UK economy is a significant task. We welcome the recent creation of new financing mechanisms through the British Business Bank.[54] But we believe that this needs to go further. It is for this reason that we set out in chapter 6 our proposal for the creation of a new National Investment Bank, which can provide long-term finance for business growth and innovation and for infrastructure.

We also believe that short-termism in equity markets and corporate behaviour needs to be addressed. In chapter 8 we argue for a change in corporate governance to help do this, ending the primacy of shareholders in the duties of directors, restricting voting rights for short-term shareholders and bringing new voices, including those of workers, onto company boards. We also argue for a change in the composition of remuneration committees and the incentive packages awarded to company executives.

At the same time, incentives need to be better aligned between investors, their intermediaries and companies. Fiduciary law requires that agents representing the interests of savers and others take every reasonable step to ensure that their actions do in fact result in the best value to the ultimate client or asset owner. This duty has tended to be interpreted narrowly. Echoing the recommendations of the Kay Review and Law Commission reviews, we believe that the current legal provision, which covers board directors and fund trustees, can be strengthened and clarified.[55] There is a strong case for the obligations and powers of fiduciary responsibility to remain with the principal corporate 'agents' or pension fund trustees, even if intermediaries are contracted to act on their behalf; and for the legal reach of fiduciary responsibility to be extended to asset managers and brokers in the investment chain. *We therefore propose that the legal fiduciary duty on pension and insurance funds should be reviewed, including its extension to financial intermediaries.* This should include a review of how more explicit environmental and social obligations might be included within fiduciary duties. The aim should be to ensure that shareholders exercise good stewardship over companies, in the long-term interests of their savers and the economy as a whole.

Improving financial stability

Since the financial crisis, international institutions have largely agreed on the need for 'macroprudential' regulation to ensure the financial stability of the whole economy, not just individual firms. The voluntary 'Basel III' recommendations – agreed in September 2010 but currently being phased in by 2019 – effectively triple the size of the capital reserves that the world's banks must hold against losses.[56] The recommendations include leverage ratios relating banks' balance sheets to their capital stocks; the implementation of 'dynamic capital' ratios and other measures to dampen pro-cyclicality (the tendency of banks to lend more when the economy is in an upswing); and a stable funding ratio requiring banks to have enough liquid assets to cover their costs for at least 30 days.

There is widespread agreement that Basel III is 'necessary but not sufficient'.[57] It was effectively designed to protect the banks from the business cycle, but not the reverse. While restricting the activities of individual banks – which itself has had an appreciable effect on their approach to risk and willingness to lend – it has neither reduced systemic risk to acceptable levels nor prevented rising debt levels and asset price inflation.[58]

We therefore propose three sets of measures to improve financial stability by curbing excessive debt levels. Our proposals cover changes to lending for housing; reforms to the banking levy to improve the resilience of the sector; and changes to how debt is treated for corporations.

A house price inflation target

We believe that the Bank of England should be able to do more to dampen asset price inflation as part of its macroprudential responsibility to counter systemic risk. *We therefore propose that the government investigate whether the Financial Policy Committee (FPC) should be given an explicit house price inflation target, set by government.* This would be analogous to the mandate of the Bank's Monetary Policy Committee to control consumer price inflation. The aim of such a target would be to set property price expectations (a critical driver of house price inflation), reduce excessive debt and control capital inflows.

We recognise that seeking to control house price inflation today is to some extent 'closing the stable door after the horse has bolted'. It would have been much better had such a measure been part of the policy framework when the Bank of England was made independent 20 years ago. We recognise the limitations of its adoption at this stage; on balance, however, we believe it may be able to play a role in limiting house price inflation in the future and is worthy of serious examination, including by the Bank itself.

The primary levers available to the FPC to act on a house price inflation target would be the controls it can impose on banks and other lenders regarding the levels of credit they can make available for property purchases. These include loan-to-value and debt-to-income ratios, and the proportion of a bank's total assets which can be lent against property. The FPC recently implemented a loan-to-income ratio limit of 4.5 for 15 per cent of new mortgages, even though the Bank of England estimated that only around 11 per cent of mortgages exceeded this ratio in 2015.[59] Implementing targets that constrain excessive lending will require a stronger mandate than at present to limit asset price inflation.

Since house price inflation is very different in different parts of the country, any such controls would need to be exercised on a regionally differentiated basis. They would also need to acknowledge the equity impacts on different groups of house purchasers, with priority given (for example) to first-time buyers over second-home and buy-to-let purchasers. The overall aim would be to reduce levels of mortgage lending and keep house prices within the new inflation target. Since house prices are also determined by supply, if the FPC were unable to hold house prices to a mandated target, it should be able to request that the government do more through supply-side measures, including house building. We discuss some such measures further in chapter 12.

Curbing systemic financial risk

In addition to exploring a new house price inflation target, we propose that the FPC should be able to impose new 'counter-cyclical' capital requirements on banking institutions and groups. Such controls, which rise and fall depending on the state of the financial cycle, have been shown to be effective in reducing leverage and limiting systemic risk in the financial system.[60]

In the run-up to the financial crisis, much of the risk that had built up in the financial system was hidden in the shadow banking sector. The growing interconnectivity between banks and non-bank financial institutions meant that a slight increase in defaults spread quickly throughout the system, creating a systemic crisis.[61] Non-bank financial institutions are still very important to the UK's financial system today, and regulation has failed to keep pace with developments in the sector.[62] There are concerns about the distribution and visibility of risks in this complex system, which ultimately can precipitate a financial crisis.[63]

At present, the UK has a bank levy based on lenders' balance sheets, and banks are also subject to a corporation tax surcharge. The latter in practice has an anti-competitive effect, with a greater proportionate impact on small and challenger banks.[64] *We therefore propose that the corporation tax surcharge be abolished, and the bank levy made into a counter-cyclical measure applied to both regular and shadow banks.* This would limit profitability at the height of the financial cycle and protect banks in downswings.

Improving company stability

While borrowing for investment is desirable, as the financial crisis exposed, companies can become vulnerable if they are excessively indebted. Very high debt levels – sometimes as much as six or seven times pre-tax profits – increase the exposure of companies to shocks, such as an increase in the cost of borrowing or a sudden downturn in revenues that means debt cannot be serviced.

The reasons for increases in corporate debt levels in the lead-up to the financial crisis were multi-faceted. Financial deregulation, combined with low global interest rates, encouraged corporations to take out more debt.[65] The emergence of the leveraged buyout model of acquisitions saw financial engineering increase company debt levels, in many cases with little or no long-term value creation in the process.[66] One of the underlying reasons has been the preferential treatment given to debt over equity financing through debt interest tax relief.[67]

The OECD guidelines on base erosion and profit shifting guidelines recommend that countries adopt reforms to cap the amount of debt interest relief at between 10 and 30 per cent of corporate annual earnings. The UK has since committed to following through with this recommendation, using the upper limit of 30 per cent. However, this will only affect a small number of very large companies.[68] *We therefore propose that the UK review whether the cap should be progressively reduced to the lower limit of 10 per cent of earnings recommended by the OECD from 2022-7.*

Tackling illicit capital flows and promoting transparency

Over recent years, increasing attention has been drawn to the role of London, and therefore sterling, in international money laundering and tax avoidance and evasion.[69] There is evidence to suggest that illicit capital flows account for a sizeable and growing portion of the capital that flows into the UK. This is reflected in the sustained positive balance in the 'net errors and omissions' (NEO) item of the balance of payments, which over the last decade has been consistently above 0.5 per cent of GDP.[70] It is likely to have contributed to sterling's appreciation and sustained its high value.

Sterling is a particularly attractive currency to use for money laundering and tax evasion for a number of reasons. The UK is a major conduit to the network of so-called 'secrecy jurisdictions', where companies can be registered without scrutiny, such as the British Virgin Islands and the Cayman Islands.[71] At the same time, the London property market is a significant destination for laundered money.[72] And until recently, sterling has been a strong currency not subject to too much volatility.

Reducing the use of sterling for illegal activities should be an aim in itself. It would also help stem the level of capital inflows into the UK, thereby placing downward pressure on sterling and helping to correct its overvaluation. *We therefore propose a series of measures to clamp down on tax avoidance and illicit capital flows into the UK.*

Transparency of company ownership is vital for the management of risk and the elimination of criminal and corrupt activity. If the authorities are to act on the latter, and if investors are to make good investment decisions based on risk, they need to know who owns what.

The UK has been pioneering the development of a searchable, free-to-access, public 'Register of People with Significant Control' of companies. In May 2018, the House of Commons voted through the Sanctions and Anti-Money Laundering Bill, which included a provision to extend the public register of people with significant control to the overseas territories. This is welcome, but there are two serious weaknesses that should now be remedied. First, the data submitted is not verified and instead relies on wholly self-reported data from companies, reducing confidence in its accuracy.[73] Proof of identity could be required, as is the case in Denmark. And other actors – such as lawyers, auditors, banks and estate agents – should be required to cross-check the data with their own records and due diligence findings and report discrepancies. Second, the threshold for declaration of beneficial ownership is currently set at 25 per cent of the shares or voting rights in a company.[74] This makes it relatively straightforward to avoid: if a family were to divide ownership between five of its members, no single person would be required to disclose their identity. *We therefore recommend that the data on the public register of people with significant control should be verifiable; that named individuals should be required to provide proof of identity; and that the threshold for inclusion on the register should be lowered from 25 per cent to 5 per cent of shares or voting rights.*

Alongside the public register of beneficial ownership, we believe the UK should create transparency on the beneficiaries of trusts. Trusts are legal arrangements in which an individual transfers assets, such as property, to a trustee to manage on behalf of someone else. By transferring control to trustees, it is possible to hide the true source of the assets in the trust.[75] *We therefore propose that trusts should be included in the public register of people with significant control.* This should include the disclosure of all parties to a trust, including the individual that established the trust, the people set to benefit from it, and the trustees who manage it.

A series of other measures are also needed. The UK should implement publicly available, country-by-country reporting to curb corporate tax avoidance and create a 'blacklist' of financial regulatory havens. Alongside increased transparency, enforcement measures should be in stepped up, and more substantial sanctions applied for those found to be undertaking illegal activity in or via the UK. Banks found to have knowingly or unknowingly facilitated illegal activities in the UK should be liable for much higher fines, and those individuals found to have engaged in or facilitated these activities should also be expected to face criminal convictions.

As the financial crisis showed, the finance sector has a significant impact on us all. We believe our proposals would help strengthen financial stability and promote productive investment.

12

Spreading Wealth and Ownership across the Economy

How much wealth people have shapes their lives: economic security affects whether they can take a risk and set up a new business, invest in their future through periods of education, or take time away from work to help or support their loved ones.

But the wealth that individuals and households own – their property, private pensions, financial assets and physical assets – is very unequally distributed. Wealth inequalities are worsening and are a particular source of injustice, since wealth is often not earned, but instead either inherited or the result of rising asset values, unrelated to effort. Many of the causes of such inequalities, particularly rising house prices, also serve to undermine prosperity.

In this chapter we examine the UK's inequalities of wealth and their causes, explain why such inequalities matter, and make a series of proposals to share wealth and asset ownership more widely.

Wealth inequality and its causes

The total wealth of households and individuals in Great Britain is estimated at £12.8 trillion.[1] It is very unevenly distributed.[2] The wealthiest 10 per cent of households own more than 900 times the wealth of the poorest 10 per cent, and five times more than the entire bottom half of all households combined.[3] Wealth is much more unequally distributed than income: whereas the median income in the top 10 per cent is around seven times the median income in the bottom 10 per cent, the median wealth of the top 10 per cent is 315 times the median in the bottom 10 per cent (see figure 12.1).[4]

Perhaps the starkest aspect of wealth inequality today is generational. In the first half of the twentieth century, wealth tended to cascade down the generations: each generation had more wealth than the previous one. But every generation since the postwar 'baby boomers' has had less wealth than the generation before them had at the same age.[5] People born in the 1980s had just a third of the property wealth at age 28 of those born in the 1970s.[6]

Wealth is very unequally distributed across the regions – both a consequence and a driver of the geographical economic imbalances

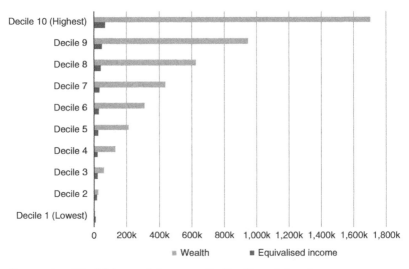

Figure 12.1 Wealth is much less equally distributed than income
Median household net equivalised income and median total net wealth by decile, Great Britain, July 2014–June 2016
Source: ONS (2018)[7]

described in chapter 15. People living in London and the South East hold much more of the country's wealth than those in other regions. The average household in the South East has more than twice the wealth (£380,600) of the average household in the North East (£163,000).[8]

There is also a clear gender divide. The average man at retirement age today has four to five times the pension pot of the average woman at retirement age, while men in their late thirties already have 60 per cent more savings than women.[9] Social class, education and ethnicity also still matter hugely. People with a degree are almost five times as likely as those with no qualifications to be in a household with wealth of £1 million or more.[10]

At the same time, low levels of savings and high levels of debt (which is effectively negative financial wealth), add to the distributional picture. One in eight adults has no cash savings at all available for a 'rainy day' or unexpected expenses.[11] One in ten households have over £10,000 of unsecured consumer debt, and 13 per cent of households spend over a quarter of their monthly income servicing debt or are in arrears on loans and bills.[12] Parents, particularly single parents, are more likely to be struggling with debt than other adults.[13]

Wealth inequality fell for most of the twentieth century, as economic growth allowed lower income groups to accumulate savings and buy homes. But since the 1980s, inequality has been rising again in almost all developed economies. As the rate of return on financial assets and property has exceeded the growth rate of economies as a whole, those with greater wealth have pulled even further ahead of those dependent primarily on their earnings from work.[14]

In the UK, the largest single driver of rising wealth inequality has been rising land and property prices, which for two decades have grown far faster than earnings (see figure 12.2). This trend has

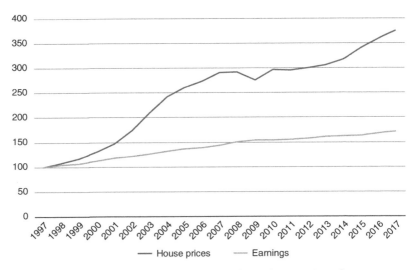

Figure 12.2 House price inflation has significantly outstripped wage growth for two decades
Median full-time earnings and median house prices in England and Wales, 1997–2017 (Index: 1997 = 100)
Source: IPPR analysis using ONS (2018b)[15]

Note: Data for annual earnings are not available before 1999. For these years the ratio of house price to earnings has been calculated using annualised weekly earnings.

dramatically reduced home ownership rates. From the 1990s to the mid-2000s, an increasing proportion of the population came to own their own homes.[16] But since the financial crash in 2007–8 this trend has been reversed, with falling rates of home ownership among those in the bottom half of the wealth distribution driving a significant increase in property wealth inequality.[17] It is a stark fact that today one in 10 adults, or 5.2 million people, own a second home, while 40 per cent own no property at all.[18]

There is a distinct generational dimension to this. In 1990, half of those aged between 25 and 34 owned their own home. But by 2017 this had fallen to one in four. By contrast, in 1990, half of those aged over 65 owned their own home, but by 2017 this had increased to three in four.[19] With land and property prices diverging markedly between different parts of the country, this is also the single largest source of regional wealth inequality: the total value of housing stock in London is now greater than the housing stock of all of Scotland, Wales, Northern Ireland and the North of England combined.[20]

Land and property prices have risen because demand has out-stripped supply. Economic and population growth, particularly in London and the South East, along with a reduction in the average size of households, has increased demand. This has also been stoked by more permissive lending practices by banks and other financial institutions, discussed further in chapter 11.[21] Increasing foreign investment in property, much of it speculative, has exacerbated these trends, particularly in London.[22]

Supply, too, has been constrained. Planning and housing policies, including the restrictions which successive governments have placed on local authority house-building, have kept new builds well below the rate needed to match increasing demand.[23] And as we discuss below, a more general failure of public policy to capture the increase in land value which arises when planning permission is given has made house-building much more expensive than it needs to be.

Though rising land and property prices are the principal cause of rising wealth inequality, other factors are also important. Individual ownership of company shares has declined markedly since the 1980s. The wealthiest 10 per cent now own over 60 per cent of the UK's financial wealth, including stocks and shares.[24]

At the same time, as we discuss in chapter 3, there are clear risks that wealth inequality will worsen in the future if automation accelerates. As technological advances substitute machines for labour in the production process, this is likely to drive rising returns to capital. If share ownership remains highly concentrated, this will tend to increase wealth inequality.[25]

Why wealth inequality matters

Wealth makes a big difference to people's life chances and their feelings of security. Those with savings and a pension have the comfort of knowing that they and their family can deal with unexpected events – such as an appliance breaking down at home, or being made redundant – and can look forward to living comfortably in retirement. Lack of savings is unsurprisingly associated with stress, relationship breakdown, and a feeling of lack of choice and control over one's life.[26]

Property wealth is particularly important in this regard. The capital stake in a home can be borrowed against later in life: to pay for social care costs, for example. But it also reduces housing costs. Those who rent generally pay more, as a proportion of income, than those who own.[27]

Wealth also confers opportunity, creating an 'asset-effect' on life chances. Those who start out in adult life with some wealth have better outcomes by their mid-thirties than those who do not, measured in terms of employment, earnings, physical and mental health, and even greater political agency.[28] Those with assets are more able to take risks and invest in new ventures: among successful entrepreneurs, the most commonly shared trait is not personality but access to capital.[29]

These advantages of wealth raise an important issue of economic justice, because a great deal of wealth is unearned. While many people's desire to pass on wealth to their children is understandable, inheritance creates a lottery of birth. The amount of bequeathed wealth as a proportion of national income is increasing: between 1977 and 2006, the total wealth gifted each year is estimated to have doubled from 4.7 per cent to 8.2 per cent of national income.[30]

Some of the return on different kinds of assets may be a reward for risk-taking, and necessary to enable people to take risks. But much is simply an 'economic rent' – the difference between what an asset actually yields and the (often much lower) investment that was needed to bring it into use. The increases in land and property values that have occurred over the last 30 years are almost entirely unearned rents of this kind.

Wealth inequality is damaging to prosperity. Rising land and property values have diverted investment and lending away from more productive uses, with banks in particular (as discussed in chapter 11) increasing the proportion of their overall lending going into real estate. At the same time, rising property wealth has encouraged consumers to borrow and to spend beyond their incomes, raising household debt and contributing towards an unbalanced pattern of overall growth. Given the importance of private wealth to entrepreneurship, it seems likely that the lack of wealth among large parts of the population is limiting entrepreneurial activity in the economy as a whole.[31]

Third, the structure and distribution of capital ownership shapes how economic rewards and power are distributed in the economy. Ownership of capital grants rights both to income and to control over how businesses are run. The concentration of business ownership means relatively few people have a significant stake in economic decision-making, including in the businesses in which they work.

So we believe government should aim to reverse the recent rise in wealth inequality and to spread wealth and ownership more widely. We set out proposals to widen the ownership of wealth and ensure more people benefit from its rising returns; to tackle the rise in land values and build more homes; and to open up the ownership of businesses to their workers. In the next chapter, we look at how wealth and land can be taxed more fairly and efficiently.

A Citizens' Wealth Fund

How can more people share in the nation's wealth? *We propose that the UK should establish a Citizens' Wealth Fund, a sovereign wealth fund owned by and run in the interests of the whole population.* We believe a fund of this kind would provide a mechanism for all of society to hold a stake in national wealth, and to benefit from the increasing returns to capital. By transforming a part of national private and corporate wealth into shared net public wealth, and stewarding it well, it would help redistribute wealth within and between generations.[32]

Over 70 governments around the world have sovereign wealth funds, including those of Norway, Australia, France, New Zealand, Ireland, Singapore and nine US states. Many, but not all, are capitalised using royalties and tax revenues from natural resources or fiscal surpluses; almost all are invested in a diverse range of global assets, including equity, property and bonds. The UK had the opportunity to create a sovereign wealth fund (as Norway did) when it began to exploit North Sea oil in the 1970s: it is estimated that had such a fund been created then, it would be worth over £500 billion today.[33]

There are a number of sources through which the UK could capitalise a Citizens' Wealth Fund, which are described in detail in the policy paper published by the Commission.[34] They range from revenues from wealth taxes to the proceeds of asset sales (planned asset sales between 2017–18 and 2022–23 are expected to raise around £57 billion, including £15 billion from the sale of RBS shares and £27 billion from the winding down of UK Asset Resolution).[35] The £14.1 billion[36] worth of assets in the Crown Estate could be included, and new options such as a 'scrip tax' (a tax on the issuance of equity) could be considered. At a time when the costs of long-term public borrowing are very low – and with a likely higher real rate of return from investments in a wealth fund – government could also issue bonds to help capitalise the fund.

We estimate that from a mixture of such sources, along with the returns from investment, it would be possible to create a Citizens' Wealth Fund worth around £186 billion over an approximately ten-year period.[37] Average real (above inflation) returns of 4 per cent per year from such a fund should be achievable; most funds around the world have comfortably reached or exceeded this rate over the long term.[38] Payouts would then be made only from annual returns, preserving the fund in perpetuity.

The governance of the fund should be structured so that the public have both control and benefit of their fund and its assets.[39] We would propose that Parliament should enshrine the fund and its structure in legislation, with a publicly appointed board. Parliament should set the investment mandate and any ethical and sustainability requirements on how the fund could invest, but the fund should then be independently managed by the board, using an asset management agency.

As the ultimate owners of the fund, and as its purpose is wealth redistribution, we believe the public should receive the monetary benefits of ownership. This could be done, for example, by providing all citizens with an annual dividend. This is currently done by the Alaska state fund.[40] But any such universal dividend would inevitably be relatively small.

We are therefore more attracted to paying a larger dividend, but focusing it on young people. At the age of 25, young people are looking to invest in their futures. They may wish to invest in their education, put down a deposit on a home or start a business. Currently only the already wealthy – generally those with wealthy parents – can do this. A fund of £186 billion would be sufficiently large to enable it to provide a 'universal minimum inheritance' of £10,000 to all 25-year-olds born in the UK from 2030.[41] The Resolution Foundation's Intergenerational Commission has supported this proposal.[42] By providing everyone with the means to invest in their future and take risks, a lump-sum capital dividend of this kind would help to equalise the 'opportunity effect' of holding assets, underpinning a more just but also a more enterprising society.

Building more homes

Enabling more young people to build up wealth by owning their own home, while enabling others to rent at affordable rates, will require significant changes to the markets for land and property. House price inflation needs to be slowed so that it no longer exceeds the growth of earnings. And we need to increase the rate at which new homes are built.

In chapter 11, we argue that the government should investigate whether the Bank of England should be given a new target to control house price inflation, by using macroprudential tools to restrict excessive lending for property. We also need to reduce the cost of new homes by reducing the cost of building them.

The high cost of land is a fundamental cause of the shortage of housing supply over the past few decades: it makes it more expensive, difficult and risky to build homes at affordable prices. A negative feedback loop has been created, in which the high cost of land is driven by the shortage of homes, but as land prices rise it becomes more expensive to build, thus driving prices up further.[43] As fewer people are able to own their own home, rising house prices benefit an increasingly small group of (generally older) homeowners – and now increasingly owners of second homes – exacerbating wealth inequality even further.

A major part of the reason why new homes are expensive is that landowners make significant gains when residential planning permission is granted. The average price of a piece of agricultural land in England is £21,000 per hectare. But for land with planning permission to build homes it is over £6 million per hectare.[44] This huge 'planning gain' is created by the state, in the granting of planning permission; but it accrues almost entirely to the landowner as an unearned windfall.

Currently local authorities can claw back some of this planning gain for the benefit of the community through use of a Community Infrastructure Levy on developers, or by obliging them to provide a certain amount of affordable housing, local infrastructure or community amenities in 'Section 106' agreements. But these powers are relatively weak and capture only a small amount of the increase in land value.[45] 'Affordability' is based on market prices rather than incomes and ability to pay. Since the cost of land determines the cost of the housing built on it, this has a significant impact on the price and quality of new homes.

To address this problem, we propose a number of reforms to the land and housing markets. First, the cap on local authority borrowing to finance house building in England should be abolished. Today, private sector developers are only building around half of the government's target of 300,000 new homes a year. To achieve the remainder, local authorities must be allowed to borrow. Given that housing investment earns a return in rents paid or sales made, it makes no sense for councils' borrowing to be capped as at present.[46]

Second, government should set new guidelines in England for the minimum proportion of new housing developments which must be genuinely affordable. Our view is that one-third of all new housing should be social housing for rent; one-third genuinely affordable (in perpetuity) for sale; and one-third for sale at market prices. We acknowledge that this may mean some private developers withdrawing from the market. But their place should be taken by local authorities, housing associations and other civic house-builders such as new town development corporations.[47]

Third, compulsory purchase laws should be reformed to allow local authorities and public bodies to buy land at its 'use value' prior to planning permission, plus a degree of compensation. This is the approach taken in a number of countries including Germany and the Netherlands. At present, under the 1961 Land Compensation Act, landowners are able to capture the 'hope value' of land – the increase in its value that would be likely to occur were it to be given planning permission. The difference in cost to the public authority can be significant, with a distorting impact on the land market.[48] In practice, compulsory purchase powers would likely be used sparingly; but the threat of them would reduce price expectations and allow the cost of land to fall.[49]

Fourth, planning authorities should be given the powers to 'zone' areas of land for development and freeze its price close to its current use value, as happens in Germany.[50] Landowners would still get a fair return, but any windfall would accrue to the state to pay for infrastructure and affordable housing to benefit the local community. Authorities would have the power to determine what would be built on the land, ensuring that these new developments deliver high-quality and sustainable communities.

Fifth, the sale of public land to the private sector for residential development should in most circumstances be ended. Public ownership offers a relatively simple way of ensuring that land is used for affordable housing. It also provides a way for the public to share in any rise in land values. The public sector owns a significant proportion of land – around 900,000 hectares, or 6 per cent of all freehold land in England and Wales.[51] And while the government has set a goal of building 160,000 homes on public sector land by 2020, only one in five of these homes is set to be 'affordable', and public land that could be developed for housing continues to be sold.[52]

Suitable public land should instead be prioritised for the delivery of genuinely affordable and high-quality developments. Government departments should be required to retain the freehold of their public land and enter into partnerships with local authorities and housing associations to develop it. There are particular opportunities for public land to be developed by community land trusts (CLTs), not-for-profit organisations that develop and hold in perpetuity affordable homes for a local community. Since access to land and finance are significant barriers to CLTs,[53] CLTs and other co-operative housing organisations should qualify for lending through the regional divisions of our proposed National Investment Bank.

Expanding employee ownership

The third area in which we believe it is possible to spread wealth more widely is in company ownership. [54] We would like to see an extension of employee ownership, to give people a greater stake and voice in their workplaces. The aim would be to give more people a share of capital and to spread economic power and control in the economy by expanding the decision rights of employees in the management of companies. The evidence shows that broadening worker owner-ship creates more committed workforces and more productive and fulfilling workplaces.[55]

One route to doing this is by expanding the number of employee ownership trusts (EOTs). EOTs are a business structure introduced in 2014 that allows employees to hold a controlling stake (51 per cent or more) of their company. The trust creates a form of employee common ownership that gives employees both a share of profits and decision rights through seats on the board. Based on well-established practice in the United States, EOTs are generally created when a business owner retires or otherwise wishes to sell the business: he or she is given the incentive to sell to an EOT by exemption from capital gains tax.

To increase the number of EOTs in the economy, we propose a number of new tax incentives and other reforms.[56] These include exempting from inheritance tax any loans which the original business owner makes to an EOT to enable it to buy its stake; exempting EOTs from corporation tax, so long as its shares are allocated to its employees on a broad basis; allowing EOTs to allocate their shares to employees as individual stakes; and allowing former employees to retain shares as well as current ones. We also suggest that employers should be able to make additional pension contributions to their employees in the form of company shares in an EOT, up to a limit to avoid the over-concentration of risk.

The number of EOTs is currently increasing by around 50 per cent a year. We believe these reforms could incentivise a major expansion. Doubling the current growth rate of EOTs would lead to over 21,000 EOT companies by 2030, with almost 3 million employee owners.[57] This would mark a significant spreading of wealth and capital ownership.

A second route to expanding employee and wider forms of ownership is through co-operatives and mutuals. These are companies wholly owned and governed by their workers or consumers. In 2017 there were 6,815 co-operatives in the UK with a combined turnover of £35.7 billion, with 13.6 million members and 226,300 employees.[58]

Common ownership ensures that every member shares in the profits of the company, and has a stake and a say in how it is managed. The evidence suggests that the co-operative model is associated with economic and social benefits, including greater job satisfaction and wellbeing, lower levels of pay inequality and higher rates of engagement and productivity.[59]

The UK has disproportionately fewer co-operatives and mutuals than most other OECD countries. Germany has a co-operative sector four times the size of the UK's as a proportion of GDP, while in France it is six times larger.[60] In the UK, many co-operatives struggle to access the finance for investment they need, due to their unconventional ownership structure. But there are opportunities for expansion, particularly in the service sector where capital requirements are relatively light.

To help support the expansion of the co-operative and mutual sector, we propose a Co-operative Development Act. Such an Act would provide statutory underpinning for the principle of 'asset-locked reserves', ensuring capital owned by a co-operative cannot be divided individually among members. In turn, this would enable co-ops to raise long-term investment capital without the threat of demutualisation. The Act could also introduce a 'right to own', giving employees the option to buy out a conventional business when it was being offered for sale, and turning it into a co-operative or EOT.

By widening the ownership of wealth, tackling the rise in land values and building more homes, and by opening up the ownership of businesses to their workers, prosperity and justice can both be served.

13

Designing Simpler and Fairer Taxes

Taxation is the primary means by which governments raise revenue and fund the public services on which a civilised society depends. While taxation will always be politically controversial, it is important that as a society we have an open and honest conversation about how much tax we need to raise to pay for the services we want, and how much different people should contribute. Over recent decades the UK tax system has become very complicated and in many respects it does not promote economic justice.

Though a comprehensive review of the tax system was beyond our scope, the Commission has examined both the overall rate of taxation in the economy and the way in which some key taxes are levied. We seek a tax system that is progressive – so that those with the greatest ability to pay contribute the most – as well as transparent and efficient. In this chapter we propose changes to the taxation of income, wealth, land and business, each of which would make the tax system both simpler and fairer.

Public spending underpins a modern society

Modern economies rely on public spending. The private sector could not make a profit, nor could any of us earn a living, without the core services provided by the public sector, including education, health and social care, transport and policing, along with the social, welfare and cultural services that sustain livelihoods and social cohesion. Through these services, the state assumes and collectivises vital risks and costs, on which the private sector relies but which it could not itself replicate. Public services are also a crucial part of the economy in their own right, employing over five million people, generating their own tax receipts, and creating markets for public procurement worth around £200 billion a year.[1] Their outputs constitute an important part of the country's prosperity.

The reduction in the UK's budget deficit since 2009–10 has been achieved largely through reductions in public expenditure; around four-fifths has come from government spending falling as a proportion of GDP, and only one-fifth from rising tax revenue.[2] This has come at a cost. It is clear now that many public services are under severe strain. This has been widely recognised in the case of the NHS.[3] But it is plainly true too in other fields: in social care, the police service, prisons and local authority services in general. At the same time, widespread hardships have been generated by cuts to benefits and tax credits, and by the freeze on public sector pay.[4] We believe there is a real question facing the country, therefore, of whether public spending can or should be cut further, as is currently planned; or should instead be increased.

By European standards, the UK is not a high-tax country. At around 33 per cent of GDP, tax revenues are significantly lower than the OECD average: they are on a par with Estonia, the Czech Republic and Poland; but are well below more comparable economies such as Germany (38 per cent), France (45 per cent) and Denmark (46 per cent).[5] Different levels of taxation partly reflect national economic conditions, but they are largely determined by the political decisions that countries have made over the quality of their public services and welfare spending. As the experience of different European economies shows, there is no simple relationship between economic performance and the levels of taxation and public spending.[6] Higher levels of taxation do not mean impaired economic performance – on the contrary, if spent on the right things, they can generate stronger growth as well as better public goods.

The UK's level of taxation is not just an issue for today. The deeper challenge we must confront is the pressure on public spending that will come in the future. Projections by the OBR show that over the next 30 years there will be a widening gap between expected public spending and forecast tax receipts. Without changes in policy, the public sector deficit is set to grow throughout the 2020s and beyond, rising to over 5 per cent of GDP in 2056-7; as a result, overall debt is projected to rise from around 90 per cent of GDP today to 172 per cent by 2056-7.[7] This 'fiscal gap' will continue to widen until 2066-7, the final year of the OBR's projections. The OBR warns starkly that this is 'an unsustainable fiscal position over the long term'.[8]

This widening deficit will be driven largely by demographic change, as the proportion of the population aged over 65 rises from 18 per cent in 2016 to 26 per cent by 2066.[9] An ageing population – particularly the much larger numbers of the very elderly – means rising demand both for public pensions and for cost-intensive health and social care. These two factors alone are expected to contribute to an increase in public expenditure of as much as 3.9 per cent of GDP between 2021-2 and 2036-7.[10] At the same time, demographic change will also reduce the proportion of the population who are in work. In effect, a proportionately smaller working-age population will be required to pay for a larger (and more costly) non-working one.

The Commission therefore welcomes the recent recognition by the government that the overall level of taxes will have to rise to pay for the improved health and social care the country needs. *We call for a serious debate about the appropriate level of both public spending and taxation which can achieve the economy and society we desire.*

Taxation of individual incomes

Taxes on individual incomes account for 42 per cent of major UK tax receipts and equate to 15.2 per cent of GDP.[11] The UK's current system of taxing incomes is complex: it combines two different tax schedules, one for income tax and another for employees' national insurance contributions (NICs), with a variety of different tax rates, bands, thresholds, allowances and reliefs. These make it both difficult to understand and less progressive than it could be.[12]

The marginal rate of taxation on incomes varies somewhat arbitrarily. While the effective rate of tax on annual earnings from employment above the tax-free allowance is 32 per cent, this is only 7.5 per cent for income paid in dividends from company profits. The marginal rate of income tax jumps from 40 per cent to 60 per cent and back to 40 as the personal allowance is withdrawn for incomes over £100,000 (see figure 13.1). For income tax payers on the lowest earnings, effective marginal tax rates – once means-tested benefits are withdrawn as a result of higher pay – can be as high as 75 per cent. This variable treatment of different sources of incomes, combined with sharp 'cliffs' in the marginal rate between tax bands, creates distorting economic incentives and is not transparent.

An important principle of any tax system is that it should be progressive – ensuring that an individual's marginal tax rate rises as their earnings rise. Income taxes are the most effective instrument for making the tax system more progressive as a whole. But overall, they are failing in this task. On average, the poorest 20 per cent of households pay 35 per cent of their gross income in tax, which is more than the top 20 per cent (indeed, more than all other quintiles).[13] This means that income taxes are not doing enough to offset the effects of other, more regressive taxes like VAT and council tax. It is notable that the UK raises less tax from earned income, as a proportion of GDP, than most other West European countries.[14]

Proposed reforms

To address these challenges, we propose that personal income taxes should be simplified and the system reformed.[15] This would have two key elements.

First, *the rates and allowances for employee NICs and income tax should be combined into a single tax schedule, and applied to all incomes on an individual, annual basis.* All income would be treated under the same rates, irrespective of whether it was sourced from labour earnings or from wealth. We discuss the implications of this for wealth taxation below.

Second, *the present system of marginal tax bands should be replaced with a 'formula-based' system.* This would abolish tax bands, applying instead a gradually rising marginal rate of tax in a smooth curve as incomes rise. There would be a new tax-free allowance and a new threshold for the top marginal rate. In practice every taxpayer's marginal rate, as well as their average rate, would depend on their own precise level of income (see figure 13.1). This is the system used in Germany.

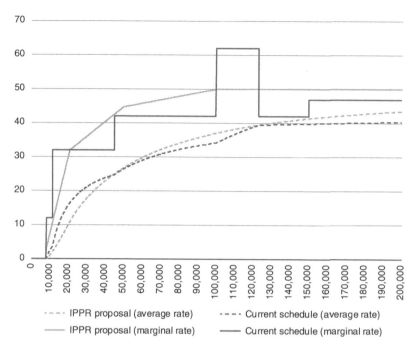

Figure 13.1 A formula-based schedule produces a more even increase in marginal and average tax rates

Effective marginal and average rates for taxation of income (%) for different annual incomes (£) under an illustrative formula-based schedule and the current schedule, 2017–18

Source: IPPR analysis using HMRC (2018)[16]

Note: The current system represents the effective tax rates from income tax and Class 1 employee NICs combined. This illustration covers only current forms of income to which income tax is applied.

Such a proposed new tax system would be more progressive and efficient, and would enable government to alter taxes more fairly and easily.[17] By improving work incentives for low earners, and removing the variable treatment of different sources of income, it would reduce distorting economic incentives and make tax avoidance less feasible.

Most importantly, it would enable the income tax system to be made more progressive. Using illustrative versions of a formula-based

tax system for the UK, a fiscally neutral reform has significant redistributive potential.[18] Such a system would allow the same level of total
revenue to be raised as at present while giving more than 80 per cent of
taxpayers an increase in their post-tax income, with gains around the
median income as high as £1,200 a year (see figure 13.1).

By eliminating distortions, such a system would make it simpler
for governments to adjust the position of the curve to meet revenue
requirements. We estimate that, were a government to want to raise an
illustrative £16 billion a year for additional public spending, a formula-
based system would allow this to be done while still increasing or
keeping constant post-tax incomes for at least 75 per cent of individual
taxpayers. Only the highest 25 per cent of taxpayers would need to pay
more.[19] Overall, we believe these reforms would therefore make the
UK's tax system more transparent, more progressive and better able to
meet the public spending challenges we will face in the future.

Taxation of wealth

Wealth is currently taxed in the UK in a number of different ways.[20]
Excluding taxes on property (which we address below), the main taxes
on wealth are capital gains tax, dividend income taxation, inheritance
tax, stamp duty reserve tax, and taxation of trusts. These taxes currently
represent 4 per cent of total tax receipts, raising an estimated £27.7
billion in 2017–18.[21] In their current form, these arrangements work
against economic justice.

There are simple ways to avoid paying many of these taxes.
Inheritance tax (currently levied at 40 per cent on bequests over
£325,000 for a single person, or £650,000 for a married couple), for
example, can be avoided by transferring wealth to others more than

seven years before death. This is generally easier to do for the very wealthy, who are less likely to need the money, than for those with assets closer to the value of the threshold.

There is a fundamental injustice in the way that income from work is taxed more highly than income from wealth. While earned income is taxed at 20, 40 and 45 per cent, capital gains are taxed at 10 and 20 per cent (and 18 and 28 per cent on property, excluding first homes), while dividends attract rates of 7.5, 32.5 and 38.1 per cent. These differences significantly benefit those with wealth, and those who can organise their income to be paid in that form. This is plainly unfair.

We believe it is time for a new approach to taxing wealth. As the returns to wealth exceed the growth of earned income, the tax system should do more to reduce wealth inequality. Much of the increase in wealth comes from unearned economic 'rents' which do not contribute to economic output or growth and can be taxed without significant economic impact.

Proposed reforms

First, *we propose that all income, whether from work or from wealth, should be taxed in the same way.* This would mean abolishing capital gains tax and the separate rates of tax for dividends altogether, and incorporating income from dividends and capital gains into the income tax schedule. Whilst we would argue that most exemptions from capital gains tax should be removed, we would maintain the exemption for capital gains on first homes. We believe these gains could be most effectively captured through a progressive replacement for council tax, although we have not explored this possibility in detail, together with reform of inheritance tax, set out below.

Taxing income from wealth in the same way as income from work was recommended by the Mirrlees review of taxation[22] as well as others.[23] It would allow for the capture of a greater proportion of the economic rents derived from wealth and would reduce the incentives for avoidance. While uncertainty around the behavioural response to such a reform makes it difficult to estimate the fiscal impact, we would expect the higher rates in our proposal to yield substantially more revenue than the present system.[24]

Second, *we propose that inheritance tax should be abolished, and replaced with a lifetime gifts tax levied on the recipient.* Inheritance tax is unpopular, and it is levied on the wrong party. Taxation should be levied on those who receive income (reflecting their circumstances), not on those who make a bequest. A lifetime gifts tax would be a tax on all gifts received throughout a person's life, above a specified lifetime allowance, which we propose should initially be set at around £125,000. Once an individual has received gifts worth over this limit, all further gifts would be classified as income for that year and taxed at income tax rates. Gifts worth a small amount, and gifts between spouses and civil partners, would be exempt from the tax.

A number of countries have gift taxes of this kind, including Ireland, Germany, France, Belgium and the Netherlands.[25] In the UK, this proposal too has been widely advocated by others.[26] It would reduce the opportunities for avoidance offered by the current system of inheritance tax. It would focus taxation on those who can pay it. And it could raise more revenue, in a fairer way, than the current system. Modelling undertaken by the Resolution Foundation indicates that taxing gifts through the income tax system in this way could raise around £15 billion in 2020-1, around £9 billion more than the current inheritance tax system.[27]

Taxation of property and land

Taxes on property and land have long been favoured by economists.[28] Fixed in supply and hard to avoid, they – and the economic rents they earn – can be taxed without distorting behaviour.[29] In the UK, the main taxes on property and land are council tax, stamp duty land tax (SDLT) and the national non-domestic rate (business rates). Council tax is levied on domestic properties and is part of the funding base for local government; SDLT is charged on residential property sales, paid for by the purchaser; business rates, also collected locally, are calculated as a percentage of the estimated rental – or 'rateable' – value of non-residential property. These combined taxes raised £72.6 billion in 2017–18, representing 10.4 per cent of overall tax receipts.[30]

None of these taxes is ideally designed. Council tax is still calculated on the estimated value of homes in 1991, leaving those whose homes have gained most in value since then significantly under-taxed. Business rates do not apply to undeveloped land, creating significant distortions in the incentives to hold and develop land. Stamp duty adds undesirable friction to the property market and makes home ownership more expensive, especially for those on low incomes.[31] None of these taxes adequately capture increases in land values, including those which occur when planning permission is granted. Overall, there is a strong case that land in the UK is currently under-taxed.[32] In turn (as we discuss in chapter 11), this contributes to the wider problem of rising land and house prices and their impact on macroeconomic stability.[33]

Proposed reforms

We believe there is a strong case for reforming the system of commercial property taxation. In particular, like others, we see significant merit in the replacement of business rates by a land value tax (LVT).[34] If these reforms were successful, they would provide useful lessons for the wider reform of council tax and stamp duty which are plainly necessary.

A land value tax is based on two principles.[35] It taxes the value of land, not the property standing on it. And the value of the land is calculated on the basis of its 'optimum use' under existing planning permission, not its current use. These principles confer several advantages over the taxation of property, such as our current business rates. By taxing undeveloped land on the basis of its use value, it penalises those who hold land without developing it, and incentivises development. Since the value of a property is excluded from the valuation of the land, it does not penalise those businesses which improve their properties, as business rates do today.

Introducing a land value tax in the UK would not be simple. There are still inadequacies in the registration of land ownership. Estimating the value of land without the property on it would require new techniques and institutional arrangements. There would also be significant transitional issues in shifting from one form of taxation to another. Nonetheless, land value taxation is already in place in a number of European countries, as well as in parts of the US, Australia and New Zealand, and each has found ways of overcoming the obstacles.

Introducing a land value tax would, we believe, be the most economically efficient means of taxing commercial land without the distorting effects of business rates. It would support, rather than deter, productive investment; and it would capture some of the unearned windfalls from the ownership of land and reduce the incentive to speculate on it. It would help rebalance the economy geographically, making disadvantaged regions with lower land values more attractive locations in which to do business. *We therefore propose that the intention should be set to replace business rates by a new land value tax on all non-residential land, and measures should be introduced for the registration and valuation of land for this purpose.*

We would see such a tax continuing to fund local government, with the rates of tax set nationally (as is the case for business rates), to allow for redistribution between local authorities. In due course, as regions converged, it might be possible to introduce some local variation.

Business taxation

Since 2008, the main rate of corporation tax paid by businesses on their profits in the UK has been dramatically reduced, from 30 per cent to 19 per cent. The UK now has the lowest rate of corporation tax in the G7, and one of the lowest rates among all developed countries.[36] At the same time, the rate of employers' National Insurance contributions (ENICs) has been raised. As a result, the relative importance of these taxes in revenue terms has been reversed: corporation tax revenues have fallen from 3.5 per cent of GDP in 2006 to just 2.7 per cent of GDP today.[37] Over the same period, revenues from ENICs have risen from 3 per cent of GDP to nearly 4 per cent.[38] The overall effect has been to reduce the tax paid by profitable but low-employment businesses and increase it for those with more employees but lower profits.

The intention behind cutting corporation tax was to increase private investment.[39] This has not happened. Corporate investment in the UK remains lower today than in economies with much higher rates of corporation tax, such as France (38 per cent) and Germany (31 per cent).[40] There is, in fact, little evidence that investment levels are significantly influenced by corporation tax rates; a whole range of other factors, particularly the overall level of demand in the economy, are much more important.[41] Shifting the relative burden of taxation from profits to payroll has changed the balance of who ultimately pays them. Broadly speaking, taxes on profits fall on shareholders, while employment taxes are paid (in the form of lower wages) by employees themselves.[42] The shift in business taxation has therefore almost certainly contributed to widening inequality.

At the same time as corporation tax rates have been cut, a proliferation of reliefs and allowances has led to the erosion of the tax base. As the National Audit Office (NAO) has observed, the 119 separate reliefs which now exist have created a highly complicated and opaque system.[43] Such reliefs distort economic incentives in arbitrary and often damaging ways, as well as providing opportunities for avoidance. A number have failed to achieve their stated purpose: as we noted in chapter 6, the patent box and R&D tax credits, for example, have significant 'deadweight' loss.[44]

These developments have taken place in the context of mounting evidence that many multinational corporations are able to avoid corporate income taxation altogether, in the UK and elsewhere. According to the NAO, 50 per cent of the largest 800 businesses in the UK paid less than £10 million each in corporation tax in 2012–13, with 20 per cent paying none at all.[45] Of course, a low or zero tax liability may be a genuine reflection of low profits earned. But it is clear that international 'profit shifting', where a company's pricing and accounts are organised so as to show profits occurring in the lowest tax jurisdictions, has become widespread.[46] It is within the business community that this is perhaps most widely considered unfair, since it effectively leaves domestic firms that cannot avoid tax paying more to compensate for the foregone revenues.

Profit shifting is a global problem, requiring international tax cooperation to solve it. The recently agreed convention on 'base erosion and profit shifting' (BEPS) – overseen by the OECD and involving more than 100 countries – has begun to address these concerns, but it has not achieved a full solution, and the UK currently only plans to implement some of the proposed reforms.[47] Recent changes to the US system of corporate income taxation – including the lowering of the main federal rate from 30 to 21 per cent – risk triggering a 'race to the bottom' between competing jurisdictions, which would result in lower tax revenues everywhere.[48]

Proposed reforms

We believe that UK corporation tax is now too low. It raises insufficient revenue, and profitable companies which are able to pay more should do so. We see no reason for the UK to be an outlier among developed countries in this respect. *We therefore propose that the UK should retain its international competitiveness by matching the lowest effective rate of corporation tax in the G7, while simplifying the system of reliefs and allowances to increase the tax base.* This would mean an increase in the UK rate of corporation tax from 19 per cent to 24 per cent. (Although the US has reduced its federal rate to 21 per cent, its effective average rate is 25.7 per cent when state corporation taxes are included.[49]) Using HMRC figures, we estimate that, if this increase were to be implemented over three years, this would raise £13.3 billion in additional tax revenue in 2020–1.[50] At the same time, there is scope to raise the level of investment allowances to tilt corporate incentives towards investment rather than dividend payments.

The Office of Tax Simplification has called for a 'roadmap' for the simplification of the corporation tax system, and we would support such a move. As we argue in chapter 6, there is a compelling case for the removal or reduction in the value of reliefs, including the patent box and R&D tax reliefs, and (among others) the depreciation of write-down allowances. We would argue that no new tax reliefs should be introduced unless it can be shown that the desired effect cannot be achieved through more transparent spending measures instead.

At the same time, to tackle tax avoidance by multinational corporations, *we propose the introduction of an Alternative Minimum Corporation Tax (AMCT)*. This would be a 'backstop tax' levied on multinational companies which consistently reported low profits in the UK and were unable to show that these were genuine.[51] Our proposal is that the AMCT should be applied when a firm declared profits below a certain percentage of its global profits for more than five years. The tax would be calculated on the basis of the company's sales in the UK, expressed as a proportion of its global turnover. That proportion would then be applied to the firm's global profits, to produce an imputed measure of profit earned within the UK. The ACMT would then be levied on that profit estimate. Firms would be able to challenge the AMCT by opening their books to HMRC to prove that the UK was a less profitable market for the firm than its global margin would suggest.

The introduction of an AMCT would, we believe, do much to tackle the unfairness of multinational profit-shifting, and would help move towards an international system in which tax is properly assigned to the jurisdictions in which the profits are made. In this regard, the government should seek to ratify and implement the BEPS Convention as soon as possible, and work hard with other countries to develop further measures to reduce international tax avoidance and evasion.

Reforming taxation is essential if prosperity is to be promoted and justice secured. As we have shown in this chapter, it is possible to make taxes both simpler and fairer at the same time.

14

Ensuring Environmental Sustainability

In chapter 2, we stated our conviction that environmental sustainability must lie at the heart of economic policy. We cannot sustain prosperity into the future if climate change continues on its present course, and if the world's environmental resources and life support systems continue to be degraded and depleted. Enhancing the integrity of the natural environment is also central to justice: both in relation to future generations, and in respect of the world's poorer citizens today, whose livelihoods and security are affected by the global impacts of the consumption and production for which we in the UK are responsible.

As a Commission, it was beyond our scope to examine and make recommendations in every area of environmental policy. In this chapter we therefore focus on the overall framework of policymaking which can enable the UK economy to become environmentally sustainable – while at the same time supporting our goals of higher productivity, stronger innovation and exports and better jobs across the country.

Sustainability and green growth

All economies are ultimately dependent on the natural environment, to provide material and energy resources and to assimilate wastes, and to maintain fundamental 'ecosystem services' such as the regulation of the water cycle and a stable climate.[1] Today, many of the natural systems that sustain human life and economic activity are under severe threat.

Unless current emissions of greenhouse gases are drastically reduced, the earth is on course for an increase in the average global temperature of at least 3–4 degrees Celsius by the end of the century. Even at 2 degrees of warming, the impacts will be severe. They include a higher incidence of extreme weather events (such as flooding, storm surges and droughts), which may lead to a breakdown of infrastructure networks and critical services, particularly in cities and coastal regions; lower agricultural productivity, increasing the risk of food insecurity; increased ill-health and mortality from extreme heat events and disease; a greater risk of the displacement of peoples and conflict; and a faster loss of ecosystems and species.[2]

Yet climate change is only one of many kinds of environmental degradation that have resulted from a growing global population and economic growth. A third of all arable land is now degraded.[3] The increase in carbon dioxide emissions has increased the acidity of the oceans by 30 per cent since the Industrial Revolution.[4] Habitat loss and species extinction are accelerating, with the current period now regarded as the 'sixth major mass extinction' in the earth's history.[5] Around 8 million tonnes of plastic are estimated to enter the world's oceans each year.[6]

To assess the risks posed by these trends, recent scientific work has developed the concept of a 'safe operating space' for humanity across a range of environmental functions. The safe space is characterised by 'planetary boundaries' beyond which environmental degradation will cross critical thresholds or 'tipping points', risking catastrophic and/or irreversible damage.[7] Analysis suggests that for biodiversity loss and the nitrogen and phosphorous cycles, human activities are already outside the safe operating space, with climate change and land use change (such as deforestation and the loss of wetlands) at increasing risk of approaching this condition. In almost all fields, the risks are rising.

As an advanced, rich economy, the UK contributes both to these global threats and to a range of national and local environmental problems, including air and water pollution, and loss of biodiversity and soil fertility. Around 40,000 deaths per year in the UK are now attributable to exposure to outdoor air pollution.[8] More than one in ten of the UK's wildlife species are threatened with extinction, and the total number of animals and plants has declined by a sixth since 1970, making the UK one of the most nature-depleted nations in the world.[9] On current trends, we may have only 30–40 years of soil fertility left.[10]

In this context, the goal of sustainability takes on critical importance. It can be defined as the reduction of the economy's environmental impacts to levels at which the capacities of the natural environment – to supply resources, to absorb wastes, and to provide life support services and amenities – are maintained over time, at stable and acceptable standards of environmental health and integrity.[11] In turn, this means defining what those standards are. This will partly be a scientific process, based on our understanding of biophysical systems and natural resource capacities. And it will partly be a social and political one, in which societies choose the levels of harm they are prepared to tolerate, and the integrity and beauty of the natural world in which they will live.

It is clear that achieving a sustainable economy will require major changes in the ways in which we use and consume resources, in this country and globally. It demands above all a huge improvement in 'resource productivity', the rate at which we use resources and generate waste per pound of economic value created. Raising resource productivity needs to become as important a source of economic growth as raising labour productivity. There is considerable potential to do this: a recent study for the United Nations Environmental Programme suggests that resource efficiency policies could boost GDP in advanced countries by around 3 per cent by 2050, with even larger global gains.[12] This is the strategy now widely described as 'green growth'.[13]

Raising resource productivity can take many different forms. The structural shift in the composition of output over recent decades, from manufacturing to services and digital products, has already generated a marked reduction in domestic environmental impact – although some of this has merely been exported to developing countries where the bulk of manufacturing is now conducted.[14] Technological innovation is driving other dramatic improvements: from renewable energy sources such as wind and solar, to 'smart' electricity systems that manage supply and demand; from new lighter materials and water-efficient industrial processes, to new forms of agricultural management that reduce greenhouse gas (GHG) emissions.[15] The development of the 'circular economy', focused on reusing and recycling materials and eliminating waste, offers particular potential to 'decouple' economic growth from resource use and environmental impact.[16] And as technologies change, so do people's tastes and lifestyles. Generational shifts in attitudes towards consumption, the growth of vegetarianism, the valuing of experiential, 'natural' and 'artisan' products and ethical consumer choices: all point to changing patterns of demand in the future.[17]

It is important, however, to recognise the scale of the productivity improvements required. The decoupling of growth and resource use has to be at a sufficient pace to bring environmental impacts down to sustainable levels. For example, to keep average global warming to below 2 degrees by 2050, global greenhouse gas emissions will need to fall by about 5 per cent per year. But with continuing economic growth of over 2 per cent per year, the carbon intensity (or resource productivity) of the global economy would have to fall by around 7 per cent per year. This is about ten times faster than it has been falling since 1990.[18] It means in effect the more or less complete 'decarbonisation' of energy, transport and industrial systems by mid-century.[19] Indeed, as the Paris Climate Agreement acknowledged, achieving the goal of limiting warming to under 2 degrees (or under 1.5 degrees, to which the Agreement aspires) will require the reduction of net greenhouse gas emissions to zero in the period beyond 2050.[20]

The policy challenge to achieve resource productivity improvements on this kind of scale – across multiple environmental issues – is therefore very large. But the economic benefits are also likely to be significant. Environmental improvement requires investment and creates demand for new goods and services, which stimulates economic growth and job-creation. Over the past ten years, environmental policies both at home and overseas have led to a significant growth in the UK's environmental goods and services sector. This contributed £30.5 billion in gross value added to the UK economy in 2015, or 1.6 per cent of GDP, and employed around 335,000 full-time employees, around 1 per cent of total UK employment.[21] The UK is already a world leader in a number of environmental industries, with growing global markets and huge potential for technological innovation.[22]

There is considerable potential, therefore, for the UK to achieve green growth. But the policy framework to achieve it on the scale necessary is not yet in place. Although the UK has been successful in decoupling its economic growth and domestic greenhouse gas emissions (see figure 14.1), the government's independent Committee on Climate Change has warned that we are not on track to meet the statutory 'carbon budgets' for the 2020s, which governments have set under

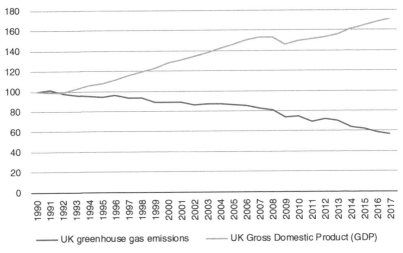

Figure 14.1 Since 1990, the UK's greenhouse gas emissions from domestic production have 'decoupled' from economic growth
UK greenhouse gas emissions compared to GDP, 1990–2017 (Index: 1990 = 100)
Source: Committee on Climate Change (2018)[23]

the Climate Change Act 2008 in order to reduce our emissions by 80 per cent by 2050 (see figure 14.2). And on many of the other major environmental indicators, progress is either too slow or the trends are adverse, with the UK's global environmental footprint significantly above sustainable levels.[24]

A Sustainable Economy Act

The UK has a comprehensive array of environmental policies, most of which have derived from our membership of the European Union and are largely devolved. Yet we are far from achieving sustainability. There are two simple reasons for this.

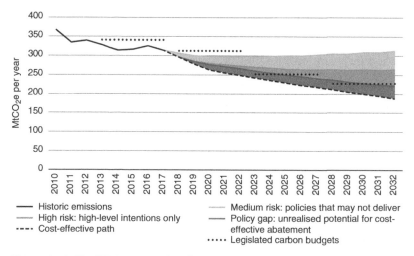

Figure 14.2 The UK is currently off track to meet its statutory carbon budgets in the 2020s

Risks around the delivery of policies to meet carbon budgets (non-traded sector)

Source: Committee on Climate Change (2018)[25]

The first is that most environmental policy has been aimed at improving the individual environmental performance of companies and products, not their aggregate impact on the environment. Products such as cars and white goods, buildings, farms and factories have been required to cut the waste and pollution they generate individually, whether through standards and regulations, taxes and charges, or incentives of various kinds. But their collective impact on the environment as a whole has not been controlled. In practice, individual product and business-level improvements have been outweighed by the overall effect of economic growth, and by the introduction of new products and economic activities. So even though almost every aspect of the economy is more environmentally efficient than in the past, air pollution has continued to get worse, soil quality is damaged, habitats and species have been lost, and resources depleted.

Second, many global impacts are barely regulated at all. There are almost no controls on plastics pollution. Though there are some sustainability standards for timber, fish and a few other products, the vast majority of globally traded resources, including foods, face few or no environmental constraints. So it is no wonder that our production and consumption patterns are not sustainable.

The major exception to this fundamental problem of environmental policy has been in the field of climate change. It is not just individual products and companies that are required to cut their greenhouse gas emissions: whole countries are. Under the Paris Climate Agreement, EU law and the UK's own 2008 Climate Change Act, we have imposed environmental limits on our entire economy. The Act requires governments to limit the total carbon emissions of the UK to target levels set in statute, derived from an assessment of the UK's fair contribution to the global goal of holding average warming to under two degrees.

The Climate Change Act effectively brings the UK economy within a 'sustainability limit'. Every five years, the government of the day is required to adopt a legally binding carbon budget, a maximum amount of GHG emissions the UK economy can emit in a five-year period. Such budgets must be set for 15 years ahead to give businesses and investors time to plan reductions, and they must lie on a plausible trajectory towards the long-term goal of an 80 per cent reduction in UK emissions by 2050 (defined relative to 1990 levels). The budgets must be set by government taking into account the advice of the independent Committee on Climate Change (CCC), which must in turn take into account a range of scientific, economic, social and international factors. And once the budgets have been adopted by Parliament, the government is legally required to produce a plan showing how it will meet them. The CCC must report to Parliament on the success or otherwise of the government's policies in achieving its targets.

Since at present we are not on track to reach the carbon budgets, it might be said that the Act has not worked. But the critical point is that the budgets are legally binding on the government, so it can be taken to court for failing to achieve them and forced to take further action until it does. In 2015 the government repealed or abandoned a whole range of climate policies.[26] But two years later, the Act forced its successor administration to come back with a new plan and new policies to meet the statutory targets. In this way the Act has therefore overcome one of the key problems for environmental policy, that of short-term political changes undermining long-term environmental goals. The Act has retained almost universal cross-party support.[27]

If the UK is to achieve a sustainable economy, not just in relation to climate change, but across the full range of its environmental impacts, the principles of the Climate Change Act need to be applied more widely. This is particularly important in the light of Brexit, which will demand a new basis for environmental law in the UK and for the devolved nations. *We therefore propose that Parliament legislates for a Sustainable Economy Act, to provide an overall framework of environmental policy for the UK, grounded in the principle of sustainability.* It would be based on the successful model of the Climate Change Act.

The core of a Sustainable Economy Act would be a legal requirement on government to set environmental limits in law, and to produce economy-wide plans to achieve them. Over time, these limits should cover all the major global and domestic environmental impacts of the UK economy. For each major environmental impact, the Act would require a long-term goal to be established, and then a trajectory of short- and medium-term targets to be periodically set. So, for example, a 25-year goal of eliminating non-recyclable plastics would be implemented through a series of five-year plans to cut annual plastic waste by a specific number of tonnes. A long-term goal of restoring biodiversity to (say) a 1970 benchmark would be implemented through successive five-year targets for individual declining species. Local air pollution targets could be set in a similar way.

As with carbon budgets, these limits and targets should be biophysically informed but politically chosen. Our proposed Act would therefore establish an independent Committee on Sustainability, made up of experts in a range of fields, drawn from different economic and social constituencies. On the model of the CCC, it would be tasked with providing advice to the government on the setting of both long-term goals and shorter term targets, based on a range of both scientific and economic and social criteria. Where the relevant limits are global (such as for plastics pollution), the Committee would be expected to define a fair UK target based on our contribution to the global problem, as with greenhouse gas emissions. As the CCC does, it would also provide guidance to government on how these targets could be feasibly achieved through technological and policy change, and would report on the success or otherwise of policy in doing so. The Committee would be accountable to Parliament.

In the same way as the Climate Change Act, a key feature of the Sustainable Economy Act would be its requirement, not just on Parliament to adopt environmental limits, but on the government to produce a plan showing how it would meet them. The combination of statutory targets and plans would be designed to ensure that the UK economy was placed on a trajectory towards sustainable levels of environmental impact in the short, medium and long term. The government needs to be held accountable in this task by a new environmental 'watchdog' body with sufficient powers to replace the roles of the European Commission and European Court of Justice.[28]

A Sustainable Economy Act of this kind would fill the two gaps in current environmental policymaking. It would require governments not just to introduce environmental standards at the level of individual products and companies, but for their aggregate environmental impact. And it would frame policy not just for domestic impacts, but for the UK's global footprint.

Green industrial strategy

Setting environmental limits is, of course, only the first stage of environmental policymaking. Ensuring that aggregate impacts stay within those limits requires an array of policies in relevant sectors designed to incentivise companies to change their production methods and products, and consumers to change their demand, in order to raise resource productivity sufficiently. Such policies may take many forms: law and regulation, taxes, charges and tradable permit systems, land use and infrastructure planning, public spending, consumer incentives and so on.[29]

Two goals should be key to the policy design process. First, policies should aim not to raise overall economic costs, but as far as possible to reduce them by encouraging innovation and shifts in demand, thereby boosting economic growth rather than retarding it. Second, in doing so, the goal should be to maximise the domestic economic advantage of achieving environmental targets, in terms of UK-based output, employment and exports.

The latter goal represents a relatively new departure for environmental policymaking in the UK. In the past, environmental policy required companies to install new, more environmentally friendly processes and equipment and for consumers to buy new greener products. But it did not pay much attention to where those things were produced. Today, we have the opportunity to use industrial strategy to ensure that as much as possible of the demand created by environmental policy is supplied by UK-based firms.

An example of integrating demand and supply in this way has already occurred since the passage of the 2008 Climate Change Act, which shifted energy policy significantly towards renewables. It was clear that this would lead to a huge demand for offshore wind turbines and associated goods and services; but at the time the Act was passed, there were no offshore turbine manufacturers located in the UK. So successive governments have sought to attract manufacturing investment, by making available land and port capacity on the North Sea coast, funding research and development, improving workforce skills and helping UK companies enter the supply chain. As a result, the UK now has nine wind turbine manufacturing and assembly plants, supplying not only the UK but the expanding European offshore wind market, with a wider supply industry estimated to employ around 13,000 people.[30]

We believe this offers a widely applicable model for combining environmental policy with industrial strategy. In chapter 6, we argue that industrial strategy should be organised in part around 'missions', in which government directs innovation and supply chain policy to meet some of the great societal challenges of the twenty-first century; and that 'green growth' should be one of these. *We therefore propose the adoption of a 'green industrial strategy', with the aim of reducing the UK's environmental footprint to levels consistent with global sustainability by 2040.*

In practice, a green industrial strategy would be likely to comprise three sub-missions:

- Decarbonisation, covering the reduction in greenhouse gas and local air pollution emissions in energy, transport, buildings, industry and agriculture

- The circular economy, covering the overall reduction in the use of materials, their sustainable sourcing, and the elimination of waste
- Sustainable natural capital, covering the conservation and enhancement of habitats, species and landscapes and the maintenance of water, nitrogen and phosphorous cycles.

Each mission or sub-mission would be implemented through three steps. On the demand side, this would include the establishment of a long-run goal and intermediate targets, and a set of environmental policies designed to meet them. On the supply side, it would comprise a set of industrial strategy policies aimed at supporting the innovation and supply chains through which the targets can be met most cost-effectively and with maximum benefit to the UK economy.

The government already has some of this framework in place. Under the Climate Change Act it has published a Clean Growth Strategy, which sets out the policies designed to achieve the carbon budgets covering the period 2023–32.[31] Separately, it has produced a 25-year Environment Plan, covering its long-run ambitions across a comprehensive range of environmental issues.[32] Between them these documents begin the process of establishing goals and targets and setting out the policies required to meet them, though many of the targets remain merely aspirational, and many of the policies as yet undefined. One of the goals of a Sustainable Economy Act would be to give these targets the statutory force that only the carbon budgets have now, and require the government to publish policy plans to meet them.

There is a particular economic importance to statutory targets and plans. They effectively tell businesses and investors where there are going to be present and future markets, and how large they are likely to be. As such they can strongly incentivise companies to invest in productive techniques and goods and services that can meet this demand, and in innovation to meet them more cheaply or in new ways altogether. It also considerably reduces the risk in doing so, since there is much greater certainty of future demand than would otherwise exist. As we argue in chapter 4, the creation of expectations and the reduction in risk and uncertainty to raise the level of investment is a key economic role that the state can play.[33]

On the supply side, the present government has started out on the road to a green industrial strategy, naming 'clean growth' as one of the 'grand challenges' towards which innovation policy will be directed.[34] We would like to see this programme considerably expanded to encompass the full set of sub-missions we have identified. The mission should become a strong organising focus both for the business department and for its agencies, notably UK Research and Innovation (which already has well-advanced programmes in some of these areas), and our proposed National Investment Bank.

One of the key elements of green industrial strategy should be to support workers and communities adversely affected by the process of change. Over recent years the international trade union movement has developed the idea and practice of a 'just transition'.[35] This acknowledges that meeting climate change targets will involve the decline of high-carbon sectors, and therefore seeks accompanying policies to enable displaced workers to acquire new skills, and communities dependent on old sectors to create new employment opportunities. We believe this should be a key focus of the partnership-based regional and local industrial strategies we propose in chapters 6 and 15.

We acknowledge that making the UK economy globally sustainable will not be easy. It will involve a transformation in the way we produce and consume resources, affecting more or less every major sector. It must become a central goal of economic policy, requiring a degree of policy commitment no government has yet shown. But we believe it offers immense opportunities for the UK to develop new world-leading sectors, and to provide high-quality employment opportunities across the country.

15

Creating a New Economic Constitution

The UK economy is often discussed as if it were a unified whole. In fact, it is several economies that are intertwined but also distinct. Scotland, Wales, Northern Ireland and the English regions each have a different history, a different mix of economic activities, and different challenges to their future prosperity. As the UK economy has changed in structure over the last 40 years, particularly through deindustrialisation, large geographic inequalities have been allowed to develop: average earnings, for example, are now a third lower in the East Midlands than they are in London.[1]

In this chapter, we discuss how devolving more autonomy over economic policymaking – to the nations of the UK and to the regional level in England – would help to address the UK's geographical economic imbalances. And we make the case more widely for a 'social partnership' approach to economic governance, in which the government consults more widely with business, trade unions and civil society – as well as with the nations and regions of the UK – on its economic plans and policies. Rethinking where and how economic decisions are made is essential to achieving prosperity and justice for the whole country.

One state, many economies

In terms of economic output per head, as we note in chapter 1, the UK is a deeply unbalanced economy. London is effectively an economy in its own right, distinct from the rest of the country: incomes, output and productivity are the highest in the UK, yet high housing costs mean living standards are below average, and the capital has the widest inequalities between the richest and poorest neighbourhoods.[2] Since devolution, Scotland's economy has performed relatively well on pay, productivity growth and employment, but since the financial crisis its growth has slowed relative to the UK as a whole. Northern Ireland, Wales and some areas in the North of England – the parts of the country where the loss of manufacturing capacity has been felt most acutely – are the UK's poorest (see figure 15.1 and table 15.1). The UK's nations and regions have had very different experiences following the 2008–9 recession, with the poorest areas taking much longer to recover. This has increased the gap between the best economic performers, and the worst.[3]

England

England is often characterised as having an economic 'north–south divide', and for the most part, this is true. London is a global centre for finance, professional services, technology and the creative industries, and is one of the world's top tourist destinations. Proximity to London has helped the South East to become the second-most prosperous part of the UK. Some parts of the East of England have similarly benefited, notably the new high-tech cluster around Cambridge, which forms a 'Golden Triangle' of innovation activity with Oxford and London.

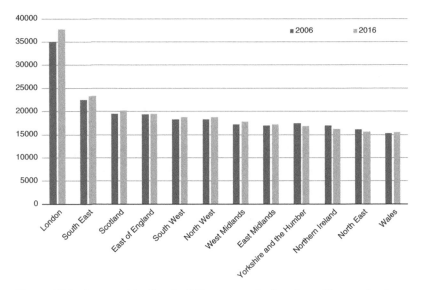

Figure 15.1 Geographically, the UK economy is deeply and increasingly unbalanced
Real gross value added (GVA) per head of population (£) for UK nations and regions, 2005 prices
Source: ONS (2017)[4] and HM Treasury (2018)[5]

In contrast, the regions in the North, Midlands and most of the South West of England have struggled to find new economic identities as their manufacturing and mining sectors have diminished. In recent decades, regional strategies in England have been almost entirely managed by central government, with (until recently) little proactive policy intervention, and there are much lower levels of infrastructure investment than in London and the South East.[6] As a result, the public sector accounts for a larger share of employment, meaning that austerity has had a proportionally greater economic impact. The lack of a high-quality replacement for manufacturing jobs means many regions in England have struggled with high levels of 'structural' economic inactivity, and much of the employment now on offer – in retail,

Table 15.1 Selected economic indicators for UK nations and regions

	Average weekly earnings (April 2017)	Manufacturing as a % of GVA (2016)	Public sector employment as a % of total (2016)	Unemployment rate (2017)	Economic inactivity rate (ages 16–64, 2017)
Scotland	£547	10.7	20.9	4.1	22.5
Northern Ireland	£501	14.4	25.9	4.4	27.7
Wales	£498	18.0	22.4	4.8	24.0
England	£556	9.8	16.2	4.5	21.4
London	£693	2.1	14.0	5.3	21.8
South East	£575	7.7	15.0	3.2	18.6
East of England	£546	11.4	15.3	3.6	19.2
South West	£520	11.0	16.4	3.3	18.6
North West	£514	16.1	18.0	4.4	23.5
West Midlands	£515	15.6	17.3	5.2	23.6
East Midlands	£499	16.6	16.1	4.4	22.4
Yorkshire and the Humber	£503	14.7	18.3	5.0	22.7
North East	£504	14.3	20.3	6.2	24.6

Sources: ONS (2018)[7]; ONS (2018)[8]; ONS (2017)[9]; ONS (2017)[10]

wholesale and health and social care – is low-paid, low-skilled, and less productive than the same industries in London.[11]

But there are important exceptions. The Midlands is a hub for high-value manufacturing, not least in the automotive sector; in the North, Cheshire East is the most productive sub-region outside of the South East, and Manchester has seen strong inward investment. And although London's aggregate economic performance is strong, this masks huge variation between inner and outer areas. London has the highest child poverty rate in the country after housing costs are taken into account (37 per cent), despite having the highest average incomes in the country.[12]

Scotland

Scotland is in many ways the strongest-performing economy outside of London and the South East. Its richest urban centre, Edinburgh, has average disposable incomes per capita (GDHI) on a par with the South East of England,[13] and over the last 20 years it has developed a multi-dimensional economy, with strengths in financial services, construction and manufacturing, as well as the oil and gas industry centred around Aberdeen.

Looking ahead, however, it faces a unique set of challenges. Though oil and gas remain a significant source of high-paid jobs and gross value added (GVA), this leaves the economy highly exposed to shocks. The sector shed 13,000 jobs between 2014 and 2017 in the wake of the 2014 oil price crash,[14] and in the longer term, the potential reduction in the industry's importance to the economy will mean Scotland needs to expand its other economic activities.

Scotland also faces a more difficult demographic outlook than other parts of the country. Its population is ageing more quickly than the rest of the UK: its over-75s population is projected to increase by 27 per cent between 2016 and 2026.[15] This will place extra pressure on health and social care services, while at the same time reducing the proportion of working-age taxpayers.

Wales

The Welsh economy has the lowest productivity of the four nations or any region of England. Wales has struggled to find alternative sources of productive economic growth since the closure of the coal mines and the decline of manufacturing, and suffers from poor internal connectivity. There are important divergences within Wales; whereas in Cardiff GVA per hour worked is only 6 per cent below the UK average, in other parts of Wales, such as Powys, it is less than two-thirds of the average.[16]

Although it has significant natural tourist attractions, energy generation capacity, and some advanced manufacturing, these industries are generally small-scale and cannot offer the employment opportunities that would make them a sufficient replacement for the manufacturing and mining capacity that has been lost. As a result, much of Wales' rural and semi-rural population remains economically isolated: working-age economic inactivity is 24 per cent, while 18.5 per cent of young people (aged 19–24) are not in employment, education or training.[17]

Northern Ireland

Across a broad range of indicators, Northern Ireland is an underperforming part of the UK (see table 15.1). It faces the twin headwinds of political instability – its devolved government has been suspended since summer 2017 – and relative geographical isolation, having no land border with the rest of the UK, and a 100-mile journey from Belfast to Dublin, the nearest major city over land. Its economy is weighted towards low-wage, low-productivity service sectors, such as retail, tourism and health, and although some manufacturing sectors have grown strongly over the past 20 years, in particular chemicals and engineering, they remain a small component of Northern Ireland's economy.

The city of Belfast is one significant exception to this picture. More than a third of Belfast's workforce are graduates and it has attracted significant inward investment.[18] As a result, its GVA per head is significantly higher than both the UK average and the rest of Northern Ireland. It has diversified sectors including financial services, creative and digital industries (notably cyber security), life sciences and clean tech.

Across Northern Ireland as a whole, economic performance is both a driver and a consequence of its skills base: 16.3 per cent of the working age population have no qualifications (twice the UK average), while only 31.9 per cent of adults have a university-level qualification.[19] At 27.9 per cent, its working-age economic inactivity rate is the highest in the country.[20]

Diverse challenges require devolved policy solutions

The Commission believes that reducing these geographical imbalances should be amongst the highest priorities of government. It violates our goal of justice that economic opportunities and life chances should differ so greatly between people living in different parts of the country. Such an unbalanced pattern of growth is also not economically efficient, since it fails to make best use of the talents and capabilities of many people and places.

Driving equitable and sustainable growth right across the country cannot be done from Whitehall. The assets and capabilities as well as the present and future challenges of different parts of the country are diverse. The requisite levels of local knowledge or commitment simply cannot be found in central government departments. The only way this can be done, we believe, is through decentralisation of economic powers and resources.

There has already been devolution to Scotland, Wales and Northern Ireland. In Scotland the assignation of tax revenue from VAT and devolution of other taxes means that by 2021 the Scottish Parliament will raise around half of its budget from taxes raised in Scotland. The education, justice and health systems have always been separate in Scotland; it has responsibility for economic development and transport; and more recently further powers in relation to employability, social security and tax have been devolved. But the Scottish government still has relatively few economic policy levers and limited (though recently increased) capacity to borrow, while labour market regulation and immigration policy, as for the rest of the UK, are set from Westminster.

The lack of economic levers is even more pronounced in Wales and Northern Ireland. In Wales, some powers over stamp duty and income tax have been devolved, and borrowing powers increased, but the Welsh government has less power over income tax than Scotland, and unlike Scotland it has no powers over air passenger duty or assignment of VAT. Northern Ireland has the lowest level of fiscal devolution amongst the nations: long-haul air passenger duty was devolved in January 2013, while the rates system (the equivalent of council tax) and business rates are also devolved.[21] Devolution *within* Northern Ireland is also minimal: councils in Northern Ireland were responsible for less than 4 per cent (£738 million) of public spending in Northern Ireland in 2015–16, compared with 27 per cent in Scotland and Wales.[22]

Over recent years Westminster has begun to devolve some economic powers within England. Nine 'combined authorities' have now been established to bring local councils together, mostly in urban areas. These have greater control over transport policy and spending, and some powers over skills and planning. But the 'devolution deals' are effectively spending allocations from Whitehall, and much of this power is in fact delegated rather than devolved.[23] The devolution process has been piecemeal and haphazard, more a function of Whitehall departments' willingness to shift responsibility, combined with variable local appetite, than economic need. There has been minimal fiscal devolution. Business rate retention is being piloted in some areas, but is unlikely to deliver much autonomy, because it requires so much redistribution to make it work.[24]

In England, two pan-regional government initiatives, the 'Northern Powerhouse' and the 'Midlands Engine', have provided new brands under which regional investment can be coordinated and promoted.[25] By spanning larger economic geographies than the traditional English 'regions', the Northern Powerhouse (15.3 million people) and Midlands Engine (10.5 million people) suggest a scale of sub-national government in line with the regional governments of other comparable countries. While still relatively informal, they have begun to take institutional form in some places: Transport for the North is England's first statutory transport body outside London, and other such organisations are planned for other regions.[26] But their coverage of England is only partial, they have little democratic scrutiny or accountability, and their remit is much narrower than regional governments in other countries.[27]

International comparisons reveal the extent to which the UK is an outlier in the degree to which economic decision-making is centralised rather than devolved. Even among countries with a unitary rather than federal governance structure, the UK makes relatively few economic spending decisions at the sub-national level, particularly given its size (see figure 15.2). It also collects the lowest proportion of tax locally of any G7 country: even taking into account the further fiscal devolution in the pipeline: just 12 per cent is set to be levied at a sub-national level, compared with close to 50 per cent in Canada (at either the local or provincial level), and 30 per cent in Germany. [28]

It is clear why other countries have more decentralised governance. Devolution of control over economic policy has multiple benefits. First, and most basic, is the superior level of attention, responsiveness and insight that sub-national policymakers can give to their economies; far

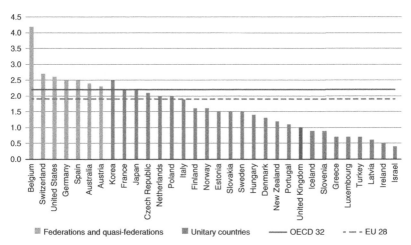

Figure 15.2 Local control of economic policymaking in the UK is low by international standards
Subnational government expenditure on economic affairs (% GDP), 2015
Source: OECD (2018)[29]
Note: Measuring fiscal devolution is complex, and interpreting these figures should be undertaken with caution.[30]

more than central government can ever achieve.[31] Second, it is easier to hold local representatives accountable, since the channels through which sub-national policy impacts on local economic outcomes are much more transparent and traceable.[32] Third, decentralisation facilitates intelligent coordination of infrastructure, public services and policy. Devolving transport policy alongside labour market policy enables integration between transport modes and the cross-subsidy of routes to improve connectivity in excluded areas.[33] Devolving education, training and labour market policy means barriers to work can be addressed more effectively.[34] And delivering land use planning policy alongside transport and housing means they can be much more aligned with economic, social and environmental objectives.[35]

There is clear international evidence that devolution works at reducing geographical imbalances.[36] In Germany, the federal system, supported by a system of fiscal transfers, has helped to raise the economic performance of many parts of eastern Germany and narrow the productivity gap with the western regions. Less than 30 years after reunification, much of former East Germany now outperforms many English regions outside of London.[37] Even countries with strong traditions of centralised government, such France and Japan, have in recent decades committed to long-term programmes of decentralisation. These have delivered significant benefits to second-tier cities such as Lyon, Bordeaux and Osaka.[38]

For policy at local level, functional 'travel to work' areas provide the appropriate scale of economic governance, particularly to integrate spatial and transport planning, and to develop education, skills and business support policies to meet the needs of local labour markets. But at present these functions are very patchily performed: most local authorities are simply too small and have too few powers and resources. In England, the 39 business-led Local Enterprise Partnerships (set up in 2010 to replace the much better-funded Regional Development Agencies) operate at a more appropriate scale, but they have limited resources and powers, and are of inconsistent quality and capacity.[39] The Local Enterprise Partnership geographies overlap with one another, and with the combined authorities in some parts of the country.

Beyond the local economy, the international evidence suggests that there is a suite of economic policies that are most effectively designed and controlled at what could be described as a 'mezzanine tier' of governance: larger than a county or city region, but smaller than the size of the UK as a whole.[40] The German Länder (which average 5.2 million residents), French conséil regionals (5.3 million) and US states (6.1 million) are all examples of sub-national units that operate their own economic policies effectively. The specific policy areas and responsibilities that are suitable at this scale are those that require coordination over a large functional economic area, such as infrastructure planning, inward investment, regional industrial strategy and public investment banking.[41]

Such a mezzanine tier of governance already exists within the UK in the devolved nations of Scotland, Wales, Northern Ireland and in London. The Northern Powerhouse and the Midlands Engine are small steps towards institutional arrangements at that scale in England. But for the rest of England, it is missing.

Devolving economic governance in England

To build an economy that achieves prosperity and justice right across the UK, we believe that much stronger economic powers and responsibilities need to be held at sub-national level. This is particularly true in England. Current devolution arrangements are simply not adequate to the task of developing regions' strengths, reviving poorer regions and towns, or allowing the regions to shape their own destinies. We need institutions with sufficient resources and capacity to make a significant difference.

Regional economic executives

We therefore propose the creation of four economic authorities or 'executives' for the regions of England, to be responsible for regional economic and industrial strategy. The Northern Economic Executive and Midlands Economic Executive would be created from the current institutions of the Northern Powerhouse and Midlands Engine respectively. In the rest of the country we propose that the government consult on the creation of an economic executive for the South West, and a South East Economic Executive encompassing London, the East and the South East regions (see figure 15.3).

The economic executives should have responsibility for a range of economic development functions at regional level, including

- regional industrial strategies, including innovation clusters, supply chains and inward investment, as set out in chapter 6
- regional infrastructure planning, including transport, energy, communications and environmental and resource management
- oversight of inter-city rail networks and franchises and the new 'major road network'
- regional immigration policy, as set out in chapter 6
- oversight of the regional divisions of our proposed National Investment Bank (NIB) in England, as set out in chapter 6
- responsibility for regional spending of the Inclusive Growth Fund we propose below.

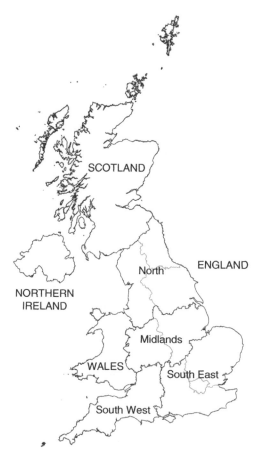

Figure 15.3 Potential geographies of regional economic executives in England
Source: IPPR

Economic executives of this kind would be able to represent their regions overseas to attract inward investment in the way that smaller existing authorities cannot. At this scale they would have the political clout to demand resources from central government, and to attract talented staff. As the Northern Powerhouse and Midlands Engine have shown, we hope that they would be able to overcome some of the rivalries between cities and towns that currently exist at the smaller regional scale. Through the regional divisions of the NIB they should have the power to borrow to invest.

We propose that each economic executive should be governed by a 'regional council' indirectly elected from their constituent local authorities, to ensure they are democratically accountable. In the first instance they should be funded by a block grant from the Treasury, but in due course might become part of a new, more devolved fiscal framework for England.

City and county regions

Beneath the regional level we also need stronger economic institutions at city region and county level. We believe combined authorities are a sensible model. *We therefore propose that combined authorities are created to cover the rest of England, in both city and county regions.* This should happen on an appropriate timetable in different areas given local circumstances.

Such combined authorities would have responsibility for many of the place-based elements of industrial strategy, including labour market planning, further education and skills and business support services, working in conjunction with the national productivity agency (Productivity UK) we propose in chapter 6. They should also have full autonomy over local transport services. We would expect combined authorities to be funded by block grants, offering the freedom to allocate funds across their areas of control, and to be able to levy some taxes of their own, including workplace parking levies, hotel bed taxes, congestion charges and business rate supplements. Once established, city-regions and county-regions should be allowed to borrow to invest in social housing and transport infrastructure.

We see particular potential in the development of 'local wealth-building' strategies.[42] In recent years a number of local authorities have sought to use their procurement policies to support the development of local businesses and supply chains (see box below). Several have combined with other 'anchor institutions' at local level, such as hospitals, universities, housing associations and major businesses.[43] The aim is to enable as much as possible of local procurement to be supplied from within the local economy, thereby supporting local employment and preventing the 'leakage' of local demand out of the local economy.[44] Combined with industrial strategy policies to support business growth and innovation, local wealth-building strategies offer an important means of reviving disadvantaged local economies. They can provide particular opportunities to develop social enterprises (businesses with social as well as commercial purposes), including community and cooperatively owned businesses of various kinds.

Examples of local wealth-building strategies

- Preston City Council has made a concerted effort towards community wealth-building since 2013. Coordinating a number of other local 'anchor institutions', it has increased the proportion of collective procurement spent in the local economy from 5 per cent to over 18 per cent in 2016–17, and in the wider Lancashire economy from 39 per cent to over 79 per cent.[45] Drawing on US experience in Cleveland, Ohio, its strategy has been theorised as a 'Preston model'.[46]

- Manchester City Council has pioneered 'progressive procurement' since 2008. Targeting organisations based in, or with a presence in, Manchester, it has increased the proportion of total procurement spent in the city from 51 per cent in 2008–9 to 74 per cent in 2015–16. At the Greater Manchester level, this has risen from 86.5 per cent to 90.7 per cent, with an estimated creation of over 5,000 new jobs.[47]

- Since the Welsh Assembly government committed to increasing procurement spend in Wales-based businesses in 2013, the proportion of public procurement expenditure won by businesses in Wales has increased from 34 per cent to 50 per cent.[48] The strategy has changed the policies of the National Procurement Service for Wales and the Value Wales organisation.

Economic policy in the devolved nations

As a UK-wide Commission, we have not sought to define economic strategies for the devolved nations. We are conscious that the devolved governments in Scotland and Wales, in particular, have been pursuing active economic development strategies.[49] In Scotland, we have seen important recent contributions to how sustainable economic growth can be delivered.[50] We therefore limit our recommendations to those areas where our proposals in this report would need to be implemented at a devolved level, and to further economic powers and responsibilities which we believe should be devolved from Westminster. In Northern Ireland, restoration of the Assembly is plainly a precondition for further devolution.

Devolved measures

For a number of the policy recommendations we have made in other chapters, it would be for the devolved governments in Scotland, Wales and Northern Ireland to decide whether and how to implement them. These encompass many of our proposals on industrial strategy, including the establishment of a new national productivity agency, skills policies and a 'good jobs standard'. Our proposal for the latter has already drawn on the Scottish government's Fair Work agenda. Where in England we propose extending the model of combined authorities to provide stronger institutions for local economic development, in each of the devolved nations there are strong arguments also to give greater powers to existing local authorities. In Northern Ireland this could involve a consideration of unitary status, and the development of 'rural economy deals'.[51]

We see a particular opportunity to devolve some aspects of immigration policy. This would allow the governments of Scotland, Wales and potentially Northern Ireland (although we recognise that the evolution of Brexit will have implications here) to develop new visa arrangements for non-EU nationals, and EU nationals following Brexit, to help tackle demographic change and align immigration with skills policy as it applies in each country. As with devolved immigration systems in Canada and Australia, the UK government would continue to issue visas (including the devolved nation visas) and undertake security vetting.

The Scottish government is already in the process of establishing a Scottish National Investment Bank (SNIB), which we welcome, and there is a Development Bank of Wales (DBW).[52] We hope that these would cooperate closely with the National Investment Bank (NIB) we propose, which we would therefore envisage operating largely in the rest of the UK. We see the NIB having a national division in Northern Ireland, under the scrutiny of the devolved government, and regional divisions in the four economic executive regions of England.

Further devolution of economic development powers

Scotland is currently able to borrow 15 per cent of its annual capital budget (around £450 million) up to a maximum of £3 billion in total. We believe there is a good case that further borrowing powers should be devolved to the Scottish Parliament, to take its annual capital borrowing limit to 1 per cent of GDP (around £1.5 billion per year) and its total capital borrowing limit to 10 per cent of GDP (around £15 billion in total). This would allow the Scottish government to capitalise the SNIB more quickly, and to boost infrastructure and business investment in Scotland.

Wales is in particular need of new transport infrastructure in order to connect its fragmented economy, and this will also require substantial additional investment. We believe there would be merit in granting the Welsh government the same power to borrow in proportion to its spending as the Scottish government. If implemented, this would raise its annual limit from £150 million (under the current arrangements) to just over £600 million (1 per cent of GDP), and its total borrowing cap from £1 billion to £6 billion (10 per cent of GDP).[53]

At the same time, given its unique labour market, we can see a strong case for the Welsh government to be given more autonomy over employment support, including the work and health programme, and the ability to top up benefit payments, bringing its powers into line with those of Scotland. This would enable the integration of the public services that support people moving into work, and it would enable more effective matching of job seekers to opportunities.

An Inclusive Growth Fund

More decentralisation of revenue-raising in the UK is desirable, but the current inequalities between different parts of the UK mean it is not feasible without retaining a significant redistributive function from the centre. For example, giving city regions the power to raise their own tax revenues without a block grant would immediately increase inequality, as most regions would be unable to raise the resources they need. Many countries have developed redistributive solutions to this problem: Germany, Sweden, France and Canada each have a different model of fiscal transfers between central and regional levels of government from which the UK can learn.[54] The functioning of Scotland's new Fiscal Framework, which attempts to balance risk between the UK and Scotland following the devolution of tax powers and revenues, will also be instructive.[55]

The UK's membership of the European Union has delivered significant targeted support to the poorest parts of the UK via the European Regional Development and Social Funds. As the UK leaves the EU, the government has pledged that this support will be replaced. *We therefore propose that the UK government should create an Inclusive Growth Fund (IGF) of £10 billion over five years, with the explicit objective of narrowing geographical inequalities within the UK.* This should be administered by the devolved nations (as the EU funds are now) along with our proposed economic executives and combined authorities in England. Given that the European structural funds are due to spend a total of €10.9 billion in the UK between 2014 and 2020, a funding level for the IGF of £10 billion over five years would act as a replacement. For further funding of economic development across the UK, consideration might be given to a 'solidarity surcharge' on some taxes, similar to that used following the reunification of East and West Germany in the early 1990s, and to the solidarity taxes introduced by Japan and France to fund the restoration of infrastructure after crises.[56]

Developing the partnership economy

In chapter 4, we expressed our desire for stronger models of social partnership in the economy. This would have important implications for economic governance.

Over the last 40 years, economic policy in the UK has been almost exclusively managed by the Treasury. (Since 1997 the Bank of England has been independent but operating under a Treasury mandate.) As an institution, the Treasury has often taken a very orthodox approach in its consideration of economic ideas and policies. We believe it would be beneficial for economic policymaking to be opened up more widely, both within government and beyond it.

First, we would like to see government engage in much broader consultation on economic policy. In particular, *we propose that public consultation should be required for all measures announced in the Budget.* Currently, the Treasury's fiscal decision-making is highly secretive, with Chancellors of the Exchequer frequently delighting in pulling out surprise 'policy rabbits' on Budget day. Most other countries (including the UK's devolved nations) have much more open budget processes, in which policies are consulted upon as in other departments of government. Although there are some 'overnight' tax changes and other policies for which this is not possible due to market sensitivities, there is no reason why most Budget measures cannot be subject to consultation. This would much reduce the risk of poor fiscal policymaking, of a kind too frequently seen in recent years.

At the same time, we would like to see government engage in a much more open public conversation about economic policy choices. Many people feel understandably ill-educated and confused about economic policy, and it should be part of the government's role to widen public understanding, as the Bank of England has been trying to do.[57] We see particular potential in citizens' deliberation processes, such as recently piloted by the Royal Society of Arts, and would like to see further exercises of this kind.[58]

Second, we believe that a much wider range of voices needs to be involved in national economic policymaking. It is no longer sufficient for the Westminster government to seek to manage the economy on its own: this should be a process of partnership with the devolved nations and regions of the UK, and with the interests of businesses, trade unions and civil society.

We therefore propose the establishment of a National Economic Council (NEC) as a forum for economic policy consultation and coordination. We see this being chaired jointly by the Chancellor of the Exchequer and Secretary of State for Business, Energy and Industrial Strategy, and to comprise in addition the economy ministers of the devolved nations, the leaders of the four economic executives in England, and the leaders of major business, trade union and relevant civil society organisations.

The NEC would have two principal roles. It would advise on economic policies. And it would draw up and agree a coordinated ten-year plan for the UK economy. The plan would provide a coordinated framework for the management of economic policy, with clear targets and specific commitments made by each tier of government and by the social partner organisations. Such a plan would be widely consulted upon, and progress against it would be reported to the UK Parliament and the devolved Parliaments and Assemblies. It would be updated every three years.

The old centralised methods of making economic policy will no longer do. We believe our proposals for devolution and partnership offer a better way to achieve prosperity and justice together.

Notes

1: The Economy Today

1 International Monetary Fund (IMF) (2018) 'DataMapper: GDP, current prices'. https://bit.ly/2JeGjPC

2 OECD (2018) 'Quarterly international trade statistics'. https://bit.ly/2uqcHcz

3 Office for National Statistics (ONS) (2018) 'BoP: trade in services balance as per cent of GDP'. https://bit.ly/2vpdbku

4 Rhodes C (2018) *Financial services: Contribution to the UK economy*, House of Commons Library. https://bit.ly/2Jik8YP

5 Brien P and Rhodes C (2017) 'The aerospace industry: Statistics and policy', House of Commons Library. https://bit.ly/2JgXikn; ONS (2018).

6 Ibid.

7 Office for Life Sciences (2017) *Life sciences competitiveness indicators*. https://bit.ly/2N8C7mH

8 TechUK (2017) 'The UK digital sectors after Brexit'. https://bit.ly/2tfNIua; Tech London Advocates, Tech UK and Centre for London (2016) *London's digital future: The mayoral tech manifesto*. https://bit.ly/2M1HwPK

9 TechCity UK (2017) *Tech nation 2017: At the forefront of global digital innovation*, Tech Nation/Tech City. https://technation.techcityuk.com/

10 Department for Digital, Culture, Media & Sport [DCMS] 'Sector economic estimates 2016: Gross value added'. https://bit.ly/2L8r4cK

11 DCMS (2018) 'DCMS sectors economic estimates 2017: Employment and trade'. https://bit.ly/2uhdRb4

12 Bakhshi H et al. (2015) *Creativity vs. robots*, Nesta. https://bit.ly/2L8WpMh

13 ONS (2017) 'Gross domestic product: Year on year growth: CVM SA %'. https://bit.ly/2KOdkaU.

14 IPPR analysis of ONS (2017) 'Gross domestic product: Chained volume measures: Seasonally adjusted £m'. https://bit.ly/2ufjiYl

15 ONS (2017) 'UK economic accounts time series dataset (UKEA)'. https://bit.ly/2L9m5Zf.

16 ONS (2018) 'UK economic accounts time series dataset (UKEA)'. https://bit.ly/2ztooVP

17 Office for Budget Responsibility (OBR) (2018) *Economic and fiscal outlook.* https://bit.ly/2GtmNz8

18 IMF 'World economic outlook: Update January 2018'. https://bit.ly/2DWDK3E

19 Bank of England (2018), 'Quantitative easing'. https://www.bankofengland.co.uk/monetary-policy/quantitative-easing

20 IPPR Commission on Economic Justice (2017), *Time for change: A new vision for the British economy.* Interim Report. https://bit.ly/2NIabYl

21 Cribb J, Norris Keiller A and Waters T (2018) *Living standards, poverty and inequality in the UK: 2018,* IFS. http://bit.ly/2mdIKss

22 Corlett A, Bangham G and Finch D (2018) *The living standards outlook 2018,* Resolution Foundation. https://bit.ly/2zH94VR

23 Ibid.

24 IPPR analysis of OECD (2018) 'Average annual wages'. http://bit.ly/2JfREyY

25 ONS (2018) 'Gross Domestic Product: Chained volume measures: Seasonally adjusted £m'. http://bit.ly/2Nca2ei; ONS (2018) 'Output per worker: Whole economy SA: Index 2016=100'. http://bit.ly/2LeAzKS; ONS (2018) Series 'SA AWE: INDEX xbxa: Whole Economy' in 'Average Weekly Earnings time series'. http://bit.ly/2Nf3a00; ONS (2018) 'RPI All Items Index: Jan 1987=100'. http://bit.ly/2zE8FDj

26 Bailey D, Cowling K and Tomlinson P (2015) *New perspectives on industrial policy for a modern Britain,* Oxford University Press.

27 Haldane A (2015) 'Labour's share', speech to the TUC, 12 November. https://bit.ly/2L5WfIU

28 Piketty T (2014) *Capital in the twenty-first century*, Harvard University Press.

29 Haldane (2015). Analysis is based on supplementary data to Piketty T and Zucman G (2014) 'Capital is back: Wealth–income ratios in rich countries, 1700–2010', *The Quarterly Journal of Economics* 129(3): 1255–310; ONS (2015) *United Kingdom national accounts: The blue book, 2015 edition*. http://bit.ly/2NfY2sq; Allen R (2009) 'Engels' pause: Technical change, capital accumulation, and inequality in the British industrial revolution', *Explorations in Economic History* 46(4): 418–35. https://bit.ly/1jQkiE3

30 ONS (2018) 'UK labour market: June 2018'. https://bit.ly/2tN8gJn

31 ONS (2017) 'EMP16: Underemployment and overemployment'. https://bit.ly/2rZlkMl

32 ONS (2018) 'A01: Summary of labour market statistics'. https://bit.ly/2ma7guy

33 Courts and Tribunals Judiciary (2016) 'Employment tribunal between Y Aslam, J Farrar & others and Uber B.V., Uber London Ltd and Uber Britannia Ltd'. http://bit.ly/2mm26vO

34 ONS (2018) 'Contracts that do not guarantee a minimum number of hours: April 2018'. https://bit.ly/2HWTlCu.

35 Bloodworth J (2018) *Hired: Six months undercover in low-wage Britain*, Atlantic Books.

36 Joseph Rowntree Foundation (2017) *UK poverty 2017*. https://bit.ly/2jd6FYe

37 Department for Work and Pensions (2018) 'Households below average income: 1994/95 to 2016/17'. https://bit.ly/2HXu4Xv

38 Joseph Rowntree Foundation (2018) *Destitution in the UK 2018*. https://bit.ly/2Joo8rI

39 Cribb, Norris Keiller and Waters (2018).

40 OECD (2018) 'Inequality'. http://www.oecd.org/social/inequality.htm

41 Corlett A and Clarke S (2017) *Living standards 2017: The past, present and possible future of UK incomes*, Resolution Foundation. https://bit.ly/2jUodXd

42 ONS Digital (2016) 'The gender pay gap – what is it and what affects it?' https://bit.ly/2ff2nyW

43 TUC (2016) 'Black workers with degrees earn a quarter less than white counterparts, finds TUC', 1 February 2016. https://bit. ly/2Kvc2ga; TUC (2017) 'Black workers with A-levels earn 10% less than white counterparts, finds TUC', 14 August 2017. https://bit. ly/2uzoLbR; Powell A (2018) *Unemployment by ethnic background*, House of Commons Library. https://bit.ly/2mcmUHu

44 ONS (2018) 'Wealth in Great Britain wave 5: 2014 to 2016'. https:// bit.ly/2GRedtB

45 World Inequality Database (2018) 'Income and wealth inequality, United Kingdom, 1896–2014'. https://wid.world/country/ united-kingdom/

46 D'Arcy C and Gardiner L (2017) *The generation of wealth: Asset accumulation across and within cohorts*, Resolution Foundation. https://bit.ly/2MFEcxr

47 ONS (2018) 'Life expectancy at birth and at age 65 by local areas in the United Kingdom: 2006–08 to 2010–12'. https://bit.ly/2L7B6hE

48 Resolution Foundation (2018) *A new generational contract.* https://bit.ly/2wikAoG.

49 Cribb, Norris Keiller and Waters (2017).

50 Eurostat (2018) 'Gross domestic product (GDP) at current market prices by NUTS 2 regions: Purchasing power standard per inhabitant'. https://bit.ly/2dItUGb

2: Prosperity and Justice: A New Vision for the Economy

1 Atkinson A (2015) *Inequality: What can be done?*, Harvard University Press.

2 Layard R (2011) *Happiness: Lessons from a new science*, Penguin.

3 Ibid.

4 Wheatley D (2017) 'Autonomy in paid work and employee subjective well-being', *Work and Occupations* 44(32): 296–328.

5 Health and Safety Executive (2017) *Work-related stress, depression or anxiety statistics in Great Britain 2017.* https://bit.ly/1omjNco

6 OECD (2018) 'Average annual hours actually worked by worker'. https://bit.ly/1J5VVPq; ONS (2018) 'EMP16: Underemployment and overemployment', May 2018. https://bit.ly/2rZlkMl

7 It might be noted that in Catholic social teaching, the concept of the Common Good covers all areas of life – the economic, political, personal and spiritual. A holistic approach to development with human dignity at its centre, founded on the principles of Catholic social teaching, is what Pope Paul VI called 'authentic development'. See Catholic Bishops' Conference of England and Wales (1996), *The common good and the Catholic Church's social teaching*. https://bit.ly/2Ns3cm4

8 Clark A et al. (2018) *The origins of happiness: The science of wellbeing over the life course*, Princeton University Press.

9 Heliwell J, Layard R and Sachs J (2018) *World happiness report*, Sustainable Development Solutions Network. https://bit.ly/2GqkBZ7

10 Jacobs M (1991) *The green economy: Environment, sustainable development and the politics of the future*, Pluto Press.

11 World Economic Forum (2018) *The global risks report 2018*. http://bit.ly/2Nw2yDb

12 Haidt J (2012) *The righteous mind: Why good people are divided by politics and religion*, Pantheon Books.

13 McGuinness F (2018) 'Poverty in the UK: Statistics', House of Commons Library. https://bit.ly/2KQgRWk; Padley M and Hirsch D (2017) *A minimum income standard for the UK in 2017*, Joseph Rowntree Foundation. http://bit.ly/2mflomh

14 Equality and Human Rights Commisson (2018) *Progress on socio-economic rights in Great Britain*. http://bit.ly/2udmaEU

15 Padley and Hirsch (2017).

16 World Commission on Environment and Development (1987) *Our common future*, United Nations. http://bit.ly/2Lczikb.

17 United Nations Development Programme (2011) *Human development report 2011: Sustainability and equity – a better future for all*. http://bit.ly/2KPaQcl

18 International Labour Organisation (2017) *Global estimates of child labour*. http://bit.ly/2zwUbFr; ILO (2017) *Purchasing practices and working conditions in global supply chains: Global survey results*. http://bit.ly/2JhDzkw

19 Stiglitz J (2012) *The price of inequality: How today's divided society endangers our future*, WW Norton

20 Berg A and Ostry J (2011) *Inequality and sustainable growth: Two sides of the same coin?*, International Monetary Fund. http://bit.ly/2Jv3HZv; Cingano F (2014) *Trends in income inequality and its impact on economic growth*, OECD. http://bit.ly/2JhPu1L; Ostry J, Berg A and Tsangarides C (2014), *Redistribution, inequality and growth*, IMF. http://bit.ly/2NUDgQd

21 Stiglitz J (2016) 'Inequality and economic growth', in Jacobs M and Mazzucato M (eds) *Rethinking capitalism: Economics and policy for sustainable and inclusive growth*, Wiley Blackwell.

22 Ibid.

23 Akerlof G and Yellen J (1986) *Efficiency wage models of the labor market*, Cambridge University Press.

24 Berg and Ostry (2011).

25 Stiglitz (2016).

26 Wilkinson R and Pickett K (2009) *The spirit level: Why more equal societies almost always do better*, Allen Lane; Wilkinson R and Pickett K (2018) *The inner level: How more equal societies reduce stress, restore sanity and improve everyone's wellbeing*, Allen Lane.

27 Easterlin R (1974) 'Does economic growth improve the human lot? Some empirical evidence', in David P and Reder M (eds) *Nations and households in economic growth: Essays in honour of Moses Abramovitz*, Academic Press.

28 Atkinson (2015).

29 Milanovic B (2016) *Global inequality: A new approach for the age of globalization*, Harvard University Press.

30 United Nations (2018) 'The sustainable development agenda'. http://bit.ly/2zzMpdS; OECD (2017) *Bridging the gap: Inclusive*

growth 2017 update report. http://bit.ly/2LdaQzg; World Bank (2012) *Inclusive green growth: The pathway to sustainable development.* http://bit.ly/2JgVebS

31 Daly H (1997) *Beyond growth: The economics of sustainable development,* Beacon Press; Monbiot G (2016) *How did we get into this mess?* Verso.

32 Jackson T (2016) *Prosperity without growth: Foundations for the economy of tomorrow,* Routledge; Raworth K (2017) *Doughnut economics: Seven ways to think like a 21st-Century economist,* Random House.

33 Ekins P (1999) *Economic growth and environmental sustainability: The prospects for green growth,* Routledge; World Bank (2012); OECD (2017).

34 Pilling D (2018) *The growth delusion: The wealth and well-being of nations,* Bloomsbury.

35 Coyle D (2014) *GDP: A brief but affectionate history,* Princeton University Press.

36 Colebrook C (2018) *Measuring what matters: Improving the indicators of economic performance,* IPPR. http://bit.ly/2LaxJTS

37 ONS (2018) 'Wellbeing'. http://bit.ly/2NiKmgj

38 OECD (2018) 'Better Life Index'. http://www.oecdbetterlifeindex. org/

39 Colebrook (2018).

40 Dwyer J (2005) 'Ethics and economics: Bridging Adam Smith's *Theory of Moral Sentiments* and *Wealth of Nations*', *Journal of British Studies* 44(4): 662–87.

41 For a longer version of this vision, see IPPR Commission on Economic Justice (2017) *Time for change: A new vision for the British economy,* Interim Report. http://bit.ly/2uvdXvk

3: Reshaping the Economy

1 IPPR Commission on Economic Justice (2017) *Time for change: A new vision for the British economy,* Interim Report. http://bit. ly/2uvdXvk

2 IPPR analysis of OBR (2018) *Economic and Fiscal Outlook – March 2018*. http://bit.ly/2mfrKlQ

3 Harari D (2018) *Household debt: statistics and impact on economy*, House of Commons Library. http://bit.ly/2LciOs8

4 ONS (2018) 'Households' saving ratio (per cent): Current price: £m: SA'. http://bit.ly/2L0dBaj

5 OBR (2018); Brazier A (2017) '"Debt strikes back" or "the return of the regulator"?', speech at the University of Liverpool, 24 July. http://bit.ly/2Lftw1m

6 Hein E et al. (2017) *Financialisation and distribution in the US, the UK, Spain, Germany, Sweden and France – before and after the crisis*, Institute for International Political Economy, Berlin. http://bit.ly/2udY7pq

7 OBR (2018).

8 World Bank (2018) 'Gross capital formation (% of GDP)'. http://bit.ly/2JdEr9T

9 Ibid.

10 ONS (2018) 'Quarterly National Accounts, Q1 2018, Time series'. http://bit.ly/2N8NF9C

11 World Bank (2018).

12 Ibid.

13 World Bank (2018a) 'Research and development expenditure (% of GDP)'. http://bit.ly/2N9trwr

14 OECD (2018) 'Gross domestic spending on R&D'. http://bit.ly/2ufLgDg

15 Hughes A (2013) *Short-termism, impatient capital and finance for manufacturing innovation in the UK*, University of Cambridge. http://bit.ly/2ufM3Ee; Jones R (2017) *Innovation, research and the UK's productivity crisis*, Sheffield Political Economy Research Institute. http://bit.ly/2mdACZm

16 Davies R et al. (2014) 'Measuring the costs of short-termism', *Journal of Financial Stability* 12: 16–25; Kay J (2012) *The Kay review of UK equity markets and long-term decision making*, HM Government. http://bit.ly/2KOVzbE

17 Haldane A (2016) 'The costs of short-termism', in Jacobs M and Mazzucato M (eds) *Rethinking capitalism: Economics and policy for sustainable and inclusive growth*, Wiley-Blackwell.

18 ONS (2017) 'Ownership of UK Quoted Shares: 2016'. http://bit. ly/2L4QATu

19 Stirling A and King L (2017) *Financing investment: Reforming finance markets for the long-term*, IPPR. http://bit.ly/2zzlmPQ

20 Haldane A (2015) 'Who owns a company?', speech at the University of Edinburgh, 22 May 2015. http://bit.ly/2JflGmw; Big Innovation Centre (2016) *The purposeful company: Interim report*. http://bit. ly/2L3GTVo

21 Lazonick W (2014) 'Profits without prosperity', *Harvard Business Review*, September 2014. http://bit.ly/2LeeZmB

22 IPPR analysis from Tomorrow's Company (2016) *UK Business: What's wrong? What's next? Creating value for shareholders and society through a focus on purpose, values, relationships and the long term*. https://bit.ly/2OOopaD

23 Shabani M et al. (2014) *The financial system in the UK*, FESSUD. http://bit.ly/2mdxKeV

24 European Central Bank (2017) 'MFI balance sheets'. http://bit. ly/2JglTpw

25 Fitzpatrick T and McQuinn K (2007) 'House prices and mortgage credit: Empirical evidence for Ireland', *The Manchester School* 75(1): 82–103.

26 Bahaj S, Foulis A and Pinter G (2016) *The residential collateral channel*, Centre for Macroeconomics. http://bit.ly/2zzdnlK

27 Ibid.

28 Bank of England (2018) *Inflation report – May 2018*. http://bit. ly/2KPHTgH

29 OBR (2017) 'Public finances databank'. http://budgetresponsi bility.org.uk/data/

30 ONS (2018) 'Gross domestic expenditure on research and development, UK: 2016'. http://bit.ly/2KT00SA; OECD (2018) 'Investment by sector – General government, % of GFCF, 2016'. http://bit. ly/2L8uxIi

31 Stirling and King (2017).
32 Summers L (2016) 'The age of secular stagnation: what it is and what to do about it', *Foreign Affairs*. http://bit.ly/2Nb6FEq
33 Griffith-Jones S and Cozzi G (2016) 'Investment-led growth: a solution to the European crisis', in Jacobs M and Mazzucato M (eds) *Rethinking capitalism: Economics and policy for sustainable and inclusive growth*, Wiley-Blackwell.
34 Rodrik D (2016) 'A progressive logic of trade', Project Syndicate. http://bit.ly/2ueZOmB
35 Centre for Labour and Social Studies (2018) *Back to basics: Trade agreements*. http://bit.ly/2L4xBs1
36 ONS (2017) 'United Kingdom Balance of Payments – The Pink Book'. http://bit.ly/2zugFqE
37 ONS (2017) 'Chapter 1: Summary of Balance of Payments, The Pink Book'. http://bit.ly/2KUt5xf
38 Burgess S and Shanbhogue R (2017) 'A prince not a pauper: The truth behind the UK's current account deficit', *Bank Underground*, 7 December 2017. http://bit.ly/2L4yssJ
39 Blakeley G (2018) *On borrowed time: Finance and the UK's current account deficit*, IPPR. http://bit.ly/2LcisC3
40 OECD (2018) 'Value added by activity'. http://bit.ly/2Jhyclz
41 Jacobs M et al. (2017) *Industrial strategy: Steering structural change in the UK economy*, IPPR. http://bit.ly/2KO576C
42 Ibid.
43 Gervais A (2013) *Are services tradable? Evidence from US Microdata*, National Bureau of Economic Research. http://bit.ly/2Lc2pEi
44 World Bank (2018b) 'Manufacturing, value added (% of GDP)'. http://bit.ly/2ufLnyH
45 Dolphin T (2014) *Gathering strength: Backing clusters to boost Britain's exports*. IPPR. http://bit.ly/2NaKlLm
46 Economist Intelligence Unit (2011), *Fostering innovation-led clusters*. http://bit.ly/2NJHjyw; Hausmann et al. (2011) *The atlas of economic complexity: Mapping paths to prosperity*, MIT Press.
47 Jacobs et al. (2017).

48 British Business Bank (2016) *Small business finance markets report 2015/16*. http://bit.ly/2KTSvuM

49 Science and Technology Select Committee (2013) 'Bridging the valley of death: Improving the commercialisation of research', Eighth report of session 2012–13. http://bit.ly/2N4O3G4

50 Leung D, Meh C and Terajima Y (2008) *Firm size and productivity*, Bank of Canada. http://bit.ly/2N72t8K

51 Kneller R and Pisu M (2010) 'The returns to exporting: Evidence from UK firms', *Canadian Journal of Economics* 43(2): 414–519.

52 Mazzucato M and Macfarlane L (2017) *Patient strategic finance: Opportunities for state investment banks in the UK*, working paper, UCL Institute for Innovation and Public Purpose. http://bit.ly/2udZF2I

53 OECD (2018) 'GDP per hour worked: Total, US dollars, 2016'. http://bit.ly/2KSJhPk

54 Jacobs et al. (2017).

55 ONS (2018) 'UK Whole Economy: Output per hour worked SA'. http://bit.ly/2LfbHT9

56 Haldane A (2017) 'Productivity puzzles', speech at the London School of Economics, 20 March. http://bit.ly/2zxCrJZ

57 Ibid.

58 Haldane A (2018) 'The UK's productivity problem: hub no spokes', Academy of Social Sciences annual lecture, 28 June. http://bit.ly/2N7yJZw

59 ONS (2018) *Regional and sub-regional productivity in the UK: February 2018*. http://bit.ly/2zHdYlJ

60 Haldane (2017).

61 Blakeley G (2017) *Paying for our progress: How will the Northern Powerhouse be financed and funded?*, IPPR. http://bit.ly/2L6FvRG

62 Bloom N and Van Reenen J (2010) 'Why do management practices differ across firms and countries?', *Journal of Economic Perspectives* 24(1): 203–24.

63 Department for Business, Energy and Industrial Strategy (2017) *Industrial digitalisation review: Interim report*. http://bit.ly/2JhgGOi

64 Haldane (2017, 2018).
65 Confederation of British Industry (2018) *From ostrich to magpie: Increasing business take-up of proven ideas and technologies.* http://bit.ly/2JhgHSm
66 Dromey J and McNeil C (2017) *Skills 2030: Why the adult skills system is failing to build an economy that works for everyone*, IPPR. http://bit.ly/2LcJdGt
67 European Centre for the Development of Vocational Training (2015) *Skills, qualifications and jobs in the EU: The making of a perfect match?*, Publications Office for the European Union. https://bit.ly/2vmi39Z
68 World Economic Forum (2018) *The global competitiveness report 2017–18.* http://bit.ly/2mhAzf7
69 Manyika J et al. (2016) *Independent work: Choice, necessity, and the gig economy*, McKinsey Global Institute. https://mck.co/2N9v8dh
70 ONS (2018) *Labour market economic commentary: June 2018.* http://bit.ly/2uiqnqQ
71 Ibid.
72 Dromey J (2018) *Power to the people: How stronger unions can deliver economic justice*, IPPR. http://bit.ly/2ugOaHD
73 Lawrence M, Roberts C and King L (2017) *Managing automation employment, inequality and ethics in the digital age*, IPPR. http://bit.ly/2uqP1ow
74 Jacobs et al. (2017); see also Bentham et al. (2017) *Manifesto for the foundational economy*, working paper, University of Manchester Centre for Research on Socio-Cultural Change. http://bit.ly/2maymBT
75 Reed H (2010) *Flexible with the truth? Exploring the relationship between labour market flexibility and labour market performance*, Trades Union Congress. http://bit.ly/2KRg07F
76 Manyika et al. (2017) *Harnessing automation for a future that works*, McKinsey Global Institute. https://mck.co/2JhPXkm
77 Frey C and Osborne M (2015) *From brawn to brains: The impact of technology on jobs in the UK*, Deloitte. http://bit.ly/2uteIVD
78 Ibid.

79 Manyika et al. (2017).
80 Lawrence, Roberts and King (2017).
81 Autor D (2015) 'Why are there still so many jobs? The history and future of workplace automation', *Journal of Economic Perspectives* 29(3): 3–30.
82 Acemoglu D and Autor D (2011) 'Skills, tasks and technologies: Implications for employment and earnings', *Handbook of Labor Economics* 4b. http://bit.ly/2NKzatR
83 Frey and Osborne (2015).
84 Burkhardt R and Bradford C (2017) *Addressing the accelerating labor market dislocation from digitalization*, Brookings Institute. https://brook.gs/2uqPY04
85 Lawrence, Roberts and King (2017).
86 Dao M et al. (2017) 'Drivers of declining labour share of income', IMF Blog. http://bit.ly/2KRofAU
87 Karabarbounis L and Neiman B (2013) 'The global decline of the labor share', *Quarterly Journal of Economics* 129(1): 61–103.
88 Lawrence, Roberts and King (2017).
89 Ibid.
90 Westerheide F (2018) 'Global artificial intelligence landscape 2018', database. http://bit.ly/2L88BQK
91 International Federation of Robotics (2018) 'Robot density rises globally', 7 February 2018. http://bit.ly/2uqBRI5
92 Goodman S (2017) 'The robots are coming and Sweden is fine', *New York Times*, 27 December 2017. https://nyti.ms/2zzUorq
93 Díez F, Leigh D and Tambunlertchai S (2018) 'Global market power and its macroeconomic implications', working paper, IMF. http://bit.ly/2udpfVu
94 Ibid.
95 Aghion P et al. (2005) 'Competition and innovation: An inverted-U relation', *The Quarterly Journal of Economics*, 120(2): 701–28.
96 Ahn S (2002) *Competition, innovation and productivity growth: A review of theory and evidence*, working paper, OECD Economics Department. http://bit.ly/2L0fMdZ
97 Díez, Leigh and Tambunlertchai (2018).

98 Corfe S and Gicheva N (2017) *Concentration not competition: The state of UK consumer markets*, Social Market Foundation. http://bit.ly/2zwQbot

99 Ofgem (2018) 'Retail market indicators'. http://bit.ly/2zwQrUt

100 Statistica (2018) 'Market share of grocery stores in Great Britain from August 2012 to August 2017'. http://bit.ly/2NLS4AK

101 Statistica (2018) 'Market share of current accounts of leading United Kingdom (UK) banks in 2014'. http://bit.ly/2N9xQiV

102 Statistica (2018) 'Market share held by mobile operators in the United Kingdom (UK) 2018, by subscriber'. http://bit.ly/2ugOwxX

103 Shoaib A (2018) 'Big Four dominate FTSE 250 audit market in Q1 rankings', *Accountancy Age*, 5 March. http://bit.ly/2uqxDQU

104 Chahal M (2015) 'Big brands left out of consumers' ideal high street', *Marketing Week*, 1 July. http://bit.ly/2L0fWlB

105 Institute of Customer Service (2018) 'The state of customer satisfaction in the UK (2018)'. http://bit.ly/2Jgkb7F

106 Fredenburgh J (2017) 'Supermarket treatment of suppliers – the good, bad and ugly', *Farmers Weekly*, 26 June. http://bit.ly/2KQlHCY

107 Azar J et al. (2018) 'Concentration in US labor markets: Evidence from online vacancy data', SSRN. http://bit.ly/2ud756u

108 Marinescu I and Hovenkamp H (2018) 'Anticompetitive mergers in labor markets', Faculty Scholarship University of Pennsylvania Law School. http://bit.ly/2zyBUYb

109 D'Arcy C (2018) *Low pay Britain 2018*, Resolution Foundation. http://bit.ly/2LcCZGz

110 Net Market Share (2018) 'Search engine market share'. http://bit.ly/2mfvqnE

111 Jumpshot (2018) 'State of the Amazon era data report: Amazon owns over 80 percent market share across product categories'. https://prn.to/2meFiy0

112 We Are Social (2018) *Global digital report 2018*. http://bit.ly/2zzR8w8

113 *Financial Times* (2017) 'Google and Facebook build digital ad duopoly', 14 March. https://on.ft.com/2ue1ZGY

114 McDaniel S and Berry C (2017) *Digital platforms and competition policy: A literature review*, Sheffield Political Economy Research Institute. http://bit.ly/2utf4LX

115 Srnicek N (2016) *Platform capitalism*, Polity.

116 McDaniel and Berry (2017).

117 Srnicek (2016).

118 Cogman D and Lau A (2016) 'The "tech bubble" puzzle', *McKinsey Quarterly*, May 2016. https://mck.co/2KNA7Ut

119 Section 25, Enterprise and Regulatory Reform Act 2013. UK Parliament.

120 Coyle D, *Practical completion policy implications of digital platforms*, working paper, University of Cambridge Bennett Institute for Public Policy. http://bit.ly/2zwwz3x

4: Partnership and Power

1 Salanie B (2000) *Microeconomics of market failures*, MIT Press.

2 Jacobs M (2013) 'Beyond the social market: Rethinking capitalism and public policy', *Political Quarterly* 84(1): 16–27.

3 Mazzucato M (2018) *The entrepreneurial state: Debunking public vs private sector myths*, 2nd edn, Penguin.

4 Griffith-Jones S and Cozzi G (2016) 'Investment-led growth: A solution to the European crisis', in Jacobs M and Mazzucato M (eds) *Rethinking capitalism: Economic policies for equitable and sustainable growth*, Wiley-Blackwell.

5 Mazzucato M (2017) *Mission oriented policy: Challenges and opportunities*, working paper, UCL Institute for Innovation and Public Purpose. https://bit.ly/2ndGBxs

6 Leijonhufvud A (2009) 'Stabilities and instabilities in the macro-economy', Vox. http://bit.ly/2ueurbx

7 McCann P (2016) *The UK regional–national economic problem: Geography, globalisation and governance*, Routledge.

8 ONS (2017) Table 1 of 'Statistical Bulletin: regional gross value added (balanced), UK: 1998 to 2016'. http://bit.ly/2z EcV62

9 Raikes L (2018) *Future transport investment in the North: A briefing on the government's new regional analysis of the National Infrastructure and Construction Pipeline*, IPPR North. http://bit.ly/2KQm68s

10 McCann (2016).

11 CBI (2016) *Time for action: The business case for inclusive workplaces*. http://bit.ly/2KZyD9H

12 MacLeod D and Clarke N (2009) *Engaging for success: Enhancing performance through employee engagement*, Department for Business, Innovation and Skills. http://bit.ly/2JisrUy

13 Lawrence M (2017) *Corporate governance reform: Turning business towards long-term success*, IPPR. http://bit.ly/2um8oA7

14 Dromey J (2018) *Power to the people: How stronger unions can deliver economic justice*, IPPR. http://bit.ly/2L7X2Wv

15 Ibid.

16 IPPR analysis using membership numbers from Heseltine M (2012) *No stone unturned: Chamber of Commerce international comparisons*, Department for Business Innovation & Skills. http://bit.ly/2LbMlSW; and ONS, US Census Bureau, and Japan Statistics Bureau for numbers of businesses.

17 Coulter S (2018) 'Social partnership in Europe in the face of the future', LSE New European Trade Unions Forum. https://bit.ly/1jymNQ6

18 Dromey (2018).

5: Time for Change

1 Lawrence M (2016) *Future proof: Britain in the 2020s*, IPPR. http://bit.ly/2JhAfGh.

2 World Trade Organization (2017) *World trade report 2017: Trade and development: Trade, technology and jobs*. http://bit.ly/2uen7wK

3 World Trade Organization (2014) *World trade report 2014: Trade and development: Recent trends and the role of the WTO*. http://bit.ly/2uvgO7w

4 PwC (2017) *The long view: How will the global economic order change by 2050?* https://pwc.to/2vZqOrl

5 Eurostat (2018) 'Population projections at national level (2015–2080)'. http://bit.ly/2LblNRH

6 IPPR analysis using ONS (2017) 'Table A1-1, Principal projection – UK summary'. http://bit.ly/2maRks3; ONS (2017) 'Table K2-1, Young age structure variant – UK population in age groups'. http://bit.ly/2maWq7J

7 ONS (2017) 'National Population Projections: 2016-based Statistical Bulletin'. http://bit.ly/2uvhWbg

8 OBR (2017) *Fiscal sustainability report – January 2017.* http://bit.ly/2ueTHhV; Darzi A (2018) *Better health and care for all: A 10-point plan for the 2020s,* IPPR. http://bit.ly/2KO6YbA

9 IPPR Commission on Economic Justice (2017) *Time for change: A new vision for the British economy,* Interim Report. http://bit.ly/2KPKmHZ

10 Parliament (2016) 'Online platforms and the digital single market'. http://bit.ly/2NbYNmr.

11 Lewis S and Maslin M (2018) *The human planet: How we created the Anthropocene,* Penguin.

12 Stirling A and Laybourn-Langton L (2017) 'Time for a new paradigm? Past and present transitions in economic policy', *Political Quarterly* 88(4): 558–69.

13 Mann G (2017) *In the long run we are all dead: Keynesianism, political economy and revolution,* Verso; Skidelsky R (2010) *Keynes: The return of the master,* Penguin.

14 Stedman Jones D (2012) *Masters of the universe: Hayek, Friedman, and the birth of neoliberal politics,* Princeton University Press.

15 Davies W (2014) *The limits of neoliberalism: Authority, sovereignty and the logic of competition,* Sage Publications.

16 Gamble A (2014) *Crisis without end? The unravelling of Western prosperity,* Macmillan.

17 World Bank (2012) *Inclusive green growth: The pathway to sustainable development.* http://bit.ly/2KQxocW; OECD (2017) *Bridging the gap: Inclusive growth 2017 update report.* http://

bit.ly/2LdaQzg; Samans R et al. (2017) *The inclusive growth and development report 2017*, World Economic Forum. http://bit.ly/2mtLgLH; IMF (2017) *Fostering inclusive growth*. https://bit.ly/2L4whGG

18 OECD (2018) 'New approaches to economic challenges'. http://bit.ly/2LwrwBH

6: Reshaping the Economy through Industrial Strategy

1 HM Government (2017) *Industrial strategy: Building a Britain fit for the future*, White Paper. https://bit.ly/2GuEuRt; HM Government (2018) 'The UK's industrial strategy'. https://bit.ly/2Bhdtup

2 Warwick K (2013) *Beyond industrial policy: Emerging issues and new trends*, OECD Science, Technology and Industrial policy paper. https://bit.ly/2Oc9beo

3 House of Commons Business, Energy and Industrial Strategy Committee (2017) *Industrial strategy: First review*. http://bit.ly/2N8bHSc

4 The analysis and proposals in this chapter are drawn from the IPPR Commission on Economic Justice paper: Jacobs M et al. (2017) *Industrial strategy: Steering structural change in the UK economy*, IPPR. http://bit.ly/2JgdAtR

5 Dolphin T (2014) *Gathering strength: Backing clusters to boost Britain's exports*, IPPR. http://bit.ly/2N9xEQL

6 Ibid.

7 Department for Business, Energy and Industrial Strategy (2018) 'Spatial clustering: Identifying industrial clusters in the UK'. https://bit.ly/2vlKg0X

8 Open Data Institute (2018) 'New rankings show UK's most innovative tech clusters'. https://bit.ly/2KrrYjv

9 Haldane A (2017) 'Productivity puzzles', speech to London School of Economics, 20 March. http://bit.ly/2zxCrJZ

10 Department for Business, Energy and Industrial Strategy (2017) *Building our industrial strategy*, Green Paper. http://bit.ly/2ufslIN

11 Mazzucato M (2013) *The entrepreneurial state: Debunking public vs. private sector myths*, Anthem Press; Mazzucato M (2017) *Mission oriented policy: Challenges and opportunities*, working paper, UCL Institute for Innovation and Public Purpose. https://bit.ly/2ng6cWT

12 Department for Business, Energy and Industrial Strategy (2018) 'The grand challenges'. https://bit.ly/2zJ50Uo

13 European Investment Bank (2016) *Impact for inclusion: 2016 activity report.* http://bit.ly/2L0hzzJ; Green Investment Bank (2016) *UK Green Investment Bank plc: Annual report and accounts 2015-16.* https://bit.ly/2vnizVl

14 Macfarlane L and Mazzucato M (2018) *State investment banks and patient finance: An international comparison*, working paper, UCL Institute for Innovation and Public Purpose. https://bit.ly/2ONiF0M

15 Stirling A and King L (2017) *Financing investment: Reforming finance markets for the long term*, IPPR. https://bit.ly/2OeK2Q8

16 Organisation for Economic Development (2016) *Green investment banks: Scaling up investment in low-carbon, climate-resilient infrastructure.* https://bit.ly/2KuZwNJ

17 Macfarlane and Mazzucato (2018).

18 Comptroller and Auditor General of the National Audit Office (2017) *The green investment bank.* https://bit.ly/2vETeFF

19 Scottish Government (2017) 'Scottish National Investment Bank', press release, 20 October 2017. http://bit.ly/2ut4Iwb

20 Greenham T and Prieg L (2015) *Reforming RBS: Local banking for the public good*, New Economics Foundation. http://bit.ly/2umbbJB

21 Scottish Government (2018) *Scottish National Investment Bank: Supporting analysis.* Table 18. https://bit.ly/2OidRiX

22 OECD (2011) *Government financing of business R&D and innovation.* https://bit.ly/2h9nvaq

23 Hatfield I (2017) *Equitable equity: Increasing and diversifying finance for high-growth SMEs in the UK's regions*, IPPR. http://bit.ly/2N77LkC

24 Longlands S, Round A and Kibasi T (2018) *Charting a course for the future*, IPPR. http://bit.ly/2KO7C90

25 Tungsten Network (2015) 'Long payment terms "crippling" SMEs'. https://bit.ly/2vGFN8q

26 Startups.co.uk (2017) 'How much does invoice factoring cost?' https://bit.ly/2LXDXuQ

27 Innovate UK (2017) *Delivery plan 2017/18*. http://bit.ly/2zzq3sW

28 HMRC (2018) 'Table: Estimated costs of principal tax reliefs (January 2018)'. https://bit.ly/1OqtXzO

29 Haltiwanger J, Jarmin R and Miranda J (2013) 'Who creates jobs? Small versus large versus young', *Review of Economics and Statistics* 95(2): 347–61.

30 HMRC (2017) 'Patent box reliefs statistics'. https://bit.ly/2y84kn0

31 HMRC (2015) *Evaluation of research and development tax credit*, working paper no 17. http://bit.ly/2maAqtD

32 Irish Department of Finance (2016) *Economic evaluation of the R&D tax credit*. http://bit.ly/2L4vgyb

33 Jacobs et al. (2017).

34 Bradley S, Dauchy E and Robinson L (2015) 'Cross-country evidence on the preliminary effects of patent box regimes on patent activity and ownership', *National Tax Journal*, 68(4): 1047–72; Griffith R, Miller H and O'Connell M (2014) 'Ownership of intellectual property and corporate taxation', *Journal of Public Economics*, 112: 12–23.

35 Innovate UK (2017) *Delivery Plan 2017/18*. https://bit.ly/2IHz4AA

36 Jacobs et al. (2017); Haldane A (2018) 'The UK's productivity problem: Hub no spokes', speech to Academy of Social Sciences, London, 28 June. https://bit.ly/2MnyDNj

37 Productivity Leadership Group (2016) *How good is your business really? Raising our ambitions for business performance*. https://bit.ly/2KveEdS

38 https://www.bethebusiness.com/

39 Lawrence M, Roberts C and King L (2017) *Managing automation: Employment, inequality and ethics in the digital age*, IPPR. https://bit.ly/2vFp5WL

40 International Federation of Robotics (2018) 'Robot density rises globally', 7 February 2018. http://bit.ly/2uqBRI5

41 Manyika J et al. (2015) *Unlocking the potential of the Internet of Things*, McKinsey Global Institute. https://mck.co/2wWQyXp

42 Ibid.

43 Dromey J and McNeill C (2017) *Skills 2030: Why the adult skills system is failing to build an economy that works for everyone*, IPPR. http://bit.ly/2usshnZ

44 Ibid.

45 Ibid.

46 Department for Education (2018) 'Apprenticeship and levy statistics: May 2018'. https://bit.ly/2IObp4p

47 Tovey A (2018) 'One year in, is the apprenticeship levy working yet?', *The Telegraph*, 7 April. https://bit.ly/2FeupmQ; Open University (2018) *The apprenticeship levy: One year on*. https://bit.ly/2ID8eZz

48 Federation for Industry Sector Skills and Standards website. https://bit.ly/2OdZzj2

49 Dromey J, McNeil C and Roberts C (2017) *Another lost decade? Building a skills system for the economy of the 2030s*, IPPR. http://bit.ly/2mejvGO

50 Ton Z (2014) *The good jobs strategy: How the smartest companies invest in employees to lower costs and boost profits*, Amazon Publishing; Taylor M (2017) *Good work: The Taylor review of modern employment practices*, HM Government. https://bit.ly/2udwhLx

51 Fair Work Convention (2017) *Fair work framework 2016*. http://www.fairworkconvention.scot/

52 These proposals are set out and explained more fully in the IPPR Commission on Economic Justice paper, Griffith P and Morris M (2017) *An immigration strategy for the UK: Six proposals to manage migration for economic success*, IPPR. http://bit.ly/2NLhZIt

7: Securing Good Pay, Good Jobs and Good Lives

1 ONS (2018) 'Number of people in employment (aged 16 and over, seasonally adjusted)', dataset. http://bit.ly/2ma Mz1N

2 Cribb J, Norris Keiller A and Waters T (2018) *Living standards, poverty and inequality in the UK: 2018*, Institute for Fiscal Studies. http://bit.ly/2mdIKss

3 Bangham G (2018) *Britain's labour market: The good (jobs), the bad (pay) and the ugly (productivity)*, Resolution Foundation. https://bit.ly/2AN4vK0

4 IPPR analysis of OECD (2017) 'Average annual wages.' http://bit.ly/2JfREyY

5 D'Arcy C (2018) *Low pay Britain 2018*, Resolution Foundation. https://bit.ly/2KDdxZW

6 Ibid. We use the living wage as a measure of low pay for regional comparisons as the cost of living is higher in London.

7 Joseph Rowntree Foundation (2017) *UK poverty 2017*. https://bit.ly/2jd6FYe

8 D'Arcy C and Hurrell A (2014) *Escape plan: Understanding who progresses from low pay and who gets stuck*, Resolution Foundation. https://bit.ly/2ALJEXz

9 ONS (2018a) 'Labour market economic commentary: June 2018'. http://bit.ly/2L5qb8c

10 Beatty C, Fothergill S and Gore T (2017) *The real level of unemployment 2017*, CRESR, Sheffield Hallam University. https://bit.ly/2LSKKpv

11 ONS (2018b) 'EMP16: Underemployment and overemployment', May 2018. http://bit.ly/2ui6bFz

12 TUC (2016) *Living on the edge: The rise of job insecurity in modern Britain*. https://bit.ly/2ONhezk

13 ONS (2018c) *Contracts that do not guarantee a minimum number of hours: April 2018*. http://bit.ly/2KTHWru

14 Darzi A (2018) *Better health and care for all*, IPPR. https://bit.ly/2NW6o8K

15 ONS (2016) 'Women shoulder the responsibility of "unpaid work" – costs 1.1 trillion'. https://bit.ly/2KBdnG9
16 ONS (2016) 'Changes in the value and division of unpaid care work in the UK: 2000 to 2015'. http://bit.ly/2mbtFrB
17 Kan MY and Laurie H (2016) *Gender, ethnicity and household labour in married and cohabiting couples in the UK*, working paper, Institute for Social and Economic Research. https://bit.ly/2M0jrK8
18 ONS (2018b).
19 Sellers P (2018) 'Work your proper hours day – tackling the culture of unpaid overtime', TUC blog. https://bit.ly/2orzW3M
20 Dillow C (2017) 'Bank holidays and productivity'. https://bit.ly/2Og1bJc
21 Roberts C (2017) *The inbetweeners: The new role of internships in the graduate labour market*, IPPR. http://bit.ly/2L3zczh
22 Colebrook C, Snelling C and Longlands S (2018) *The state of pay: Demystifying the gender pay gap*, IPPR. http://bit.ly/2Lp02y5
23 Business in the Community (2017) *Race at work 2015–2017: Survey insights*. http://bit.ly/2KTyrZo
24 Brown A and Powell J (2018) *People with disabilities in employment*, Briefing paper, House of Commons Library. https://bit.ly/2vsO4xx
25 Dolphin T, ed. (2014) *Technology, globalisation and the future of work in Europe: Essays on employment in a digitised economy*, IPPR. http://bit.ly/2NLo5J5
26 Low bargaining power also has a negative impact on productivity, as if wages are low, firms choose labour-intensive business models over investing, leading to a high-employment, low-wage labour market.
27 Bryson A and Forth J (2017) *The added value of trade unions*, TUC. https://bit.ly/2ObDnpV
28 Dromey J (2018) *Power to the people: How stronger unions can deliver economic justice*, IPPR. http://bit.ly/2uAmcHl
29 Ibid.
30 Ibid.

31 Haldane A (2015) *Labour's share*, speech to the TUC, 12 November. https://bit.ly/2L5WfIU

32 Jaumotte F and Osorio Buitron C (2015) 'Inequality and labour market institutions', IMF staff paper. http://bit.ly/2LfqKJc

33 World Inequality Database (2018). 'Income inequality, United Kingdom, 1918/2014'. http://wid.world/data/

34 Department for Business, Enterprise & Industrial Strategy (BEIS) (2017) 'Trade union statistics 2016'. https://bit.ly/2sddLPa

35 Hudson-Sharp N and Runge J (2017) *International trends in insecure work: A report for the Trades Union Congress*, National Institute of Economic and Social Research. http://bit.ly/2JeNc3j

36 Onaran Ö and Guschanski A (2018) 'The causes of falling wage share: Sectoral and firm level evidence from developed and developing countries – What have we learned?', GPERC policy brief, University of Greenwich. https://bit.ly/2OOHIR8

37 Bivens J, Mishel L and Schmitt J (2018) 'It's not just monopoly and monopsony: How market power has affected American wages', Economic Policy Institute. https://bit.ly/2ObRRWL

38 D'Arcy (2018).

39 The Resolution Foundation currently performs the calculation, overseen by the Living Wage Commission. The rate is calculated based on a 'minimum income standards' approach, to identify everyday living costs through public consensus. The wage is calculated based on full-time hours.

40 Low Pay Commission (LPC) (2017) *A rising floor: the latest evidence on the National Living Wage and youth rates of the minimum wage*. http://bit.ly/2uJRWZQ; LPC (2017a) *LPC Research Summary 2017: Appendix 2*. https://bit.ly/2AK132D. A full report on the impact of the national living wage on employment and hours will be published by the LPC in October 2018.

41 The reduction in ENICs would have a negative impact on the Exchequer's finances. In chapter 13, we suggest several new or increased taxes, funds from which could be used to offset the cost of the transition phase, including increases in corporation tax.

42 LPC (2017a); Rizov M and Croucher R (2011) *The impact of the UK national minimum wage on productivity by low-paying sectors and firm-size groups*, Low Pay Commission. http://bit.ly/2zB2rUO

43 LPC (2017a).

44 Taylor M (2017) *Good work: The Taylor review of modern working practices*. BEIS. https://bit.ly/2udwhLx

45 Williams J et al. (2018) *Stable scheduling increases productivity and sales*, University of Chicago. https://unc.live/2KwoEDv

46 Dellot B and Reed H (2015) *Boosting the living standards of the self-employed*, RSA. https://bit.ly/2MklzYZ

47 Mor F and Brown J (2018) *Workers underpaid the minimum wage*. Briefing paper. House of Commons Library. https://bit.ly/2LUcPg5

48 Ibid.

49 The proposals in this section are elaborated more fully in the IPPR Commission on Economic Justice paper, Dromey (2018).

50 D'Arcy (2018).

51 These rights would be enforced by the Central Arbitration Committee.

52 Colebrook, Snelling and Longlands (2018).

53 Ilgner A (2018) 'Is the ethnicity pay gap the next form of mandatory pay gap reporting?', inews. https://bit.ly/2L2ZpKO

54 Stephenson M (2018) 'Transforming equality', IPPR. http://bit.ly/2NWiijZ

55 Eurofound (2012) *Working time and work–life balance in a life course perspective*. http://bit.ly/2uki3qA

56 All couples, regardless of sex, would have the same rights to parental leave so as not to disadvantage same-sex couples.

57 BEIS (2018) 'New "share the joy" campaign promotes shared parental leave rights for parents'. https://bit.ly/2BmhwJb

58 Ben-Galim D, Pearce N and Thompson S (2014) *No more baby steps: A strategy for revolutionising childcare*, IPPR. https://bit.ly/2ALQo7P

59 As recommended by the HoC Women and Equalities Select Committee (2016) 'Second report of session: 2015-16'. http://bit. ly/2KUQeQ0

60 Tucker J (2017) *The austerity generation: The impact of a decade of cuts on family incomes and child poverty*, Child Poverty Action Group. https://bit.ly/2zn212L

61 Standing G (2017) *Basic income: And how we can make it happen*, Pelican.

62 OECD (2018) 'Average annual hours actually worked by worker'. http://bit.ly/2KQLnQ2

63 Dillow (2017).

64 ONS (2018b).

65 Stirling A and Lawrence M (2017) 'Time banking: Bank holidays, the four-day week and the politics of time', IPPR. http://bit. ly/2mgjpyi

66 TUC (2003) *It's about time to end the long-hours opt out*. https:// bit.ly/2OfiwSB

8: Turning Business towards Long-Term Success

1 These arguments are developed more fully in the IPPR Commission on Economic Justice paper, Lawrence M (2017) 'Corporate governance reform: Turning business towards long-term success', IPPR. https://bit.ly/2LVACfG

2 IPPR calculations using ONS (2017), based on method in Tomorrow's Company (2016) *UK business: What's wrong? What's next?* https://bit.ly/2OOopaD

3 Bank of England (2017) *The financial system and productive investment: New survey evidence*. https://bit.ly/2vmFDUh

4 Big Innovation Centre (2016) *The purposeful company: Interim report*. http://bit.ly/2L3GTVo. Based on analysis using data from Share Centre in 2015. http://bit.ly/2NamPy0

5 Office for National Statistics (ONS) 'Blue Book 2017'. http://bit. ly/2NTuC4D

6 Tomorrow's Company (2016).

7 Big Innovation Centre (2016) based on analysis using data from Share Centre in 2015.

8 Lazonick W (2014) *Profits without prosperity: How stock buybacks manipulate the market, and leave most Americans worse off,* Institute for New Economic Thinking. https://bit.ly/2KB5TPo

9 Lazonick W (2014) 'Profits without prosperity', *Harvard Business Review,* September 2014. http://bit.ly/2LeeZmB

10 Mazzucato M (2018) *The value of everything: Making and taking in the global economy,* Allen Lane.

11 Haldane A (2015) 'Who owns a company?', speech to University of Edinburgh Corporate Finance Conference, 22 May. https://bit.ly/2KxuC7v

12 ONS (2015) 'Ownership of UK quoted shares: 2014'. https://bit.ly/2vigqsv

13 Kay J (2012) *The Kay review of UK equity markets and long-term decision-making,* HM Government. https://bit.ly/2M2AUkc

14 Big Innovation Centre (2016).

15 Davis A et al. (2014) *Takeovers and the public interest: Responsible capitalism in practice,* Policy Network. https://bit.ly/2Mjku3I

16 Ibid.

17 MacLeod D and Clarke N (2009) *Engaging for success: Enhancing performance through employee engagement,* Department for Business, Innovation and Skills. http://bit.ly/2JisrUy

18 European Trade Union Institute (ETUI) (2017) *Benchmarking working Europe.* https://bit.ly/2LSqzbj

19 Ibid.

20 OECD (2016) 'Income distribution and poverty'. http://bit.ly/2uqBHR7

21 High Pay Centre (2017) *Executive pay: Review of FTSE 100 executive pay packages.* http://bit.ly/2zzlChN

22 Big Innovation Centre (2016).

23 Department for Business, Energy and Industrial Strategy (BEIS) (2017) *Building our industrial strategy,* Green paper. https://bit.ly/2iVIGyl

24 These arguments are more fully developed in Lawrence (2017).

25 ETUI (2017).

26 Lawrence (2017).

27 For specific wording, see ibid.

28 TUC (2016) *All aboard: Making worker representation on company boards a reality.* http://bit.ly/2NKIT3a

29 Department for Business, Innovation and Skills (2011) *Women on boards.* http://bit.ly/2mpFLNX

30 Colebrook, Snelling and Longlands (2018). https://bit.ly/2OKliQO.

31 Davis et al. (2014).

32 BEIS (2017).

33 Open Contracting Partnership (2018) *Opening up public contracting.* https://bit.ly/2MbicqN

34 Public Services (Social Value) Act 2012. http://bit.ly/2L9aJ7H

35 White C (2017) *Our money, our future: Chris White's review of the Social Value Act's effect on public sector spending,* Social Enterprise UK. https://bit.ly/2LU0Qz8

36 Butler J and Redding D (2017) *Healthy commissioning: How the Social Value Act is being used by clinical commissioning groups,* Social Enterprise UK and National Voices. https://bit.ly/2ojj3IN

9: Promoting Open Markets in the New Economy

1 Corfe S and Gicheva N (2017) *Concentration not competition: The state of UK consumer markets,* Social Market Foundation. http://bit.ly/2NXMbjU

2 Seely, A. (2016) *The UK competition regime,* HoC Briefing Paper 04814. http://bit.ly/2usGykJ

3 Chisholm A (2014) 'Public interest and competition-based merger control', speech to the Fordham Competition Law Institute Annual Conference, 11 September. https://bit.ly/1lWSG6l

4 National Audit Office (NAO) (2016) *The UK competition regime.* https://bit.ly/2Ktyw0R

5 Ibid.

6 Wilks S (2010) 'Competition policy', in Coen D, Grant W and Wilson G, eds, *The Oxford Handbook of Business and Government*, Oxford University Press.

7 Díez F, Leigh D and Tambunlertchai S (2018) 'Global market power and its macroeconomic implications', IMF working paper. http://bit.ly/2udpfVu

8 The analysis and recommendations in this and the following sections are drawn from the IPPR Commission on Economic Justice paper, Lawrence M and Laybourn-Langton L (2018) *The digital commonwealth: From private enclosure to public benefit*, IPPR. http://bit.ly/2NwVs1o

9 Coyle D (2018) *Practical competition policy implications of digital platforms*, working paper, University of Cambridge Bennett Institute for Public Policy. https://bit.ly/2M0pe2k

10 Srnicek N (2016) *Platform capitalism*, Polity.

11 Ibid.

12 Stoller M (2017) 'The return of monopoly', *The New Republic*, 13 July. http://bit.ly/2zIjO6d

13 Select Committee on European Union (2016) *Online platforms and the digital single market*, House of Lords. http://bit.ly/2NbYNmr

14 Reynolds M (2017) 'If you can't build it, buy it: Google's biggest acquisitions mapped', *Wired*, 25 November. https://bit.ly/2MoMpPI; Toth S (2018) '66 Facebook acquisitions: The complete list (2018)!', *TechWyse*. https://bit.ly/2nhgJRC

15 Coyle (2018).

16 Perrin W and Woods L (2018) 'Reducing harm in social media through a duty of care', LSE Media Policy Blog. https://bit.ly/2niEZm5

17 Srnicek (2016).

18 Bria F and Morozov E (2018) *Rethinking the smart city: Democratizing urban technology*, Rosa Luxemburg Stiftung. https://bit.ly/2n5GlB8

19 Transport for London (2018) 'Open data users'. https://bit.ly/1SQhpZH

20 Berry C and Srnicek N (2018) *The social wealth fund: The social wealth of data and a different direction for the fund*, Autonomy. https://bit.ly/2AGvqHg; Morozov E (2015) 'Socialize the data centres!' *New Left Review*, 91:1. https://bit.ly/2vsVK2P

21 Bria and Morozov (2018).

22 Mazzucato M (2018) 'Let's make private data into a public good', *Tech Review*, 27 June. http://bit.ly/2No1Doi

23 OECD (2018) *Fostering greater SME participation in a globally integrated economy*. https://bit.ly/2MlFJSs

24 Ibid.

10: Raising Public Investment in a Reformed Macroeconomic Framework

1 IPPR calculations using annual average chained-volume GDP growth rate per head of population for 2008–2017 inclusive. ONS (2018) 'Gross Domestic Product: Chained volume measures: Seasonally adjusted £m'. http://bit.ly/2utkTZT; ONS (2018) 'Population estimates time series dataset (pop)', dataset. http://bit.ly/2NcB4SV

2 OECD (2018) 'Gross domestic product (GDP) (indicator)'. https://bit.ly/1lPMK0p

3 Kirsanova T, Leith C and Wren-Lewis S (2009) 'Monetary and fiscal policy interaction: the current consensus assignment in the light of recent developments', *Economic Journal* 119(541): F482–96.

4 OBR (2018) 'Table 4.15 of Economic and Fiscal Outlook – March 2018'. https://bit.ly/2IvzKJo

5 OBR (2018) 'Para 1.24 and Table 1.2 of Economic and Fiscal Outlook – March 2018'. https://bit.ly/2IvzKJo

6 OBR (2018) 'March 2018 Economic and fiscal outlook – speaking notes'. https://bit.ly/2vpISu0

7 Hood A and Waters T (2017) *Living standards, poverty and inequality in the UK: 2016–17 to 2021–22*, Institute for Fiscal Studies. https://www.ifs.org.uk/publications/8957; Wren-Lewis S (2017)

'A self-fulfilling expectations led recession?', Mainly Macro, 2 March. https://bit.ly/2KBdNs2

8 Bank of England (2018) 'Official Bank Rate history: Data from 1694'. https://bit.ly/2ONYcJ1

9 OBR (2017) *Economic and Fiscal Outlook – March 2017*. https://bit.ly/2LYEUmm

10 Harari D (2018) *Household debt: Statistics and impact on economy*, House of Commons Library. https://bit.ly/2OgvaRo

11 Haldane A (2015) 'How low can you go?' speech to Portadown Chamber of Commerce, 18 September. https://bit.ly/2vG4Kk9

12 Bunn P, Pugh A and Yeates C (2018) *The distributional impact of monetary policy easing in the UK between 2008 and 2014*, staff working paper, Bank of England. https://bit.ly/2MjozF4

13 Yates T (2017) *Effectiveness and impact of post-2008 UK monetary policy*, evidence submitted to Treasury Committee by Professor Tony Yates. https://bit.ly/2LYF8tI

14 Summers L (2013) 'US economic prospects: Secular stagnation, hysteresis, and the zero lower bound', *Business Economics* 49(2): 65–73; Summers L (2016) 'The age of secular stagnation: What it is and what to do about it', *Foreign Affairs* 95(2).

15 Teulings C and Baldwin R (2014) *Secular stagnation: facts, causes, and cures*. http://bit.ly/2uFJrik

16 Bank of England (2018) 'Official bank rate, end quarter – IUQLBEDR'. https://bit.ly/2Og6wQV

17 ONS (2018) 'Gross domestic product: q-on-q4 growth rate CVM SA %'. http://bit.ly/2JqwgqD

18 Chen P, Karabarbounis L and Neiman B (2017) *The global corporate saving glut: long-term evidence*. http://bit.ly/2LtJZic

19 Barrett P (2018) *Interest-growth differentials and debt limits in advanced economies*, working paper, IMF. https://bit.ly/2LULDOv

20 HM Treasury (2018) Chart A4 and Chart B1 from *Debt Management Report 2018–19*. https://bit.ly/2nhaXiW

21 HM Treasury supplementary guidance to the Green Book makes reference to social infrastructure, and suggests that its guidance could be applied to social as well as economic infrastructure: HM

Treasury (2015) *Green Book supplementary guidance: Valuing infrastructure spend.* https://bit.ly/2ALQtIy

22 The KfW in Germany, for example, is not included in the definition of 'general government gross debt'. See Macfarlane L and Mazzucato M (2018) *State investment banks and patient finance: An international comparison*, working paper, UCL Institute for Innovation and Public Purpose. https://bit.ly/2Og6Miy

23 IPPR calculations based on ONS (2018) 'An international comparison of gross fixed capital formation'. https://bit.ly/2OiAS5l and OBR (2018) Table 1.2 from 'March 2018 Economic and fiscal outlook – supplementary economy tables'. https://bit.ly/2IvzKJo

24 IPPR analysis of OECD (2017) 'Government expenditure by function (COFOG)', dataset. http://bit.ly/2Ndemdd

25 Yates (2017).

26 HM Treasury (2018) 'HMT Monetary policy remit'. https://bit.ly/2vG5WE9

27 HM Treasury (2013) *Review of the monetary policy framework.* https://bit.ly/2vG7zlf

28 Blanchard O and Gali J (2005) *Real wage rigidities and the new Keynesian model*, working paper, National Bureau of Economic Research. http://bit.ly/2uj6P5D

29 Bank of England (2011) *Minutes of the MPC meeting held on 6 and 7 April 2011*, monetary policy summary and minutes. https://bit.ly/2Mo2kOm

30 Bunn, Pugh and Yeates (2018).

31 Turner A (2015) *The case for monetary finance – An essentially political issue*, conference paper. http://bit.ly/2ujhPjz

32 Bernanke B (2016) 'What tools does the Fed have left? Part 3: helicopter money', The Brookings Institution. https://brook.gs/2cmfDyA; Wren-Lewis S (2015) 'Can helicopter money be democratic?'. https://bit.ly/2nf44hS

33 This proposal is explored more fully in the IPPR Commission on Economic Justice paper, Stirling A (2018) *Just about managing demand: Reforming the UK's macroeconomic policy framework*, IPPR. http://bit.ly/2uoS9kE

34 See, for example, the Minutes of the May 2018 MPC meeting: https://bit.ly/2OfujjF

11: Strengthening the Financial System

1 Rhodes C (2018) *Financial services: Contribution to the UK economy*, House of Commons Library. http://bit.ly/2KUgrhK

2 Haldane A (2010) 'The contribution of the financial sector: Miracle or mirage?', speech at the Future of Finance Conference, 14 July. https://bit.ly/2vloM4h; Rhodes C (2016) *Historic data on industries in the UK*, House of Commons Library. http://bit.ly/2JiE8uo

3 ONS (2018) 'UK gross domestic product (output approach) low-level aggregates'. http://bit.ly/2Nc9zc2

4 Ibid.; ONS (2018) 'Gross domestic product: Chained volume measures: Seasonally adjusted £m'. http://bit.ly/2Nca2ei

5 The analysis and proposals in this chapter are drawn from the IPPR Commission on Economic Justice papers: Stirling A and King L (2017) *Financing investment: Reforming finance markets for the long term*, IPPR. https://bit.ly/2OeK2Q8; and Blakeley G (2018) *On borrowed time: Finance the UK's current account deficit*, IPPR. http://bit.ly/2LmO76S

6 HM Treasury (2017) *Financing growth in innovative firms: Consultation*. http://bit.ly/2L7jO3Z

7 Philippon T (2014) 'Has the US financial industry become less efficient? On the theory and measurement of financial intermediation', *American Economic Review* 105(4): 1408–38.

8 Ibid.

9 Ibid.

10 Pitt-Watson D and Mann H (2017) *The purpose of finance: Why finance matters – building an industry that serves its customers and society*, Pension Insurance Corporation. https://bit.ly/2jyqcp5

11 Eurostat (2018) 'Gross fixed capital formation by AN_F6 asset type'. http://bit.ly/2NbH8ee

12 Stirling and King (2017).

13 Ibid.

14 British Bankers' Association (BBA) (2017) *Bank support for SMEs – 1st Quarter 2017.* https://bit.ly/2MpUOCr

15 BBA (2017) *Bank support for SMEs – 4th Quarter 2016.* https://bit.ly/2LUmrY8

16 British Business Bank (2017) *Small business finance markets reports 2016/17.* http://bit.ly/2Lg7vz9

17 HM Government (2017) *Patient capital review: Industry panel response.* http://bit.ly/2JiZuYB.

18 European Central Bank (2017) 'MFI balance sheets'. https://bit.ly/2voZUbE

19 Ibid.

20 Bank of England (2017) 'Bankstats: Monetary & financial statistics (B1.4 and C1.2)'. http://bit.ly/2Ncb3TE

21 Kay J (2012) *The Kay review of UK equity markets and long-term decision making,* HM Government. http://bit.ly/2KOVzbE

22 Davies R et al. (2014) 'Measuring the costs of short-termism', *Journal of Financial Stability* 12: 16–25.

23 IPPR calculations using ONS data based on method in Tomorrow's Company (2016) *UK business: What's wrong? What's next?.* https://bit.ly/2OOopaD

24 Brett D (2017) 'What "dividend cover" says about the safety of stock market income', *City AM,* 8 March. https://bit.ly/2AGoTwe

25 Lazonick W (2014) 'Profits without prosperity', *Harvard Business Review,* September. http://bit.ly/2LeeZmB

26 Kay (2012).

27 World Federation of Exchanges (2013) *Understanding high frequency trading.* https://bit.ly/2nVuIQ2

28 Stirling and King (2017).

29 Davis S, Lukomnik J and Pitt-Watson D (2016) *What do they do with your money? How the financial systems fails us and how to fix it,* Yale University Press.

30 The Investment Association (2016) *Supporting UK productivity with long-term investment.* https://bit.ly/2AM71jL

31 Nationwide (2018) 'Nationwide's house price index'. https://bit.ly/2NJTISt; ONS (2018) 'Dataset: Consumer price inflation time series'. http://bit.ly/2LgukCM

32 Harari D (2018) *Household debt: Statistics and impact on economy*, House of Commons Library. https://bit.ly/2OgvaRo

33 Barwell R and Burrows O (2010) *Growing fragilities? Balance sheets in the great moderation*, Bank of England. https://bit.ly/2vJsuno

34 Nationwide (2018).

35 Bank of England (2018) 'Household credit'. https://bit.ly/2Mr8RYM

36 OECD (2018) 'Financial corporations debt to equity ratios'. https://bit.ly/2Of721c

37 Avgouleas E (2015) *Bank leverage ratios and financial stability: A micro- and macroprudential perspective*, Levy Institute. http://bit.ly/2urSi6X

38 Langfield S, Liu Z and Ota T (2014) *Mapping the UK Interbank System*, Bank of England. https://bit.ly/2vIWbFl

39 Adrian T and Ashcraft A (2012) *Shadow banking: A review of the literature*, Federal Reserve Bank of New York. https://nyfed.org/2zwKwyH

40 Crotty J (2009) 'Structural causes of the global financial crisis: A critical assessment of the "new financial architecture"', *Cambridge Journal of Economics* 33(4): 563–80.

41 Nesvetailova A (2018) *Shadow banking: Scope, origins, theories*, Routledge.

42 Bank of England (2017) *Financial Stability Report* 42, November. https://bit.ly/2ndC7XE

43 OECD (2018) 'Current account balance'. https://bit.ly/2LZjQME

44 Blakeley (2018).

45 ONS (2017) 'United Kingdom balance of payments – The Pink Book'. https://bit.ly/2OMsV9u

46 ONS (2018a) 'Monthly average, Effective exchange rate index, Sterling'. http://bit.ly/2NMQajk

47 Ibid.

48 Harari (2018).

49 ONS (2018b) 'Mergers and acquisitions involving UK companies time series'. http://bit.ly/2utt602

50 Burgess S and Shanbhogue R (2017) 'A prince not a pauper: The truth behind the UK's current account deficit', *Bank Underground*, 7 December. https://bit.ly/2Bc4Kxx

51 Kaminska I (2016) 'Brexit and Britain's Dutch disease', *Financial Times*, 12 October. https://on.ft.com/2nfg3vS

52 Standing G (2016) *The corruption of capitalism: Why rentiers thrive and work does not pay*, Biteback Publishing.

53 Jacobs M et al. (2017) *Industrial strategy: Steering structural change in the UK economy*, IPPR. http://bit.ly/2NcEtRH

54 British Business Bank (2018) '£2.5bn British patient capital programme launched to enable long-term investment in innovative companies across the UK', 13 June. https://bit.ly/2y7aJTz

55 Kay (2012); Law Commission (2014) *Fiduciary duties of investment intermediaries*, House of Commons. https://bit.ly/2vnJ7Gd

56 Byres W (2012) 'Basel III: Necessary, but not sufficient', speech to Bank for International Settlement, 6 November. http://bit.ly/2NJ9Jc1

57 Ibid.

58 Schwerter S (2011) 'Basel III's ability to mitigate systemic risk', *Journal of Financial Regulation and Compliance* 19(4): 337–54.

59 Chakraborty C, Gimpelewicz M and Uluc A (2017) *A tiger by the tail: Estimating the UK mortgage market vulnerabilities from loan-level data*, Bank of England. https://bit.ly/2ONsqvD

60 Galati G and Moessner R (2011) *Macroprudential policy – a literature review*, Bank for International Settlements. http://bit.ly/2uuHftX

61 Adrian and Ashcraft (2012).

62 Bank of England (2017).

63 Adrian T (2017) 'Shadow banking and market based finance', speech to the International Monetary Fund, 14 September. https://bit.ly/2vkjIge

64 Barber A and Hunt T (2016) *The UK banking sector and the corporation tax surcharge*, SPERI. https://bit.ly/2ALqvEV

65 Blakeley (2018).

66 Hudson M (2015) *Killing the host: How financial parasites and debt bondage destroy the global economy*, Nation Books.

67 Palley T (2008) *Financialization: What it is and why it matters*, working paper, Levy Economics Institute. https://bit.ly/22UFSzM

68 Blakeley G (2018a) *Fair dues: Rebalancing business taxation in the UK*, IPPR. http://bit.ly/2uGU0lc

69 European Network on Debt and Development (EURODAD) (2017) *Tax games: The race to the bottom: Europe's role in supporting an unjust global tax system*. https://bit.ly/2MrmKWU

70 ONS (2017).

71 Shaxson N (2012) *Treasure islands: Tax havens and the men who stole the world*, Vintage.

72 EURODAD (2017).

73 Global Witness (2017) '10 Lessons from the UK's public register of the real owners of companies', 23 October. https://bit.ly/2y65i2b

74 Department for Business Energy & Industrial Strategy (2017) *Register of people with significant control: Guidance*. https://bit.ly/2kziwQE

75 Knobel A (2017) *Trusts: Weapons of mass injustice?*, Tax Justice Network. https://bit.ly/2AMPY0Y

12: Spreading Wealth and Ownership across the Economy

1 ONS (2018) 'Wealth in Great Britain wave 5: 2014 to 2016'. http://bit.ly/2uhTb2X. All data in this section comes from the ONS Wealth and Assets Survey, which covers Great Britain rather than the United Kingdom as a whole.

2 This analysis is drawn from the IPPR Commission on Economic Justice paper: Roberts C and Lawrence M (2017) *Wealth in the twenty-first century: Inequalities and drivers*, IPPR. http://bit.ly/2uqGO3L

3 ONS (2018).

4 Ibid.

5 D'Arcy C and Gardiner L (2017) *The generation of wealth: Asset accumulation across and within cohorts*, Resolution Foundation. https://bit.ly/2rWzDhn

6 Ibid.

7 ONS (2018).

8 Ibid.

9 Chartered Insurance Institute (2016) *Risk, exposure and resilience to risk in Britain today*. https://bit.ly/2KyP4Vn

10 IPPR analysis using ONS (2018a) 'Total wealth: Wealth in Great Britain'. http://bit.ly/2La8IrH

11 Financial Conduct Authority (2017) *Understanding the financial lives of UK adults*. https://bit.ly/2xWsYdV

12 Hood A, Joyce R and Sturrock D (2018) *Problem debt and low-income households*, Institute for Fiscal Studies. http://bit.ly/2LbkAtw

13 Thompson S et al. (2017) *Stuck in debt*, Citizens Advice Bureau. https://bit.ly/2vrtn6M

14 Piketty T (2014) *Capital in the twenty-first century*, Harvard University Press.

15 ONS (2018b) 'House price to workplace/based earnings ratio'. http://bit.ly/2LieZoU

16 Corlett A and Gardiner L (2018) *Home affairs: Options for reforming property taxation*, Resolution Foundation. https://bit.ly/2ALUmNJ

17 Ibid.

18 Resolution Foundation (2017) '21st century Britain has seen a 30 per cent increase in second home ownership', 19 August 2017. http://bit.ly/2zKg2cD

19 Resolution Foundation (2017) 'Home ownership in the UK'. http://bit.ly/2NcW4ZZ

20 Savills (2017) *Residential property focus 2017: Issue 1*. https://bit.ly/2LUOWFb

21 Ryan-Collins J, Macfarlane L and Lloyd T (2017) *Rethinking the economics of land and housing*, Zed Books.

22 Sà F (2016) *The effect of foreign investors on local housing markets: Evidence from the UK*, Centre for Macroeconomics. https://bit.ly/2OLyZip

23 Griffith M and Jeffreys P (2013) *Solutions for the housing shortage: How to build the 250,000 homes we need each year*, Shelter. https://bit.ly/2OcgeDE

24 IPPR analysis using ONS (2018c) 'Financial wealth: Wealth in Great Britain'. http://bit.ly/2zG61ge

25 Lawrence M, King L and Roberts C (2017) *Managing automation: Employment, inequality and ethics in the digital age*, IPPR. http://bit.ly/2L0Ua1M

26 Bynner J and Paxton W (2001) *The asset-effect*, IPPR. https://bit.ly/2M7zPHN

27 Ministry of Housing, Communities & Local Government (MHCLG) (2018) *English housing survey 2016 to 2017: Headline report.* https://bit.ly/2DEiymk

28 McKnight A (2011) 'Estimates of the asset-effect: The search for a causal effect of assets on adult health and employment outcomes', CASE Paper, London School of Economics; Bynner and Paxton (2001).

29 Bahaj S, Foulis A and Pinter G (2016) *The residential collateral channel*, discussion paper, Centre for Macroeconomics. https://bit.ly/2vkjhmu; Blanchflower D and Oswald A (1998) 'What makes an entrepreneur?', *Journal of Labor Economics* 16(1): 26–60.

30 Atkinson A (2013) *Wealth and inheritance in Britain from 1896 to the present*, CASE paper, London School of Economics. http://bit.ly/2NKYjo8

31 Schmalz M, Sraer D and Thesmar D (2017) 'Housing collateral and entrepreneurship', *The Journal of Finance* 72(1): 99–132.

32 This proposal is elaborated more fully in the IPPR Commission on Economic Justice paper, Roberts C and Lawrence M (2018) *Our common wealth: A Citizens Wealth Fund for the UK*, IPPR. http://bit.ly/2L4x9u1

33 Lansley S (2016) *A sharing economy: How social wealth funds can reduce inequality and help balance the books*, Policy Press.

34 Roberts and Lawrence (2018).

35 OBR (2018) 'March 2018 economic and fiscal outlook – charts and tables: fiscal'. https://bit.ly/2IvzKJo

36 The Crown Estate (2018) *The Crown Estate integrated annual report and accounts, 2017-18*, http://bit.ly/2JfXWi4

37 Roberts and Lawrence (2018).

38 Lansley S, McCann D and Schifferes S (2018) *Remodelling capitalism: How social wealth funds could transform Britain*, Friends Provident Foundation. https://bit.ly/2rx5sPk

39 Cummine A (2016) *Citizens' wealth: Why (and how) sovereign funds should be managed by the people for the people*, Yale University Press.

40 Ibid.

41 Roberts and Lawrence (2018).

42 Resolution Foundation. (2018). *A new generational contract*, https://bit.ly/2wikAoG

43 Bentley D (2017) *The land question*, Civitas. http://bit.ly/2KULha9

44 MHCLG (2015) *Land value estimates for policy appraisal 2015.* https://bit.ly/1V3v2lP

45 Royal Town Planning Institute (RTPI) (2018) 'RTPI response to HCLG Select committee inquiry on land value capture, March 2018'. https://bit.ly/2Mo3rgY

46 House of Commons Treasury Committee (2017) *Autumn Budget 2017, Fifth Report of Session 2017-19.* https://bit.ly/2KxhAqd

47 Jeffreys P and Lloyd T (2017) *New civic housebuilding: Rediscovering our tradition of building beautiful and affordable homes*, Shelter. http://bit.ly/2NbOuP4

48 RTPI (2018).

49 Jeffreys and Lloyd (2017).

50 Falk N (2018) *Capital gains: A better land assembly model for London*, URBED. https://bit.ly/2ndkQy2

51 Savills (2016) *New homes on public sector land: Accelerating delivery.* https://bit.ly/2Ml4iit

52 Brett W (2017) 'Selling public land is making the housing crisis worse', NEF. https://bit.ly/2KwmIek

53 Heywood A (2016) *Local housing, community living: Prospects for scaling up and scaling out community-led housing*, The Smith Institute. https://bit.ly/2Bh5A8S

54 This section draws on the IPPR Commission on Economic Justice paper, Lawrence M and Mason N (2017) *Capital gains: Broadening company ownership in the UK economy.* http://bit.ly/2uuWNh0

55 Freeman R, Blasi J and Kruse D, eds (2010) *Shared capitalism at work: Employee ownership, profit and gain sharing, and broad-based stock options*, University of Chicago Press.

56 More detail on these proposals can be found in Lawrence and Mason (2017).

57 Ibid.

58 Co-operatives UK (2017) *Annual Report 2017.* http://bit.ly/2zy0lF4

59 Mayo E, ed. (2015) *The co-operative advantage*, Co-operatives UK.

60 Ownership Commission (2012) *Plurality, stewardship and engagement: The report of the Ownership Commission.* https://bit.ly/2AJZ2DD

13: Designing Simpler and Fairer Taxes

1 Cram C (2016) 'The impact of Brexit on UK's £200bn public procurement spend', *The Guardian*, 13 June. http://bit.ly/2ujlyh3

2 OBR (2018) 'Public finances databank: 23 May 2018'. http://obr.uk/data/

3 Charlesworth A and Johnson P (2018) *Securing the future: Funding health and social care to the 2030s*, Institute for Fiscal Studies (IFS). http://bit.ly/2NKwRqJ; Darzi A (2018) *The Lord Darzi review of health and care: Interim report*, IPPR. https://bit.ly/2r0ZINL

4 Oxfam (2013) *The true cost of austerity and inequality: UK case study.* https://bit.ly/2vCjgJM

5 OECD (2018) Table: tax revenue as % of GDP within 'Revenue Statistics – OECD countries: Comparative tables' (database). http://bit.ly/2Nb1Ye5

6 IMF (2017) 'Unproductive public expenditures: A pragmatic approach to policy analysis'. http://bit.ly/2ujmcet

7 OBR (2017) *Fiscal sustainability report – January 2017.* https://bit.ly/2vjYtvm

8 Ibid.

9 OBR (2017) Chart 3.2 of *Fiscal sustainability report – January 2017.*
https://bit.ly/2vjYtvm

10 Ibid., Table 3.7.

11 IPPR calculations based on 2016–17 out-turn as presented in
Table 4.5 of OBR (2018a) *Economic and fiscal outlook – March
2018.* https://bit.ly/2OOeu4K

12 The analysis and proposals in this section are based on the
Commission on Economic Justice paper, Stirling A (2018) *Tapering
over the tax: Reforming taxation of income in the UK,* IPPR. http://
bit.ly/2ugXzPw

13 Ibid.

14 Ibid.

15 Since income tax rates are devolved in Scotland, separate decisions would need to be made on this by the UK and Scottish
governments.

16 HMRC (2018) 'Rates and allowances'. https://bit.ly/2Kujnwh

17 Stirling (2018).

18 Ibid.

19 Ibid.

20 The analysis and proposals in this section are based on the IPPR
Commission on Economic Justice paper, Roberts C, Blakeley G
and Murphy L (2018) *A wealth of difference: Reforming the taxation of wealth,* IPPR. http://bit.ly/2OO4SmS

21 IPPR analysis using HMRC (2018) 'Tax and NIC receipts: statistics
table' (April 2018) and OBR (2018a). http://bit.ly/2ufqiUK; HMRC
(2018) 'UK income tax liabilities statistics'. http://bit.ly/2NIZwfE;
HMRC (2018) 'Trust statistics'. http://bit.ly/2KVWWpa. Figures
are for 2017–18. To estimate tax revenue from trusts, we use
2015–16 data, the latest available at the time of writing.

22 Mirrlees J et al. (2011) *Tax by design,* IFS Oxford University Press.
https://www.ifs.org.uk/publications/5353; OECD, *Tax policy
reform and economic growth,* November 2010.

23 Glennerster H (2016) *A wealth of options: Shifting tax away from
earned incomes,* Fabian Society.

24 Roberts, Blakeley and Murphy (2018).

25 Dolphin T (2010) *Death and taxes: Why inheritance tax should be replaced with a capital receipts tax*, IPPR. http://bit.ly/2LcRcmS

26 Glennerster (2016); Corlett A (2018) *Passing on: Options for reforming inheritance taxation*, Resolution Foundation. https://bit.ly/2ANJPBC

27 Corlett (2018).

28 This section is based on the IPPR Commission on Economic Justice discussion paper, Murphy L (2018) *The invisible land: The hidden force driving the UK's unequal economy and broken housing market*, IPPR. http://bit.ly/2zWbX5a

29 Mirrlees et al. (2011).

30 IPPR analysis using OBR (2018), OBR (2018a) and ONS (2018) 'Public sector current receipts: Appendix D'. http://bit.ly/2zzgqKS

31 Mirrlees et al. (2011); Scanlon K, Whitehead C and Blanc F (2017) *A taxing question: Is Stamp Duty Land Tax suffocating the English housing market?* LSE. http://bit.ly/2Jgu1X6

32 Ryan-Collins J, Macfarlane L and Lloyd T (2017) *Rethinking the Economics of Land and Housing*, Zed Books.

33 Carney M (2014) 'Rising house prices pose biggest risk to recovery', *The Guardian*, 19 May. https://bit.ly/2Ohec5m; Zhu M (2014) 'Housing markets, financial stability and the economy', speech to the Bundesbank/German Research Foundation/IMF Conference, 11 June. http://bit.ly/2KTVlQr

34 Mirrlees et al. (2011); Adler D (2017) *Home truths: A progressive vision of housing policy in the 21st century*, Tony Blair Institute. https://bit.ly/2jcURVL

35 Ryan-Collins, Macfarlane and Lloyd (2017).

36 Blakeley G (2018) *Fair dues: Rebalancing business taxation in the UK*, IPPR. http://bit.ly/2uGU0lc

37 HMRC (2018) 'Table 11.1A Corporation tax, bank levy and bank surcharge net receipts'. http://bit.ly/2LtWCNS

38 ONS (2017) 'Time series: CG: Employers social security contributions (accrued)'. http://bit.ly/2LdJadt

39 The analysis and proposals in this section are based on the IPPR Commision on Economic Justice paper, Blakeley (2018).

40 Ibid.

41 Ibid.

42 Ibid.

43 National Audit Office (2013) *Tax reliefs*, report by the Comptroller and the Auditor General, HC 1256, NAO, London. https://www.nao.org.uk/report/tax-reliefs-3/

44 Jacobs M et al. (2017) *Industrial strategy: Steering structural change in the UK economy*, IPPR. http://bit.ly/2JgdAtR

45 National Audit Office (2013).

46 Ylönen M and Teivainen T (2015) 'Politics of intra-firm trade: Corporate price planning and the double role of the arm's length principle', *New Political Economy* 23(4): 441–57; Tax Justice Network (2015) *Ten reasons to defend the corporation tax*, Tax Justice Network. https://bit.ly/2OPxWhE

47 Spoors C (2017) *Ending the tax scandals: Five actions the UK government can take to tackle tax avoidance*, Oxfam UK. http://bit.ly/2zBBdxq

48 EURODAD (2017) *Tax games: The race to the bottom: Europe's role in supporting an unjust global tax system.* http://bit.ly/2KPMfUR

49 Blakeley (2018).

50 IPPR calculations using HMRC (2018) 'Direct effects of illustrative tax changes'. https://bit.ly/2rdiYdn. This calculation does not take into account any macroeconomic effects.

51 Blakeley (2018).

14: Ensuring Environmental Sustainability

1 Jacobs M (1991) *The green economy: Environment, sustainable development and the politics of the future*, Pluto Press.

2 Intergovernmental Panel on Climate Change (2014) *Climate change 2014: Impacts, adaptation, and vulnerability.* http://bit.ly/2mgh5Hn

3 Gibbs H and Salmon J (2015) 'Mapping the world's degraded lands', *Applied Geography* 57: 12–21.

4 World Meteorological Organization (2014) 'Record greenhouse gas levels impact atmosphere and oceans', press release, 9 September. https://bit.ly/2vC76R8

5 Pimm SL et al. (2014) 'The biodiversity of species and their rates of extinction, distribution, and protection', *Science* 344(6187). http://bit.ly/2NN1vzK

6 Geyer R, Jambeck J and Lavender Law K (2017), 'Production, use, and fate of all plastics ever made', *Science Advances* 3(7). http://bit.ly/2uuFqgz

7 Rockström J et al. (2009) 'Planetary boundaries: Exploring the safe operating space for humanity', *Ecology and Society* 14(2): 32. http://bit.ly/2zA2Ned

8 Royal College of Physicians (2016) *Every breath we take: The lifelong impact of air pollution: Report of a working party.* https://bit.ly/1PUBD09

9 RSPB (2016) *State of nature 2016*, RSPB. https://bit.ly/2m8SJz0

10 *The Guardian* (2017) 'UK is 30–40 years away from "eradication of soil fertility"', warns Gove', 24 October. https://bit.ly/2h5bhP0

11 Ekins P (1999) *Economic growth and environmental sustainability: The prospects for green growth*, Routledge.

12 United Nations Environment Programme International Resource Panel (2017) *Resource efficiency: Potential and economic implications.* https://bit.ly/2nwnwJ4

13 World Bank (2012) *Inclusive green growth: The pathway to sustainable development.* https://bit.ly/1jymNQ6; OECD (2015) *Towards green growth: Tracking progress.* https://bit.ly/1C6atjt

14 United Nations Environment Programme International Resource Panel (2015) *International trade in resources: A biophysical assessment.* http://bit.ly/2L4yPDP

15 MIT News (2013) 'Innovation in renewable-energy technologies is booming', 10 October. https://bit.ly/2KvK8kb; European Commission (2016) *Transforming the European energy system through innovation.* https://bit.ly/2gpdOkL; McKinsey Global

Institute (2017) *Beyond the supercycle: How technology is reshaping resources*. https://mck.co/2zYLQGq

16 Business and Sustainable Development Commission (2017) *Better business, better world*. http://report.businesscommission. org/report; Webster K (2017) *The circular economy: A wealth of flows*, Ellen MacArthur Foundation. https://bit.ly/2vHA5CZ

17 Perez C and Murray Leach T (2018) 'A smart green "European way of life": The path for growth, jobs and wellbeing', working paper, BTTR. https://bit.ly/2AMYmO0.

18 Jackson T (2017) *Prosperity without growth: Economics for a finite planet*, 2nd edn, Routledge.

19 Zenghelis D (2016) 'Decarbonisation: Innovation and the economics of climate change', in Jacobs M and Mazzucato M (eds) *Rethinking capitalism: Economics and policy for sustainable growth*, Wiley-Blackwell.

20 United Nations Framework Convention on Climate Change (2015) *The Paris Agreement*. https://bit.ly/2EVSoXT

21 ONS (2018) 'UK environmental goods and services sector (EGSS): 2010 to 2015'. http://bit.ly/2miCUXb

22 Harper A (2012) *Green economy: A UK success story*, Green Alliance. https://bit.ly/2vGxwBe

23 Committee on Climate Change (2018) *Reducing UK emissions – 2018 Progress Report to Parliament*. https://bit.ly/2Ku6CWw

24 DEFRA (2017) *England natural environment indicators*. http:// bit.ly/2KSrx6Z (England only); Global Footprint Network (2018) 'Country trends: UK'. http://bit.ly/2JitofI.

25 Ibid.

26 BBC (2015) 'Government energy policies "will increase CO2 emissions"', 9 November. https://bbc.in/2LqZJmn

27 Fankhauser S, Averchenkova A and Finnegan J (2018) *10 years of the UK Climate Change Act*, Grantham Research Institute on Climate Change and the Environment, LSE. https://bit. ly/2MpkFdM

28 *The Guardian* (2018) 'Campaigners attack plan for new watchdog to protect environment after Brexit', 10 May. https://bit.ly/2Kb3dYW

29 Ekins (1999); Grubb M with Hourcade J-C and Neuhoff K (2014) *Planetary economics: Energy, climate change and three domains of sustainable development*, Routledge.

30 Renewable UK (2018) 'Offshore wind'. https://bit.ly/2LYcbyk

31 HM Government (2017) *The clean growth strategy.* https://bit.ly/2N1NPkb

32 HM Government (2018) *A green future: Our 25-year plan to improve the environment.* https://bit.ly/2r0iV1Z

33 Zenghelis (2016).

34 Department for Business, Energy and Industrial Strategy (2018) *The grand challenges.* https://bit.ly/2zJ50Uo

35 Just Transition Centre (2017) *Just transition: A report for the OECD.* https://bit.ly/2IZb387

15: Creating a New Economic Constitution

1 ONS (2018) 'EARN05: Gross weekly earnings of full-time employees by region'. http://bit.ly/2md46WX

2 Cribb J, et al. (2017) *Living standards, poverty and inequality in the UK: 2017*, IFS. https://bit.ly/2v85fpp

3 Haldane A (2016) 'Whose recovery?', speech at Port Talbot, 30 June. https://bit.ly/2KBRJ0q

4 ONS (2017) Table 1 of 'Statistical bulletin: Regional gross value added (balanced), UK: 1998 to 2016'. http://bit.ly/2zEcV62

5 HM Treasury (2018) 'GDP deflators at market prices, and money GDP June 2018 (Quarterly National Accounts)'. https://bit.ly/2vKTqmO

6 Jacobs M et al. (2017) *Industrial strategy: Steering structural change in the UK economy*, IPPR. http://bit.ly/2NcEtRH

7 ONS (2018) dataset: 'X03 Regional labour market: Estimates of economic inactivity by age'. http://bit.ly/2NaurQV

8 ONS (2018) 'Public sector employment'. http://bit.ly/2uijBS5

9 ONS (2017) 'Regional accounts', accessed via Nomis. https://www.nomisweb.co.uk/

10 ONS (2017) 'Annual survey of hours and earnings', accessed via Nomis. https://www.nomisweb.co.uk/

11 ONS (2017) 'Regional firm-level productivity analysis for the non-financial business economy: Jan 2017', data. http://bit.ly/2uu1XtF

12 Cribb J, Norris Keiller A and Waters T (2018) *Living standards, poverty and inequality in the UK: 2018*, IFS. http://bit.ly/2mdIKss

13 ONS (2018) 'Regional gross disposable household income (GDHI): 1997 to 2015'. http://bit.ly/2Na2lFu

14 Oil and Gas UK, *Economic Report 2017*. https://bit.ly/2MrHldH

15 National Records of Scotland (2017) *Projected population of Scotland (2016-based): National population projections by sex and age, with UK comparisons*. https://bit.ly/2M3SYdG

16 ONS (2018) 'Regional gross value added (balanced), UK: 1998 to 2016', statistical bulletin. http://bit.ly/2zEcV62

17 ONS (2018) 'Annual population survey Jan–Dec 2017', accessed via Nomis, www.nomisweb.co.uk/; Welsh Government (2018) 'Young people not in education, employment or training (NEET)'. https://bit.ly/2vJDkdn

18 Belfast City Council (2018) *Belfast facts and figures 2018*. http://bit.ly/2Lmv6BH

19 ONS (2018) 'Annual population survey Jan–Dec 2017'.

20 ONS (2018) 'Regional labour market statistics in the UK: June 2018'. http://bit.ly/2zIMRXt

21 HM Treasury (2017) *Block grant transparency: December 2017 publication*, HM Government. http://bit.ly/2ujdAo1

22 New Policy Institute (2018) *Devolution within Northern Ireland*, report for Northern Ireland Local Government Association. https://bit.ly/2vJEmWN

23 Sandford M (2018) *Devolution to local government in England*, House of Commons briefing. http://bit.ly/2mb6L3o

24 Stirling A and Thompson S (2016) *Better rates: How to ensure the new business rates regime promotes growth everywhere*, IPPR. http://bit.ly/2mnPPa7

25 https://northernpowerhouse.gov.uk/

26 Transport for the South East (2018) 'Partners launch Transport for the South East to transform travel and enhance economy', 4 March. https://bit.ly/2nixFai

27 OECD United Cities and Local Governments (2016) *Subnational Governments around the world: Structure and finance.* https://bit.ly/2LYqHGk

28 Institute for Government (2018) 'Tax and devolution'. https://bit.ly/2vHK6QB; OECD (2016) *Revenue Statistics 2016 Tax revenue trends in the OECD.* https://bit.ly/2ngWZh1

29 OECD (2018) *Subnational governments in OECD Countries: Key data 2018 edition.* https://bit.ly/2M5X9FX

30 OECD (2016) *Subnational governments around the world: Structure and finance.* https://bit.ly/2LYqHGk

31 Cox E, Henderson G and Raikes L (2014) *Decentralisation decade: A plan for economic prosperity, public service transformation and democratic renewal in England,* IPPR North. http://bit.ly/2utpkoa

32 Lyall S, Wood M and Bailey D (2015) *Democracy: The missing link in the devolution debate,* New Economics Foundation. http://bit.ly/2NbaIAN

33 Raikes L (2016) *Connecting lines: How devolving transport policy can transform our cities,* IPPR North. https://bit.ly/2viitOT

34 Round A (2018) *Skills for the North: Devolving technical education to cities,* IPPR. http://bit.ly/2Jsngl3; Davies B and Raikes L (2014) *Alright for some: Fixing the work programme, locally,* IPPR. https://bit.ly/2LTpEaq; Raikes L and Davies B (2016) *Welfare earnback: An invest-to-save approach to designing the new Work and Health Programme,* IPPR North. http://bit.ly/2LgfijW

35 European Commission (2014) *Thematic research summary: Land use and transport planning.* https://bit.ly/2OceZo7; OECD (2015) *Governing the city.* https://bit.ly/2jIqvrt; OECD (2017) *The governance of land use in OECD countries: Policy analysis and recommendations.* https://bit.ly/2AM0NjK

36 McCann P (2016) *The UK regional–national economic problem: Geography, globalisation and governance,* Routledge.

37 Ibid.

38 Cox, Henderson and Raikes (2014).

39 Pike A et al. (2013) *Local institutions and local economic growth: The state of the Local Enterprise Partnerships (LEPs) in England – A national survey*, SERC discussion paper. http://bit.ly/2NPLLfs

40 McCann (2016); Cox E (2017) *Taking back control in the North: A council of the North and other ideas*, IPPR North. http://bit.ly/2L9aQTS

41 Cox E and Raikes L (2015) *Transport for the North: A blueprint for devolving and integrating transport powers in England*, IPPR North. https://bit.ly/2LWTISN; IPPR North and the Northern Economic Futures Commission (2012) *Northern prosperity is national prosperity: A strategy for revitalising the UK economy*, IPPR North. https://bit.ly/2LV4mJz; Jacobs et al. (2017); Macfarlane L and Mazzucato M (2018) *State investment banks and patient finance: An international comparison*, working paper, UCL Institute for Innovation and Public Purpose. https://bit.ly/2Og6Miy

42 Centre for Local Economic Strategies (CLES) 'Local wealth building'. http://bit.ly/2NndsLu

43 Jackson M (2015) *Creating a good local economy: The role of anchor institutions*, CLES. https://bit.ly/2vJyoVB

44 Calafati L, Jackson M and McInroy N (2017) 'Improving the social efficiencies of local markets is not protectionism', CLES. https://bit.ly/2M6Xrfx

45 CLES (2018) 'The Preston model'. http://bit.ly/2zNBI7r

46 Singer C (2016) 'The Preston model', The Next Systems Project. http://bit.ly/2L2ucuS

47 Jackson M (2017) *The power of procurement II*, CLES. http://bit.ly/2NYkpE2

48 Drakeford M (2017) 'Written statement: repositioning of the National Procurement Service and Value Wales', Welsh Government. https://bit.ly/2AM1jOP

49 Welsh Government (2018) *Prosperity for all: Economic action plan*. https://bit.ly/2JzJ9mw; Scottish Government (2015) *Scotland's Economic Strategy*. http://bit.ly/2KStGQ5

50 SNP Sustainable Growth Commission (2018) *Scotland – the new case for optimism: a strategy for inter-generational economic renaissance.* http://bit.ly/2mummLX

51 Cox E, Murray C and Round A (2017) *Forgotten opportunities: The dynamic role of the rural economy in post-Brexit Britain,* IPPR North. https://bit.ly/2KCqEKQ

52 Scottish Government (2018) *Scottish National Investment Bank Implementation Plan.* http://bit.ly/2LjPmE6

53 IPPR analysis of HM Treasury (2017) 'Country and regional analysis 2017: interactive tables in Excel format'. https://bit.ly/2Odgxyg

54 McGough L and Bessis H (2015) *Beyond business rates: How increasing local tax-raising powers can incentivise cities to grow,* Centre for Cities. https://bit.ly/1T4a70M

55 HM Treasury and Scottish Government (2016) *The agreement between the Scottish government and the United Kingdom government on the Scottish government's fiscal framework.* https://bit. ly/1XPrcOE

56 EY (2015) *Wealth under the spotlight 2015: How taxing the wealthy is changing.* https://go.ey.com/2KPWloO

57 Bank of England (2015) 'One Bank research agenda launched today', press release, 25 February. https://bit.ly/2AM5N87

58 RSA (2017) 'Building a public culture of economics'. https://bit. ly/2vkaQYk